DEDICATION

This book is dedicated to the memory of my sister Deborah Ann Bucchi-Haigh. Her jubilance and youthful nature brought joy to all who knew her. Her inviting character transformed everyday encounters into lasting friendships. Although her life was cut short at 37, she found eternal salvation in Jesus Christ, and it is with that knowledge that I persevere.

CIA

COCAINE IN AMERICA

CIA

COCAINE IN AMERICA

Ken Bucchi

BOOKS
A Division of Shapolsky Publishers

CIA: Cocaine In America

S.P.I. BOOKS
A division of Shapolsky Publishers, Inc.

Copyright © 1994 by Ken Bucchi

ISBN 1-56171-322-8

For any additional information, contact:

S.P.I. BOOKS/Shapolsky Publishers, Inc.
136 West 22nd Street
New York, NY 10011
212/633-2022 / • FAX 212/633-2123

Manufactured in Canada

10 9 8 7 6 5 4 3 2 1

ACKNOWLEDGMENTS

Thanks to my mom and dad (Dorothy & Ben) for their eternal support, guidance and love. To my brothers Danny and Benny, and my sister Tammy for their love and support. To Robin and Mark Rizzo for their unwavering spiritual guidance and tireless work. To George F. Buckley for his love and direction. To the Gevedens for their lasting faith. To John and Pam Daly for their enduring trust. To Jim McKimmey for his expert tutelage. To Ann and Don Farber for their resilience. To Robert Edelstein and Dr. John Faughn for their support. To Mr. Hamilton for his guidance and motivation. To Mike Fisher for his spiritual mentorship. To Colonel Morris and Colonel Lewandowski for their leadership. To Marlowe Churchill and Jason Rowe for their faith and persistence. To Colonel Ray for his support and trust. And, most of all, to all the above for their friendship.

And a special thanks to actress Barbara Eden for reaching out across the ocean to my sister Debbie in her time of need. For that, I am eternally grateful.

Chapter 1.

Leaving my Gull-winged Delorean and first lieutenant's Air Force uniform behind, I climbed into an unmarked six-passenger single-engine Cessna 210 at Kelly Air Force Base in Texas. It was piloted by a man I'd never seen before. He and the three other passengers also wore casual civilian clothing. They were all strangers and I would probably never see any of them again. Central Intelligence compartmentalizes its people in such a way that they can never be linked to one another.

During the flight I was briefed on this new covert assignment. My group was to intercept a drug shipment from South America at an undisclosed destination. We were to confiscate the entire shipment, which represented half of the Medellin Cartel's export for a designated period.

This was the unique concept of the *Pseudo Miranda*, whose operations we'd been carrying out for years. We'd worked in cooperative agreement with many major cocaine distributors in the world, confiscating tons of drugs that would never reach American streets.

It was a dangerous business, but we'd become accustomed to the danger and worked around it. But there was a special tension in the air on this particular May morning in 1987. I had an eerie feeling that something was going to go very wrong this time. I put it to my long experience in the field. I now had enough experience to know how easily a mistake could happen.

Hondo Airport, located about ninety miles west by southwest of San Antonio, was a familiar landing spot for us. I looked down at a barren runway. Grass grew between the cracks and gravel filled grounding points. The facility was now used only for refurbishing aircraft and to accommodate CIA missions such as ours.

Abandoned aircraft hulls and smaller parts were visible behind the hangars. Outside the fenced-in containment was a golf course.

We landed and I joined five people with whom I'd worked during the past few years in a hangar where vintage World War II fighter aircraft had been stored. All of us used AKA names; mine was Anthony VesBucchi.

Joey was black-haired with Italian features. His slender body was defined with muscle. He was a go-get-'em, gung-ho kind of guy, yet he had an almost feminine aura about him. Although he didn't appear to be athletic, he was wiry and almost cat-like.

Quinn was a woman you wouldn't want to get into a fight with; you might get beat. Her dirty-blond hair was cut short. Of medium height, she could match her muscles with any man. She hid her innate sentimentality very well beneath a layer of bogus masculinity.

Jesus Rivas was Hispanic. Of medium height, his long wavy hair and splendidly groomed mustache portrayed his cockiness, but he tempered it with a sense of humor.

Lourdes was a natural blonde even though she was also Hispanic. She had a dark tan, good legs, and a washboard stomach. She had a face like a doll, cute and shiny. She was extremely honest and direct, which I decided was probably due to naivety. Like Rivas, she had a sense of humor, but it was slow. She never grasped any sort of complex issue.

Ming was a six-foot, athletic Asian who spoke three languages. He'd trained with us in Tonapah, but usually worked out of our sister operation in Thailand. He was disciplined and reserved, but lacked the ability to improvise.

There was a sixth person in the hanger. The sixth person who would normally have been there was missing. He was an important omission. Box for Boxer had been my handler from the beginning, a good-looking, 6' 2", smoothly muscled black man in his early thirties. A lover of rock-'n'-roll, he was a moralistic person who always did what he had to do. We'd worked shoulder to shoulder. But, on this assignment, our complete team had been split and he'd been required to accompany the other half to another interception in southern Florida.

The sixth man was a new addition to the team, which had never happened before. I was concerned about that.

I called the guy Fossil due to his apparent age and because he wouldn't reveal his name. In his mid fifties, perhaps five-nine tall, gray-haired, in good shape, he owned a distinctively raspy voice. He immediately took charge, demanding and authoritative, to the point of being dictatorial.

The group was usually a talkative bunch, but today near-silence prevailed. Perhaps, I thought, the others are feeling the same premonition I am.

We collected our weapons in the hangar. I attached a side-holstered, 45mm Colt automatic pistol to my belt and added two grenades as well. When the group was ready, we boarded two small Bell helicopters for a flight to the interception point.

It was three o'clock in the afternoon when we landed in a clearing densely surrounded by live oaks. We started walking carefully through the hilly wooded area of Texas, crossing occasional dirt paths leading to small residences, many of which were mobile homes. One resident owned an exotic collection of what appeared to be pet cougars and peacocks.

Finally, as we moved into the last patch of forest, there were no more homes in sight.

❖ ❖ ❖

The white house stood by itself on a hill. The building was a two and one-half story frame structure with a wooden deck around the perimeter. Surveillance disclosed a four-foot iron fence enclosed a treeless area at the rear where windows ran across the entire upper floor. The front featured a large picture window.

We could see people inside.

We hunkered down at the mouth of the trail leading up to the house and waited tensely. Something about the situation wasn't right.

"It'll take a hell of a pilot to make a successful drop in this terrain, especially with the limited drop zone," I said to the old man.

"The intelligence report indicates that the shipment has already been made. The mules inside transported the drugs from the drop zone to here and should be waiting for a second-level transfer. That's why we need to move swiftly and precisely."

"Whoa, whoa, hold it," I pulled back. "What kind of bullshit is this? Look! I don't know exactly what's going on here, but I do know this. We don't get involved with the affairs of the DEA. If this coke has already been received at the first level, then we're outa here."

"I don't give a rat's ass what you think," Fossil snapped. "And I don't personally give a flying fuck what you do or don't want to get involved with. I'm running the show. And you'll do exactly what you're told to do! Not that you deserve an explanation. But you were told at the start of Pseudo Miranda that first-level interceptions would be made, and a code word would be used to facilitate it." He paused, altering his tone dramatically. "Oh. Which reminds me. The code word is `Shangri La.'"

By now we were both talking in low, angry whispers.

"That reminds you?" I countered. "Now, let me tell you something. If so much as a shot is fired here today, the next one will separate your head from your shoulders. Now, go ahead and run your fuckin' show."

He hesitated, sweat began to run off his forehead.

"When I'm convinced those guys in the house have got the message that we're here to take their drugs, you'd better be ready to move!" he blustered.

"Okay. Joey, you and I'll go right up the pipe." Joey knew that I meant the two of us would go straight in the door. "Lourdes, you and Rivas flank us. Quinn, you and Ming stay positioned right here."

"Any particular marching orders?" Quinn asked.

"Yeah," I motioned toward the old guy with the automatic Colt in my hand. "If he does anything but support us, do that head-shoulder thing."

Forty-five minutes passed before the old man picked up his megaphone.

"Shangri La!"

Joey and I stood up and started walking along the path toward the house.

It seemed like an eternity. I could feel my muscles tightening. I reached out with my left hand, embracing Joey's right arm. He glanced back with heavy eyes and forced a smile, as if to tell me good-bye. He also knew the fate that lurked on the other side of the door. He grasped my hand like a vice as we neared the house. I squeezed back, wanting to remember the warmth of his skin. "Love you," I said, and moved toward the door, Joey at my side.

We climbed to the deck. The front door was opened and we stormed inside.

The room stretched before us. Probably 500 kilos of drugs were lined up on the floor. I began to feel better. This made it look like a legitimate and sizeable interception.

People were standing in front of us. Half of them looked to be American, the others Hispanic. To the left, the room raised one level and disappeared into another room. On the wall facing us was a large mirror. To the right, a spiraling staircase led upstairs to a corridor.

The majority of the people in front of us were on our right, I yelled for them to move to the left and signalled in that direction for the benefit of the Hispanics.

They all moved right.

I got a gnawing sensation in my stomach.

Something flashed in the mirror and I looked to my left. We'd been wrong. We'd thought that all of them were in the front room. But there were more, with guns, coming around the corner from the room on the left. Pulse racing now, I realized that was why the group had moved right instead of left.

I yelled, "Grenades!"

Joey immediately pulled one off his belt, yanked the pin and lobbed it toward the newcomers into the smaller room. The explosion ripped our ears. Debris came at us from all directions. Roaring from the smaller room into the larger one, the explosion reacted like it would in a wind tunnel. A tremendous force followed the blast. I bent my body in half, ducking the impact. Behind me, the scene looked surrealistic, debris flowed slowly toward me like snow flakes in the gentle breeze.

We were trapped. Our ambushers had only to fire in our direction and we'd be dead. Instinctively, I fired into the room and heard other guns near me. A confusing melee of shooting, shouting and debris filled the room. I couldn't tell what was happening in the smaller room. I didn't know what was happening outside.

"My God," I thought. "Is Joey still alive?

Unable to deal with what had happened, a strange detachment came over me. "Dear God," I pleaded. My mind turned back to myself in an earlier, more naive time when I was an easy-going student on a peaceful campus in Murray, Kentucky.

Chapter 2.

In 1984 I was still a 21-year-old senior at Kentucky's Murray State University, a pretty little campus in a small tranquil village called Murray. It had 10,000 students.

A major in criminal justice, I was an Alpha Tau Omega, but didn't live in the fraternity house. I had leased a compact, three-bedroom house at 208 Poplar Street. It was a quiet neighborhood where everyone kept to themselves and I rented two of the bedrooms to fellow fraternity brothers. There was a tiny front yard and a larger back yard with tall brush following its borders, concealing it from outside view. On one side, at the street corner, was a repair business. On the other side was a house occupied by an elderly deaf woman.

I had many friends both my own age in the fraternity and good older friends as well. I dated a lot, but rarely allowed myself to be tied down in a serious relationship. My buddies and I spent a good deal of time partying at Kentucky Lake and often traveled to Tennessee and, occasionally, as far as New Orleans in search of a good time.

The last thing I would have considered happening to me was being recruited by the CIA. Actually, my recruitment had begun over a year before; I just hadn't been aware of it.

My friend Mike, a part-time student who commuted from Paducah, was a good-looking guy who was attractive to both sexes. We started hanging out together. Eventually, Mike introduced me to this mind game and we started to play on a regular basis.

The idea was to convince someone, usually a stranger, of some crazy possibility. For example, I once posed as a health inspector dedicated to enforcing the "blue law" statutes which governed good

hygiene and was convincing enough that a young
lady showed me her undergarments in public. Both
Mike and I would kick ten bucks into a pool. Whoever
got away with the scam, got the money. If you couldn't
pull it off, you owed double.

Later, I would learn that the whole thing was rigged
so that Mike could observe how I handled people,
including when they were antagonistic. But I had no
inkling, even a year later when Mike dropped by at my
house. He was unusually curious.

"You're really interested in what you're studying,
aren't you? Criminology?"

"Yeah. Corrections. Various agencies."

"CIA?"

"Well...I don't know."

"They're going to test for employees in Chicago."

"How do you know that?"

"It was in the *Louisville Courier-Journal*."

I was amazed. "You mean they're actually adver-
tising in a newspaper?"

"Yeah."

"That doesn't make any sense. They're... they're...
what, what is that word? Clan...clandestine. They're
too clandestine."

"No. They've got a lot of jobs that have nothing to
do with that. Logistical things, secretaries, positions
like that. But maybe a lot of their secretive jobs are
hired that way too. Who knows? There's a series of
tests you have to go through."

"How the hell do you know so much about it?"

"It was in the paper."

He showed me the paper. He was right. Suddenly,
taking those tests seemed both interesting and promising. It might even be a good time. We drove to
Chicago.

The Federal Building was at the southern part of the Loop, on Dearborn. The offices were on the 7th floor. The letters on the front door announced them as also belonging to the FBI.

We were directed to another room for the test.

I expected hundreds of people, but there were, instead, just two. Both were in their middle 30s, mustached, trim, neatly dressed and politely cordial. The one who introduced himself as Salter did all of the talking and showed me a badge which identified him as belonging to the Department of Defense. I noticed that he had a Chief Master Sergeant's insignia on his pen, which indicated that he might have had prior duty with the Air Force. But he identified himself as being with the CIA.

"Tell me a little bit about yourself," he said.

I gave him a short autobiography: the type you give when you stand up on the first day of class.

He then took a file with my name on it from a briefcase and started talking about an old high-school friend of mine, Jim. I suddenly realized that they had been expecting me.

Jim had been into selling cocaine, primarily to rebel against his parents, whom he felt treated him badly. He'd once told me that his family went to Europe and left him at home. But I was never involved with drugs. My parents were really against all that stuff and so was I.

One night in 1978, when his parents were away, Jim had a really big cocaine party at their house. He was basically giving away a lot of the profit. It was a mess, with people trashing the house.

During the party he disappeared and I went looking for him. When I finally found him, a bunch of people were playing with him, throwing him back and forth. He was nearly passed out from the stuff he'd taken.

I got the people out of the room, but I didn't know what to do with Jim. I didn't want to call an ambulance. The minute it arrived, he'd be locked up for the rest of his life, I thought. There was over a kilo of cocaine in that house.

What I finally did do was call the police and report a disturbance on the street at another address. I figured that when the cops showed on the street, people would discretely get the hell out of Jim's house.

The ploy worked. People left, and I was able to get Jim to vomit profusely.

In Chicago, I found out how my file got started and this incident got into it. I'd known someone at the party named Levine. He'd ended up with either the DEA or FBI and had created a file on me. Apparently neither of the agencies had ever had use for someone of my peculiar talents. But the file had now found its way to the CIA. What happened on that night and during numerous other tight spots with Jim meant that I was someone who could get close to drugs and deal with the people involved and yet not get dirty myself. In the CIA's estimation, I'd done a lot of things in 1978 which were good for a guy my age.

It was a surprise to me.

Salter also talked to me about my father's stepfather being in the Mafia. I didn't know that.

Then he told me that my high-school friend, Jim, had been selling cocaine for a guy named Delvechio who was dealing for a guy named Hood who was peddling for a guy named Patriarca who was the head of the Mafia in all of New England. The chain was there. And I was thinking I was in big trouble.

"How would you like a job?" Salter asked.

It wasn't as though I had a lot of leeway to say no.

At the same time he'd made it sound interesting. And it would probably pay an inordinate amount of money; it's going to be in my line of work; it's a

clandestine organization; and, as all men can appreciate, it offers the perfect pick-up line.

But all I was really told was that the organization
was the Central Intelligence Drug Enforcement, simplified CITY, and that, if I went for it, I would be
contacted.

I went for it by nodding yes.

Eventually, I took a written test, which involved
such things as creating a language, but I never got the
results of it.

Eventually, I met the black man called Boxer, a
training agent. When I went back to college and played
"school" he appeared at my house several times. I was
put through scenarios with drug deals. I didn't know
if they were real or not. I'd work a week in that
fashion, then there was nothing for a month or so.

Then, in the spring of 1984, I was scheduled to
attend a secret meeting. I had no idea, at the time, that
Bill Casey would be there.

❖   ❖   ❖

Box would be going to the meeting with me, so I met
him in Chicago. Cars were made available to us and I
chose a black Pantera DeTomaso, a sports car with
European curves, yet with the distinct roar of an
American pedigree created by the power of its 351
Cleveland engine, Ford's greatest creation. As Box
and I drove from Illinois to Maryland, he made no
secret that my choice of the flamboyant Pantera was
something he worried about every mile of the way. He
also talked enough to lead me to believe that he was
married with kids.

Cumberland, Maryland was our goal. We checked
into the Holiday Inn on George Street, a street accurately remembered because it was the name of my late,
favorite uncle, George Buckley.

The next day we gathered at the house, a confiscated Drug Enforcement Administration structure.

The secret meetings were termed Commission
Meetings as a joke with reference to the Mafioso commission meetings. The group consisted of mid-level
officials from different government agencies including the DEA, the Defense Intelligence Agency, the
FBI, the Department of Defense, the CIA, and one
high-ranking official from one of the major agencies of
the Commission, who was technically the chairper-
son.

The object was to facilitate cooperation between
agencies. The meetings took place in remote locations
in order to avoid public knowledge of the petty con-
flicts which seriously hindered individual agencies
from functioning efficiently. Eventually, they degen-
erated into basic finger-pointing and ass-kissing among
the agencies.

Before we went into the house, I discovered that
Box wasn't the only one disturbed about my choice of
the Pantera. Two men, one of them wearing a very
loud sports shirt, approached us. They were obviously
angry.

"Why didn't you just announce your arrival to the
whole damned neighborhood?" The one in the sports
shirt snarled.

"I thought I'd let your shirt do it instead," I replied.

"You're one of those funny guys. You must be with
the Central Ignorance Agency."

"You have no sense of humor. You must be with the
FBI."

"DEA, asshole!"

"I thought you had to pass a test to get in the DEA."

"What kind of an idiot drives a Ferrari to a meeting
like this?" The second man chimed in.

"You need to get out of your office more often," I
said, "That's a Pantera, not a Ferrari. Anyhow, who
dresses like that to go hunting?"

"Hunting? What the hell makes you think I'm going hunting?"

I nodded toward the second one. "You brought your dog, didn't ya?"

We walked away toward the house.

"How could anyone have fallen for that old joke?" Box shook his head in disbelief.

I was acting like any 21-year-old college kid. Obviously, that was the image the agency liked so that was the way I would continue to act.

Entering the building and finding that Bill Casey was in attendance, however, made me acutely aware of the severely dramatic turn my life was taking.

Chapter 3.

The room had been enlarged by taking out a wall. At one end was the speaker's platform with a large screen flanked by easels. In front of the platform a long veneered table, narrowed at either end, ran down the room. The two DEA men were seated along one side, two from the FBI and one from the Defense Intelligence Agency on the other. Box and I were seated at the end. To our immediate right, at arm's length, was Bill Casey. The chairs swiveled and were covered with plastic, except for Casey's, which was upholstered with black leather and had a high executive-style back. Security guards were positioned on both sides of the door leading into the room..

Casey, of course, was the focal point. He was gray-haired, about six feet tall, with two and a half chins on a sagging face. Large round glasses were perched on his nose. His shoulders were slumped into a rounded posture. He wore a large school ring on one finger. Although he appeared highly intelligent, he mumbled a lot. Most of what he said could not be understood — except when he wanted it to be. Then he was very coherent. He was easily agitated. He obviously wanted the focus of the meeting to be on himself and he wanted absolute control.

Among the speakers, one of the DEA representatives spoke of an individual named Carijuana and the man's partner, Bolero, a Massachusetts attorney. Carijuana was a drug trafficker and dealt marijuana in Florida. He was literally thumbing his nose at the DEA because they'd been unable to stop him.

The DEA wanted cooperation from the CIA because they'd discovered that Carijuana had connections to Cuba. Since the CIA also had connections to Cuba, the DEA felt they could perhaps facilitate something.

At the end of this discussion, a small intermission was called. We went outside and walked around the house and ate donuts and chatted.

Box and I found ourselves reunited with the two DEA agents. We joked with them again. Then the DEA men started discussing the problem they'd been having with Carijuana and Bolero.

The moment seemed ripe for some humor.

"Why do you people waste countless tax dollars building a case against a guy you know is a drug dealer, only to arrest him after you've allowed him to dump tons of drugs onto the street?" I said. "The moment you throw him in jail, someone's there to step in and take over without skipping a beat. It's the people below who make it difficult for you. They're like assembly-line workers. Their jobs don't change regardless of who's at the top. So, if you arrest Carijuana, they'll simply replace him."

I could see that what I was saying was bothering the DEA pair, which was exactly what I'd intended in response to the way they'd jumped on me earlier about the car.

"Why don't you just suspend Carijauna's Miranda rights? Don't give him any of his constitutional guarantees. When you know he's done something illegal, simply kick his door in. Take all his money. Take all his drugs. Then let him go on his merry way."

Now, I knew, they were getting heated.

"What's he gonna do? Go to the media and say, 'They stole my five million dollars worth of mari-juana?'"

I could hear Box chuckling.

"You know Carijuana's not going to do that. So eventually you'll run him out of business. All right. It's illegal. But you're not making any arrests. So no one's hurt. No one's going to complain. And you accomplish more. Because if you just have these long-term investigations costing millions of dollars, when you finally nail the guy on some stupid hokey charge, all that'll happen is you'll have someone else taking over. You didn't really interrupt the business. But, if you interrupt it by taking money and drugs, no one else will take the business over because it won't be profitable. Call the operation *Pseudo Miranda*."

The DEA men were genuinely angry now. Both Box and I were laughing. We went back to the meeting.

The next speaker was one of the FBI representa-tives. He was entirely professional. But what he was saying was so boring that I didn't even pay attention. When he finally finished, I was practically asleep. That was when Bill Casey leaned past Box and slapped my shoulder and mumbled. He was hard to under-stand, but he was saying something in reference to the Miranda thing I'd talked about outside. I realized that he'd probably overheard the conversation I'd had with the two DEA guys at break time.

"Get up and tell us about it, Mr. VesBucchi," Casey said to me.

"It was a joke," I replied.

"No, no...give us a briefing on the merits of it."

"There aren't any merits. I was just kidding."

He was beginning to become agitated.

"Do what I'm telling you!"

I went to the podium. I figured as long as I sounded intelligent, I was going to be all right in this job. Sound smart, I thought, don't sound realistic. So I talked, telling them what I'd decided they wanted to hear.

When I'd finished, Casey mumbled for a few moments.

"All right. Fine. But it's not practical. It can't be done. They're too many complications. You can sit down, Mr. VesBucchi."

I returned to my chair. It was going to be okay. The whole thing was over. The meeting ended. We went back to the Holiday Inn. Box was obviously relieved, thinking, too, that everything was going to be all right now.

We decided that what they'd been trying to do was bleed us for anything, figuring that Box and I had been talking about the Miranda business for months, which we hadn't, and had the whole thing drummed up with these great ideas, which we didn't.

But there was nothing to worry about now.

Five hours later the call came.

❖   ❖   ❖

Box hung up and looked at me accusingly.

"Good going, Ace. Guess who has to return to the Commission. Gooood going!"

"Are you serious? What do you think it means?"

"Our asses, you moron!"

"Take a chill pill, Box. I can handle this."

"You can, huh?"

"If Case Face wanted to tear me a new asshole, he would have done it earlier."

"I hope you're right. And drop the Bill Casey pet names before you use one in front of him!"

"How in God's name have you survived the pressures of a decade in this line of work?"

"Mostly by not associating with people like you."

"Thanks for the support and encouragement."

"I'm not being paid to pad your ego, Bucchi!"

"What exactly are you being paid to do?"

"Let's just go. And I'm driving!"

"Which obviously means you're not in any hurry to get there."

At the house, we were confronted with all sorts of people: computer types, logistic types, communication types. By now I'd decided that some of the stuff I'd presented had made sense to Casey. The only reason he'd dismissed the ideas earlier was probably because he didn't want everyone else in the room at the time to know he was going in the direction I'd indicated, something he'd probably been considering for years.

I was asked to repeat the plan. This time I tried to present it both smartly and realistically:

It was essential to isolate the biggest cocaine distributors in the world, primarily in Peru, Bolivia and Colombia. They would be empowered to destroy the many smaller competitors, giving the whole market to those biggest distributors. At that point the overall market size would not be increased. Instead, that market would be concentrated in just a few hands, which could be more easily controlled. Then, because those select few would have had their markets increased perhaps ten fold, you would have them offer half of their drug shipments to you.

Now you're stopping fifty percent of the cocaine coming into the country. And the biggest distributors still have fivefold over what they would have had previously. On top of that, you wouldn't make any arrests. So they would no longer have any fear of that. You would set up corridors where the distributors could fly into the country safely under the umbrella of the radar systems that aided the DEA and Custom squads. Because they would be undetected by anyone else, you would be the one to stop half of those shipments and let half go on through.

I went on with the details we'd concocted.

Driving back to Chicago, I got the feeling that maybe Box was now a little jealous over my speech. He kept insisting we'd still get in trouble over it. But then he, as a trainer, had rules to follow that I didn't. Besides, we were very basically different people. For example, he liked Pink Floyd and Led Zeppelin. I hated both. We didn't worry, however, about bigger differences such as color or religion or where we came from. We never looked for trouble that didn't exist. Not once did he and I ever have a discussion about any of that.

❖ ❖ ❖

In Chicago we took a break by staying at a yacht club which was on Lake Shore Drive. We stayed there two days and a night, wondering what would develop next.

In a cabin of the *Down Easter*, Box broke out the Wild Turkey. I was playing Alice Cooper's *Only Women Bleed*.

"Can you believe that we could soon be involved with this new operation?" he said. "We could really make a difference in the war on drugs. Of course, the downside is that we could easily get ourselves dead doing it."

"Just a few days ago you were calling my ideas loony tunes."

"I was afraid to admit I believed your ideas made sense for fear people would think we thought alike."

"Think, thank, thunk...let's get to the booze and crank some more tunes."

We eventually worked our way to chairs on the deck of the ship.

"Believe it or not," Box said gravely, "it's the reason I originally became an agent."

CIA: COCAINE IN AMERICA   29

"It, meaning to consume grotesque amounts of alcohol?"

"No, you bone-head. To make a real and tangible difference! You know. To live a little on the edge for a real purpose. God, I hope I'm not getting too enthused about the possibilities! I hate being let down when my expectations get too high. By God, I'm glad I hooked up with you. Although you'll probably end up getting me killed. Aren't you going to say something?"

"You're doing fine for the both of us. Anyhow, I don't like to mix important discussions with alcohol."

"Me neither."

"You don't drink much, do you?"

In late June, Box joined me again at my place in Murray with more details on the arrangements.

"Well," he said, " You wanted to be part of something really big. It looks like you're going to get your chance."

"So tell me everything. Do I get to carry a gun...I'm just kidding."

"Actually you will be carrying a gun. But not before you finish training. It looks like you and I will be going to a remote and undisclosed locale. Here's a complete list of the things you'll need. Don't bring any of your Big Daddy Cane clothes with you!"

"I'll have you know women love the way I dress."

"I've seen the women you go with. Okay. You'll be departing from Paducah Airport. You know where that is. You won't be able to tell anyone what you're doing. You'll simply tell your family and friends in Massachusetts that you'll be attending the summer semester here. Tell your friends in town that you've graduated and you'll be keeping residence here while you travel around the country looking for a job. Are you following me?"

"I think so," I said with deliberate moronic sarcasm.

"Look. I know I sound condescending. But it's just that I want everything to go smoothly. So please bear with me. Believe it or not, I actually think we'll make a good team. Atypical, but, none the less, effective. Because the big news is that we're going to be participants in *Pseudo Miranda*."

"You mean they're actually going to use the name I came up with?"

"Did I forgot to mention that."

"Hey, wow! I can't believe they named it that! That's great! Can you believe they did that? Holy shit! How long have I been working for them? And now they've named a program after my idea!"

"Enough already! The name's insignificant. What's important is what we'll be doing."

"You're jealous, Box. You've been working for the Company for over a decade. And they've never named a program for one of your ideas."

"Company! Nobody calls it that. Don't get too cocky. So they named the program *Pseudo Miranda*. But the idea's been kicked around by Mr. Casey for a long time. It just happens that you, by sheer luck, happened to express some views and ideas that he liked."

"Jealous!" I said.

❖   ❖   ❖

The Paducah Airport was located in extreme Western Kentucky, far removed from populated areas. There were no terminals. A T-39 aircraft flown in from Wright Patterson Air Force Base in Ohio had stopped on the runway.

I walked out onto the tarmac to board, feeling only excitement that I was heading for my training base in Tonopah, Nevada.

Chapter 4

The T-39 appeared to have made several stops on route to my location as evidenced by the three other passengers on board who seemed to be unfamiliar with one another. We continued to make pit stops to board and off-board passengers as we lethargically traversed our way to Nevada. I was instructed by Box not to speak to anyone concerning the purpose of our visit to Nevada. I'd guessed this was the same directive given to all the passengers. "So. What's your name?" I asked the woman sitting opposite me.

"Davarra. How 'bout yours?" She replied with a grin. I knew she was lying. We all lied. It was the nature of this business to lie about anything dealing directly with your background.

"Davarra. That's a beautiful name. Any significance?"

"Yeah. Quite a bit," She snickered. "It's Arravad spelt backwards."

"Arravad! That's Turkish isn't it?

"Turkish! Yeah. Right. Turkey." She knew perfectly well that I knew she'd made up the name Davarra. "Actually it's Greek. At least it was at the time, when my parents were in Davarra, Cyprus. It's the most beautiful town in all of…an extremely small town in Cyprus. Almost microscopic. You can't blink. You know. So? You never told me your name. Mister..?"

"Tuscadero. Levon Tuscadero."

"Your parents Elton John fans?"

"No." I said abruptly, concealing my ignorance of rock-'n'-roll history. "My mom just wanted a novel name."

"And Tuscadero? Was your father a demolition driver partial to women's pink clothing" She interjected with a reference to a *Happy Days* classic.

"How about you?" The woman nodded her head toward Box. "What's your name?"

"No, thank you." Box snapped, pointing to his head. As if indicating he had a headache.

"I think he's telling us that his name is Head. Is that his name do you think?" She said sarcastically.

"Yeah. I do. Come on Richard. Why don't you wanna play?"

"Very funny asshole." Box moaned, with his head tucked beneath a newspaper.

Midnight was approaching as we entered the pattern over Nellis Air Force Base, Nevada. The city below sparkled angelically, revealing a softened image of the pagan vulgarity that is Las Vegas.

Davarra departed our company at Nellis. After the plane taxied to the end of the tarmac, Box and I were escorted by two Military Policemen of the 4450th (a top secret squadron) to a secure staging area. From there, we were hastily shuttled to a helicopter under armed guard. My sense of amusement was gone. The blood to my brain hammered at my temples. I tried to analyze Boxer's reaction to the events, but he was expressionless, almost to the point of shock. Realistically, I knew that he had no more information than I, but there was a certain comfort in knowing that I wasn't in danger alone.

"Is it always this hot out here?" I asked one of our escorts.

"No talking sir!" The Chief Master Sergeant shouted over the noise of the helicopter rotor blades.

The fact that he called me sir alleviated a lot of my stress. You don't call someone sir and then kill them, I thought. My ignorance served me well. It gave me a sense of security.

I knew that Tonopah, located northwest of Nellis, was engulfed by mountains, but my sense of direction was distorted by my inability to see outside the aircraft. Once on the tarmac, we were blindfolded and traveled in a bus with blackened windows. The driver, I would later discover, worked for a company called San Dia Industries. It certainly humbled me to know that I didn't own enough security clearance to drive a bus in Tonopah. When we exited the vehicle and the blindfolds were removed, we were struck by an incredible sight. We were looking out upon a six hundred foot by three hundred foot crater. It stood as a beacon among the impenetrable darkness. My initial impression was that I was at the sight of the final scene of *Close Encounters of the Third Kind*. The enormity of it was startling, but its contents were even more impressive. It was like a massive Hollywood sound stage. Complete with temporary buildings, alley ways, running water and electricity. The structures were supported at the rear by wood scaffolding bonded to beams that ran along the perimeter of the crater. At either end were long metal staircases, also temporary, with armed guards from the 4450th posted at their base. The fact that the guards were at the bottom of each stair case and not the top, told me they were there to keep people from leaving, not entering. The border, where we were presently standing, was lined with bracing that functioned as dirt retainers.

Looking out over the edge, I saw several people in civilian clothing gathered around a few men in camouflage fatigues. One of the men signaled with a swirling arm for us to enter. This was immediately followed by a radio transmission to the guard, telling him that we were cleared to enter.

Descending, I felt a sense of importance. I couldn't help but wonder if much of what I was seeing came by way of the meeting I attended in Cumberland, Maryland. The staircase clanged and reverberated as we sunk gradually downward. Buildings slowly gained depth and dimension, appearing more whole than facade. The world fell away.

Box began to advise me on the appropriate protocol
for such an alien environment.

"Listen first. Speak only when asked to. And for
God's sakes, no grandstanding!"

"What'd I say?"

"This is some serious shit! Look at this place. This is
some serious shit." Box nervously repeated.

"Yeah. I gotta agree with you on this. This is some
real serious shit." I said in awe struck tone.

"Just no repeats of Maryland. Okay?"

"Yeah. No repeats." I spoke as if in a trance.

As we exited the staircase some four stories into the
earth, a man, about 6'5" tall with athletic build, greeted
us with a welcoming hand shake.

"VesBucchi and Boxer, I presume. You'll refer to
me heretofore as Instructor Jones."

"Do I look that Italian?" I said sarcastically .

"No you don't." He stood between us, placing his
hands on our shoulders, "But this guy looks a lot like
a dog I once ran over."

He continued, "You two gentlemen have a meeting
with the commandant. After that, I'll show you where
you'll bunk."

"So. What's this meeting about?" Box asked.

"Don't know. What I do know is that there's forty
plus people scheduled to arrive here this evening and
only two scheduled to meet with the man." He turned
to face us but continued walking backward, pointing
index finger like a cameraman cuing the actors of a
live television show. "You two."

Box and I looked at one another. His face filled with
accusation, mine with guilt. Box uttered, "Now what?"

"Why you looking at me? We've been together all
day! This has been one of my better days. It has."

Instructor Jones, dressed in desert fatigues and
jungle boots, led us up a short wooden stair case to

the smallest structure on the block, located exactly half way up the gravel street. The Commandant excused our escort and invited us to sit down. The Commandant was without a doubt a CIA refugee. I recognized what was once a strong and invincible man. More than a shell of his former self, he seemed to come with a disclaimer. I felt he wanted those whom he first met to know of his infamous past, but that his pride prevented an explanation. His stomach muscles needed reminding as he would catch himself feeling fiftyish. His hair, grey and groomed tight, had a line more covering than my own. A long scar curved in an elongated "S" shape from the top of his cheek to the base of his chin. I wondered how he could have received such a wound. I was always paranoid about any facial deformities. I knew that I would prefer a bullet to the stomach than a cut to the face. My vanity would eventually take a much lower priority.

"You two were specifically remanded to this assessment program by Director Casey. Before you get all puffed up, realize my only instructions are to evaluate you with the others. You'll mention the nature of what you're being evaluated for to no one. You're the only ones who know what the selectees will be involved with at the completion of training. This obviously places a special burden on you to succeed."

He paused, exhaled, and completed with a cliché. "Well. Good luck. That'll be all."

As Box and I departed, I wondered aloud, "What do you suppose he meant by 'A special burden to succeed'?"

"I'm not sure. I just hope it doesn't mean what I think it means."

"Yeah. What's that?"

"Nothing. Just work hard, that's all!"

"No. Tell me. What do you think it means?"

"Okay, gentlemen. Let me show you where you'll be bunking and introduce you to the others." Instructor Jones interceded.

"How did the commandant receive that scar to his cheek?" I asked.

"No one around here really knows. There are a whole shitload of theories, though. I personally think it happened in Nam during the Phoenix project."

"Really!" I pretended to be impressed. Leaning in toward Box, I whispered. "I think it's where the coat hanger nearly snagged him."

"What's that?" Jones asked with a bewildered smile on his face.

Box interrupted quickly.

"He was just saying how they probably tried to coat-hang...him." His voice diminished as he floundered for a plausible answer that sounded a lot like my coathanger crack. He was pathetic. "You know. In Vietnam. Nam! When they would hang people by their coats to publicly humiliate them. He was just saying about that."

"And you found that funny?" Jones probed.

"Yeah, Box. What's funny about a man being tortured for his country." I stirred the proverbial pot. Box just grunted in frustration.

Forty of us slept in a barracks built for twenty. Everyone who would eventually become *Pseudo Miranda* team members were present but, for now, they were just anonymous faces in a crowd. Except for Box of course. He bunked in the cot next to me. The clothing we traveled with was replaced with military drab, provided by our gracious host. Toiletries were the only items we were allowed to keep. Personal belongings and identification were all collected by the trainers. Jones left and after telling us to anticipate a 5:00 AM wake up call. That was in three hours. Everyone

else was already asleep, so introductions would have
to wait.

❖   ❖   ❖

I expected a rude awakening, something to do with
noise and cold water. What I got was a friendly "Okay,
ladies and gentlemen. Time to get up."

"Ladies!" I thought aloud. "Holy shit! Hey, Box
man. Check out the ladies."

"Yeah. I've seen women before. You mean to tell me
you didn't smell the perfume last night?"

"Not over that shit you're wearing." I said as I
signaled to the instructor who awakened us. "Instructor..?"

"White. That should be easy for you to remember,
huh?" Sarcastically referring to his African American
ethnicity.

"Yes. Instructor White. The men's shower?"

"It's in the same place as the women's. Next building over. Five stalls."

"Thank you, Instructor White!" As he left, I said in
a voice loud enough for all to hear. "White. I'll bet his
middle name is Ain't." Everyone chuckled.

Instructor White stood about 5' 11" tall with rounded
posture. Too much neck and shoulder development
folded his shoulders about his chest. His forearms and
calves showed neglect, a sign of vanity. He had apparently developed only those muscles that conveyed the
essence of strength, but not those muscles that had
practical application. With a freckled face and dimples,
White seemed almost cartoon-like.

The showering situation wasn't a problem. Obstructions between each stall provided sufficient privacy.

Everyone was anxious about what the training
would encompass. Would it be predominately classroom instruction or would they concentrate on condi-
tioning? And how about weapons training and defense techniques?

I met my first training mate on the way to roll call. He introduced himself as Joe, and attempted to give me advice on everything from handling people to hand-to-hand combat. I shared little more than my name when we were instructed to form up in military fashion outside the barracks.

As we gathered, the Commandant addressed us on what to expect over the indefinite course of our training.

"Everything that happens here is real!" He paused, as if about to render a lengthy speech, and then retreated back to his office.

"That's it!" I thought.

A stocky man of Spanish descent stepped forward and introduced himself as Mr. Smith. His sleeves were rolled beyond the forearm, displaying a string of tattoos that flowed into his fatigues. A wide mustache covered his upper lip, but stopped abruptly at the corner of his mouth. Hairs grew wildly out of his nose and ears, compounding his rogue image. He began to speak, calling out names of potential trainees.

"Charlene Gregory!"

"Yes sir. Here!" Charlene acknowledged.

"Charlene. You're cut from the program. Step out of formation please."

"What? Why? What'd I do?"

"Stop babbling and move your ass, damn it!" Smith said furiously.

"Mike Alvarez! Mike Alvarez! Is there a Mike Alvarez here? Speak up, damn it! We don't have all day."

"Here! I'm right here." Alvarez muttered.

"You're gone, asshole. Step out."

"Anthony VesBucchi! VesBucchi! Come on people! This isn't a name you'd forget. Anyone! If I don't get an Anthony VesBucchi real soon," he screamed, "everyone's gonna pay a dear price!" Box looked over at me. He agreed with my decision not to speak.

Neither of us knew what was going on, but we knew that to answer meant certain dismissal from training. I was anxiously waiting for some sort of explanation as to what was happening when Joe raised his hand.

"Yes sir? Do you know our VesBucchi?" Smith reacted.

"Well. I'm not sure exactly. I do know a guy named Anthony. I met him a few minutes ago."

"Point his deaf ass out to me." Smith said angrily.

"Right there. He's right there, sir."

He pointed to me. Smith walked over to where I was standing and faced me off. He spoke softly:

"Are you Anthony?"

"Yes, sir."

"You're dismissed." He said routinely.

"Not Anthony what's his face though!" I followed quickly.

"Anthony who then, might I ask?"

"Just Anthony."

Smith then motioned to Joe to join our conversation. Joe approached with artificial confidence, acting as if he knew something the rest of us didn't. Smith placed his arm around Joe and began to gently interrogate.

"Is this the guy you met ah …" Smith snapped his finger a couple times as if hunting for Joe's name.

"Joe, sir!" Joe asserted.

"Joe ah …"

"Joe Thompson. Joseph Thompson!"

"Joe. Joseph. You have a nice trip home. Now move your chump ass!"

Instructor Jones grabbed Joe by the fatigue collar and hauled him away. Smith retreated to the front of the formation and continued his psychological hazing.

"Okay, people. Just Anthony has decided your collective fate for the next 24 hours. While the staff and I are laying on our posturepedics, you'll be resting in one of these." Smith pointed to a single wooden box that stood 7 feet tall by 3 feet wide. "We'll provide as many

as necessary in just a few minutes. Now let me continue
this roll call. A simple answer to a simple question will
preclude you're having to endure this agony. So listen
up!" He called out the remaining names.

Only four people bowed out by responding to their
names.

"Everyone will be going to bed now except for
VesBucchi. Let me correct that. Except for *Just* Anthony."

While everyone looked on, Smith asked me another
simple question:

"Do you like walnuts, Anthony?"

"On brownies."

"You know. The Vietnamese love their walnuts.
Take your fuckin' shoes off, smart ass."

I shot back. "Bring your little pint size ass over here
and take 'em off for me."

With his 9mm automatic raised and pointed at my
head, he countered: "Keep three things in mind when
making your next decision. I work for the CIA. No one,
but no one, knows where the fuck you are at this
moment. And I would take exceedingly great pleasure
in shooting your hairy ass." Smith then fired a round
at my feet.

I took my shoes off.

White escorted me to the front of the group, cuffing
my hands to my back with a thick plastic tie. Jones
proceeded to pour hundreds of walnuts on the ground
before blindfolding me. Smith called out for my apol-
ogy in exchange for not having to endure this torture.
I vacillated for a short period, concluding finally that
I had to resist. I wished I hadn't insulted Smith, but I
realized that there was no turning back. To acquiesce
now would only demonstrate that I could be manipu-
lated with threats of violence. I couldn't let that happen.

Before I was led barefoot over the nuts, Box cried
out in support with tension breaking humor.

"Attica! Attica! Attica!" Everyone soon chimed in.

White struck a baton blow to the back of my knees without warning. Crashing face first into the walnuts, I came to the frightening conclusion that torture was more art than science. I attempted to regain my feet, but discovered that there was no position among the walnuts that wasn't excruciatingly painful. The genius behind this torment is that the tormented inflicts more pain upon himself with every attempt to relieve pain from another part of his body. When my back would become overwhelmed with pain, I would roll to my stomach in an effort to regain my feet, shocking my knees in the process. My feet would soon become agonized, forcing me to fall backwards into my inanimate tormentors.

The chants of support diminished as reality set in. No one wanted to follow in my foot steps. I heard murmuring from the audience as I grunted in distress. The nuts sent daggers of pain up through the arches of my feet to the rest of my sensory system. Smith asked coldly:

"What is it that you know about us?"

"What!" I screamed out in dismay.

White struck another blow to the back of the legs, crashing me back unto the walnuts.

"What have you learned!"

"I've learned that you're all lifetime members of the Ferrari Club!"

"Come again?" Smith seemed confused.

"If you own a Ferrari, you don't need a big dick," I said while wincing in pain.

"Lift him." Smith demanded.

White and Jones lifted me by my arms, and tossed me back down onto the nuts.

"You're CIA. Ah. Ah. Oh shit! I don't know! What the fuck do you wanta know! Animal, vegetable, mineral! Shit. Give me a damn clue!"

"Anything you know to be true about us." Smith said calmly.

I tried to replay all that had happened over the last 18 hours. Nothing seemed juxtaposed.

"What doesn't fit?" I thought. The pain my body was enduring seemed remote as my mind raced. Then, as I felt a pair of hands grip my shoulder blades, it struck me.

"You're Vietnamese!" I rolled around on my back and laughed, because I didn't get a negative response. "That's it. You're the fucking Cong! I'm right. You do have small dicks."

❖ ❖ ❖

With everyone looking on, I was carried to the box and placed inside. The cuffs and blindfold were removed, providing me with a claustrophobic view of my coffin-like bedroom. The first thing I noticed was that I was unable to fully squat. My six foot stature and bad left knee restricted my mobility, and would eventually cause me great pain. Slits in the wood provided adequate oxygen, which, during the cooler evenings, was not such a benefit.

I soon realized that the others had also been placed in boxes around me. For a moment, my mind was snatched away from my own tribulation by their screams for exoneration. I felt no empathy for their pleas. Begging for commutation only served to validate their methods and exacerbate the situation.

After a while, my legs and back collapsed under the strain, as I folded into a ball at the base of the box. I could feel the grinding in my calcified knee, a joint that had deteriorated since high school when it had been irreparably damaged during a football game. I knew that I would not be able to endure the pain for long, so I decided to trade off positions periodically. I could stand, but squatting was an impossibility. I simply couldn't deliberately bend my leg beyond the threshold of pain.

Through a narrow crack in my casket, I witnessed

the parade of rejects who attempted to negotiate their way out of the box. Instead, they negotiated their way onto the next flight home. There were now twenty-four candidates left.

As we moved into the evening, panic subsided. Those who remained understood the sacrifice that needed to be made. We were given water intermittently, enough only to prevent dehydration. The sweat off our bodies by day turned to chill in the cool night air. Pain and discomfort gave way to fatigue as we tried to sleep.

When morning came, I awoke to the faint moans of stiffened bodies attempting to regain their natural form. Only now could I appreciate the full extent of the abuse from the day before. Oddly enough, yesterdays wounds served to distract me from the aches I should have felt from my cramped sleep. I wondered how Box was holding up. I worried because he was too old for this physical abuse. He was in his mid-thirties. For a twenty-two year old like myself, that seemed ancient. I wanted to call to him, but I couldn't risk our adversaries knowing his name. Finally, it occurred to me that he may have forgotten that he could safely call me Just Anthony. I addressed him innocuously, hoping that he would immediately recognize my Massachusetts accent. "Hey Holme! It's Just Anthony! Are you all right, bubba?"

"Yeah. I'm okay. How 'bout yourself? You must be dying from that heinous shit yesterday."

"Look. We probably can't talk long. From now on, everyone will refer to you as Number One. When we all get out, we'll assign everyone a number. I'll have to go by Just Anthony, I guess. Do you copy?"

"Roger that." Box whispered hastily.

"There'll be no talking!" Smith hollered as he pelted his baton against the side of our coffins.

"Screw you!" Box began. "Three hours sleep! Standing all night in a box. Freezin' my black ass. Come down here and tell me to shut up. You candy ass, can't get a real job, Ferrari driving, nut sucking, motha fucka! Rap your stick against my bed? Shit."

"Number one. Chill out, Holme. Shit ain't worth it man." I advised.

"Shit." Box said nervously.

"What? What's goin' on? What's happening?" I anxiously pressed.

"I don't know! But I hear 'em behind me!" Box began to panic. "Damn!"

"What's happening!" I demanded.

"It's cool! They just doused me with H-Two-Oh! It'll dry. I'm okay!"

"Water? Oh shit." I said quietly.

"What's that?" Box asked with uneasy anticipation. "Ahhhh! Ahhhh! Shit! Ahh, shit!" Box screeched in pain. "They shocked me. Holly shit! The sons of bitches fried my ass!"

"Are you okay bubba?"

"Shit! Thank God my hair's naturally curly." Box said flippantly.

"Quiet!" Smith interrupted.

Box and I heeded the warning. But, at the opposite end of the line of caskets, I could hear the dampened cries of an angered women. She insisted upon "The immediate release of all prisoners." Although I absolutely agreed with her demand, I couldn't help but feel she took this prisoner of war thing much too serious. Soon there were a number of voices mingled in discussion. Unaware of the precise words spoken, I knew they were deciding her fate. The cracks in our collective boxes allowed for an unobstructed view of her humiliation as an ominous calm fell over the crater, broken only by her frightened screams as she was stripped of her clothes by three men. I couldn't watch beyond the initial tearing. I repeated endlessly the words "God, no" to myself, as my head hung on the ventilation cracks. They quickly tossed her back into the box without sexual intrusion. I sensed that they were looking for a reason to assault a woman. This brutality conveyed that there were no boundaries outside which they wouldn't cross.

Several hours later we were released into the late afternoon heat. The naked woman was not given any covering as she stood sobbing at the end of the line. No one dared assist her, worrying that it would only provoke our adversaries to further action. There seemed to be a collective conscience among us not to look at her.

Smith, now flanked by several armed guards dressed in North Vietnamese clothing, ordered us to surrender our true identities to him. He insisted that our treatment would only worsen if we resisted.

Five more trainees, all women, departed. No one felt surprise or condemnation for their decisions. To our astonishment however, the woman who was assaulted was not among them. Instructor White handed her some new fatigues, with instructions to re-enter the box to dress. Her name was Christina Dawn Wells.

Nicknamed Seedy for her first two initials, she was a walking dichotomy. She had an innate wholesomeness that veiled the hard knocks of life. Her Californian hair, soft and naturally blond, flowed thick and evenly across her face, shadowing her drawn and darkened eye sockets. She was older than she looked, but the years were softened by a plump face that featured high cheek bones and puffy lips. She stood 5' 10" tall, with visible definition in her stomach and legs. Her arms were remarkably thin and feminine, her figure fit by manner of work not exercise. Her violet eyes were her greatest asset.

"Come on people. I know you must realize the hopelessness of your situation. If you don't bug out now…" Smith said in a fading voice. "How 'bout you, Spic?" He taunted Jesus Rivas. "Shouldn't you be home in the Barrio, cruising in your purple raked

Cadillac with the furry dice, curb feelers, and leopard skin seat covers? Huh! Beaner!"

Rivas stared back in disbelief. He then countered by pointing to his own chest and, in a befuddled manner, stating, "I'm Lebanese."

"Good. 'Cause I hate the dune-coon, camel-jockey, rag-headed, mother-fuckers more than I do the Spics! Comprende?" Smith retaliated. He withdrew and regained his composure. Now strolling casually down the line, he randomly assaulted trainees with club jabs to the abdomen and swipes to the chest. He laughed, sinisterly, as he returned to the front of the formation.

"People! People! Is this shit really worth it? Huh?" Smith bent at the waist and swirled his trunk in a circular direction as he spoke. "One last time before I torture the ever livin' shit outta ya. Who wants to give me their name? I'll give you ten minutes to mull over it. After that... I'm gonna hurt ya. I'm gonna hurt ya real bad."

"So. What do ya think Number One?" I asked Box as I knelt to tie my boot.

"Fuck that shit man! My name's Box. Damn!" Box knelt along side me and grabbed a stone. As he was about to give it a toss, he continued: "Damn it! I'm a training agent. I don't make a good prisoner of war." He then proceeded to heave the stone, accidentally shattering the Commandant's window. "Tell me that didn't happen." Box said in disbelief. "I'm a dead man. You're looking at a dead man. I'm dead. That's all there is to it."

Smith returned abruptly. With baton in hand, he scampered down the Commandant's stairs. As he once again moved briskly down the line, he poked us gently in the chest and spoke in cadence. "So-do-we-have-a-prankster-among-us? Huh? Do-we? Do-we? Huh? Huh? Huh? Well, people! Well, people!" Smith then calmed and repositioned himself to the front of the formation. "You people don't seem to be getting the message." Smith suddenly became animated. Using a full range of physical gestures, he continued: "This is a prisoner of war camp! You're in Viet-Fuckin'-Nam! You're all gonna talk! It's only a question of when. So. To hasten the process… You know. Because we're pretty busy fellas. We're gonna kill one of you. So! Before we get this little formality out of the way. Do we have any more names?"

"Don't! He's bluffing! They'd never go that far!" Debara (pronounced De-Bear-a) Allen cried out.

Debara was a strikingly beautiful women. Standing almost 5' 8" tall, she commanded attention. She owned thick milky brown hair that ran rich and straight. Debara's emerald green eyes drew you in past her chiseled face and brush stroked brows. She was without question the most attractive woman I'd ever laid eyes on.

"And you would be?" Smith inquired softly.

When Debara refused to respond, Smith continued: "Jane Fonda. Oh. That makes it all complete. Okay, Jane. You decide who we should not kill next." A desperate pause ensued. "This bitch!" Smith grabbed a woman by the hair as she pleaded for her life.

"My name is Fawn Sanders!" The women shouted in hopes of being spared certain death.

"Sorry bitch. Jane says there's no mistreatment of prisoners at this camp." Smith yanked Fawn to the front of the formation and stepped a few paces back from her. He pointed his 9mm automatic at her chest as she begged for her life. He then fired two shots. Fawn hurled backwards, blood spewing from her chest. "Now. Who would like to give me their name?"

I stared transfixed at the limp, bleeding body. Her saliva mingled with dirt and blood and collected on her chin. Her limbs twisted in a lifeless manner. There is something about a dead body that leaves you feeling cold and empty. Something that can't be reproduced or faked. I suppose it's the lack of a soul. Whatever it is, this body didn't have it. I felt life.

At that moment, it also occurred to me that dead people lose an element of self-control—their bowels. I drew a deep breath, and thought with a smile. "Yup! Her's are intact."

I would simply tell everyone that it was all fake. "But what if I'm wrong? And if I'm right, do I really want this many gullible people working with me?" I thought.

"Shoot me next butt head!" I hollered instinctively. My attention abruptly drawn from the pool of blood to Mr. Smith.

"How 'bout I blow apart your fat friend here." Smith said with a smirk. He took Box by the back of the head and placed his gun to Boxer's throat. "Blow his brains — what little he has —all over the…"

"Fat! Little brain! Go ahead, asshole! Shoot!" Box retaliated with confidence.

"Ahhh, Box. I don't think that's such a good idea." I hemmed, pointing to Smith's gun.

"What do ya mean! What? What was all that `shoot me' bullshit? What have ya gotten me into now?"

"No! There're blanks in the gun, that's for damn sure. They're blanks all right. But a blank will blow ya apart at that range. Back up! Then yell at 'em!" I signified with clenched fist.

"Ohhh, right," Box said, then snapped back and clocked Smith with an overhand right, sending him unconscious to the desert mat.

"Now go wake that bitch up!" Box added, motioning to Fawn who was still sprawled out on the ground.

Rivas shook the woman violently and turned quickly toward Box with a look of horror in his face.

"She's dead! Oh my God, Number One. She's really dead."

"What!" Box responded.

"Oh, shit." I followed.

Everyone gasped.

"Just kidding," Rivas shouted joyfully. "She's a fake!"

The Commandant reentered the picture. He walked to the base of the staircase and informed us that the prisoner of war portion of the curriculum was over. He confirmed this in our collective skeptical minds by calling out our names in the order in which we stood, acknowledging us each with a nod of his head. "I count eighteen," he announced. "That's good. Better than I expected. My boys are slipping. We'll now begin the main training portion of our program. You won't see any more of Smith. I'm certain that'll break all your hearts. But, before we go any further, let's fill those guts of yours. Chow time! Oh! One more thing. Congratulations — so far."

The training became much more conventional and structured. We met our newest trainer as we re-assembled in front of the barracks. His name was in keeping with the originality of the others. Instructor Black was the quintessential athlete. A formidable figure at 6' 4" tall and 210 pounds, he was rippled in muscle.

At first, he seemed quite reasonable. His job was to dispense pain in an effort to teach us a crash course in self defense. As with all the training we would receive, I couldn't imagine its applicability. Nonetheless, I did what was asked.

After Black conducted a few demonstrations using a long, hollow, wooden pole; he proceeded to batter a few trainees into submission — not the least of which was myself. We trained with him off and on over the next few weeks. He would knock us around and then indulge himself in a dissertation about how pathetic we were, and how "The Enemy" wouldn't show us any such mercy. Through all this, I noticed a conspicuous few whom he never chose to do battle with. Namely, Briant Boxer, Rick Chavez, and Jerimiah

Robinson. Their common denominator? Brute strength.

Rick Chavez was a tall Native American with appropriate features. His skin was lightened somewhat by the inescapable reality of the melting pot. He wore his long hair, which was black and silky, in a pony tail. Rick possessed legs that were proportionately larger than his upper body, and his feet were big. His razor sharp facial contours hearkened to an era he would never let us forget. Rick laid no false claim to his heritage, though. He never proclaimed an insight that we lacked, or a way of life that we needed. Chavez lived very much in the present, offering mere historical perspective to his indigenous past. His subtle melding of then and now was played out in his favorite song, *Cheyenne Anthem*, by the rock-'n'-roll group *Kansas*.

Jerimiah Robinson was an impregnable figure, and arguably the most physically capable of all the trainees. He was a dark black, tall, with elongated muscles. He wore his hair in a flat top. Like Chavez, Jerimiah was sculpted from head to toe. Unlike Chavez, he would remind you of his alleged ancestry whenever it suited him. Although his lineage brought him by way of Europe, he asserted that all African Americans had a claim to slavery. As intelligent as he was powerful, it amazed me that he never let the facts get in the way of any discussion dealing with this one subject. Notwithstanding, he was at the center, a very descent and caring individual.

Our training from this point was handled by Instructors White, Jones, and Black. Jones conducted weapons training, and White rendered classroom instruction on logistics, while providing field training on precision drug interdiction and deadly confrontation.

The weapons training ranged from hand guns to assault rifles and included the use of explosives, such as C-4 and grenades. Our resident expert on the use of explosives was little Joey Bali. On our first day of live fire, we handled a wide range of assault and hunting weapons. I preferred the 30/06 (spoken 30 odd 6) and 45mm automatic to all other weapons, which included the M-16, MAC 10, Uzi, and AK-47, to name a few. Once we found weapons that suited us, we began to train for proficiency. When the final scores were tallied, it was apparent that Joey was the crowned king of marksmanship. Lourdes (this was her complete name) remained only a breadth behind, qualifying as an expert in all weapons except hand guns.

When we were instructed on the technical nature of *Pseudo Miranda*, I was awed by its logistical complexity. A cache of prolific drug lords would be given the means by which to destroy the numerically larger amount of smaller drug traffickers. Means, in this instance, is best described as intelligence on the exact locations of competing cocaine laboratories, and weapons to destroy these labs and any resistance found therein. This was designed to centralize the Colombian drug trafficking operation and bring about more control. The Peruvians and Bolivians would be offered a fail-safe way of remaining lucrative partners in the drug trade. This would not, however, include affiliates of the Shining Path. Peru and Bolivia would become the primary distributors of cocaine paste to Colombia, and were essentially out of the American distribution network.

Cuba was also neutralized by one Carlos Lehder. From Norman's Cay, Lehder's personal Bahaman Island, he facilitated the distribution of Cuban cocaine to America. This cocaine originated in Colombia, and was already accounted for in the 48 percent authorized into the country via operation *Pseudo Miranda*. Therefore, eliminating any additional cocaine that Cuba would have shipped to America outside the parameters of this operation.

Pseudo Miranda aircraft, originating from Colombia, and carrying large quantities of cocaine, would lock onto CIA Long Range Navigation (LORAN) radar. Flying at low level, they could evade US Customs and Defense radar detection systems. This became known as operation *Light House*. When this was not feasible, a shadow aircraft, typically US Air Force with a scheduled flight plan, was used to conceal the radar signature of a drug aircraft flying in close proximity. This compartment of Pseudo Miranda was termed Olympic Victor for the OV-10 reconnaissance aircraft. Once over American soil, they would be intercepted by CIA aircraft and led over Inertial (Instrument) Landing Systems (ILS) radar. Positive identification was established with Identify Friend or Foe (IFF) transponders, that were installed on both trafficker and CIA aircraft. The CIA chase aircraft, having taken the helm, would lead the drug aircraft over a drop zone. The drug plane would then track on the ILS radar beam, typically associated with landing, and release his cargo to agents on the ground. We were those agents.

Once we gathered up the cargo, we would transport it to a pre-designated area and fly it to Mena, Arkansas. Immediately after our departure, a special team would arrive at the drop zone and hastily tear down the ILS radar system. The cocaine would eventually arrive at its final destination in Tonopah, Nevada, where it would be stored securely, several stories below the ground.

This was a brief overview of the operation that would become Pseudo Miranda. Initially, however, we were oblivious to all this information. In fact, none of this would be conveyed to us until we were into our final days of training. There were tests yet to be passed.

Chapter 5

We'd been in training for a couple weeks and had become acclimated to the routine. The anticipated scratches and bruises — and the inevitable sleepless night — from Instructor Black's "Circle of Death" had become palatable for most of us.

"Hands up! Watch your adversaries eyes!" Black directed. "Why are you looking at my feet? Look at my eyes damn it! My eyes!"

Personally, I always watched his feet. He never once struck me with his eyes. Black was absorbed in the pretentious philosophy of Kung Fu and, for that matter, all forms of martial arts. Although I had no personal knowledge that he'd ever applied his craft practically, I lived with the reality that he could kick the crap out of me any time he pleased.

Black had just laid a side kick into Christina's trunk, collapsing her rib cage like so much silly putty. She buckled over in agony, as he struck her again unmercifully with a round house kick to the temple. Christina flew in the direction of her broken ribs, crashing to the earth.

Black knelt at her side and bellowed, "Ooow milly that felt good!"

"Lay off her! She's had enough." Box demanded.

"Why? Cause she's a woman? She'll let 'em know when she's had enough." Debara said defensively.

"She's gonna have a difficult time speaking with her skull fractured! Get off your damn Gloria Steinam kick, Jane! This is the real world. And this asshole doesn't give a hoot about equality." I said, livid and confrontational.

"And I don't need yours and Boxes macho bullshit!" Debara said, disgusted, as she leaned in toward the circle.

"Can you get up Seedy? Do you need help? Just say when you wanta quit, okay."

"Gee Jane. She doesn't seem too responsive." I said sarcastically.

"Call me Jane one more time and I'll see how responsive your nuts are to my boot."

"If you two love birds are through, I'm gonna finish what I've begun here." Black declared as he took a hop step toward Christina, who had gathered herself to her knees. He placed a fluid drop kick to her face. His shoe landed flush to the bridge of her nose, crushing it like an aluminum can. Everyone leaped to her aid, restraining Black from committing further damage.

An alarm sounded. It wailed loud and constant, trailing off suddenly before continuing another blast. The training ground became a melee. Armed agents scrambled in support of Instructor Black. Then, without prior conference, we formed a circle around Christina and affixed ourselves in a defensive stanch. Although we were mortally threatened by Instructor White to step away from Christina, we held firm in our common defense. We were protecting a fallen team member, but more importantly, we were standing together.

The Commandant interceded in the dispute. He ordered immediate medical attention for Christina. He then told everyone to disperse to their respective quarters.

Instructor Black couldn't resist one last attempt at demoralization as Christina left the field.

"Every time you look in the mirror, you'll be reminded of how you couldn't cut it."

"I don't recall her begging for mercy, asshole!" I retaliated.

"What did you call me, you little prick?" Black hollered combatively.

I knew he was bent on making me cower, so I sought to gain the psychological edge. I had a bad habit of initiating such things, so I could always see them coming before they arrived.

"Do you only beat up on women?" I replied. "No. Don't.. I think I know the answer to that question."

"You just wrote your epithet, buddy." Black asserted as he spread his arms for everyone to back off. The Commander withdrew to watch from his staircase. I interjected one last comment to insure Black understood the ground rules.

"If you start this. Realize it ain't over until someone begs for mercy."

Box took hold of my shoulders as he faced me. "This guy's psychotic. I can kick your ass, and this guy can kick mine. Use your fuckin' head. That's why you're here, damn it! Not because of your damn fighting skills. Now tell him you didn't mean it."

I stared coldly through Box, directly at my adversary, hardly noticing what he was saying. I walked through Boxer's grip and into the dreaded circle. Initially, I stood in an appropriate martial arts pose. Black fired off several misdirected kicks and punches before landing an effective kick to the back of my head. I collapsed after a few more assaults to the legs, chest, and head. Inexplicably, the pain momentarily subsided and my focus returned. I reeled to my feet and observed Instructor Black withdrawing from an aggressive stance. He was taken back by my lucidity. Without hesitance, I attacked with flailing appendages. He swung ineffectively at my ever changing target, as I tackled him around the waist. I knew that I would be victorious the moment I felt my shoulder make firm contact with his gut. I twisted and contorted my body in an effort to cast him to the ground in a swirl. Once on his back, I proceeded to articulate a barrage of punches to his side face and head. As he rolled toward me, I kept up the onslaught and placed several carefully plotted punches to his nose. Before I could extract a plea for mercy, however, the Commandant ordered us separated.

At best, it was a draw. But I'd made a promise. I'd

told Instructor Black that the fight would end only
when one of us pled for mercy. With my right arm
slung around Box as we walked toward the barracks,
I shuffled to a halt. Spinning reluctantly in the direction of Black, I reminded him of the ground rules.

"Hey Black! This ain't over! Don't fall asleep!" I
warned.

I knew that Black had to go through his daily ritual
of meetings and briefings, so I'd be able to grab a brief
rest. Christina was taken for medical attention somewhere within the San Dia confines. By the time I
awakened, She had returned, her nose now reset. The
physical pain was far less than her belief that she
somehow hadn't measured up. As my own cob webs
began to subside, I could make out the patronizing
words directed toward Christina. Words designed to
bolster Christina's failing morale. There words were
contrived, and Christina knew it. Realistically, she
understood that she would fail the program if she
couldn't excel in all major evaluations.

"Seedy. Don't get down on yourself." Lourdes began. "You'll practice. We'll help you."

"Yeah, Christina. We're here for ya." Chavez added.

"You're here for her? Where the hell were you
when she was getting her face mangled? Why weren't
you here for her then?" I got up from my cot and
walked to Christina. "She doesn't need you now! She
needed you out there! That's where we win and lose
this game! Out there! Not here! They don't give a crap
about our support for one another in here! It's out
there! They only care what we do when the chips are
down and there are no rules! You're here for her.
Right."

Chavez was steaming, but remained seated on an
overturned trash can at the foot of Christina's cot as I
continued.

"Face it Seedy. Your gone if you don't do well. All
the mincing we do with the facts won't change that

simple truth. You're not gonna beat that Nazi sonuvabitch. I don't care how long you train. Now what are we gonna do about it?

"Oh. But I suppose one of you big men will protect her." Quinn said acidly.

"Watch it Quinn. Or he'll be calling you Gloria Alred and blaming you for the disintegration of the American family" Jerimiah embellished.

"Who?" Everyone said in virtual unison.

"You're kidding me. Right?" Jerimiah responded in dismay.

"She must be a radical feminist," I surmised. "I'm surprised Debara doesn't know who she is." I shifted gears slightly. "Give it a rest, for pete's sake." I turned in the direction of the door and began to walk away with Box trailing after me.

"Where you goin', man?" Box asked

"What the hell's it all about then!" Debara barked.

I looked over my shoulder and said simply: "It's about giving your word." I walked out to the front of Instructor Black's personal quarters. He had just laid down for the evening when I rapped on his door.

"Sleep tight Adolph! I'll be waiting for your snore!"

He exited his quarters and ordered me back to the barracks.

"I'm sorry sir. But I can't accept that order until our verbal contract is resolved."

"What! You're whack-oh! Get your ass out of here or else."

"Or else what! Come on! You want some of this? I'm ready! Let's settle this now! Let's do it! Come on! Come on!" I yelped in a crazed manner. I really didn't want to fight, and I was betting that he didn't either.

"You're mental. That's it. You're...you're... You've lost your mind. Pack your bags, nut case. You're gone tomorrow." Black said bewilderedly.

"That's tomorrow. Tonight I'm gonna camp outside your door and wait for you to fall asleep. Sweet dreams."

"Suit yourself. But you better be ready tomorrow at oh-five-hundred."

I waited patiently by his door for the distinct sounds of slumber. As he dozed off, I banged on his door and awakened him. Black then stumbled to the door in a rage, hoping to find me standing there. I fled into the still, dark night with Black in irresolute pursuit. I was surprised to find that no one attempted to control my movement as I crouched behind some structural bracing.

Black cried out in frustration, "Damn it! Where are you! You pussy! Where the hell are you! Where the hell is security?"

This routine continued throughout the evening. Neither of us received any sleep, but it was easier on me because I'd stolen a little shut-eye earlier that day. The commitment to fulfill my promise and demonstrate my leadership provided me with the extra adrenaline I needed to stay one step ahead of him.

The following day, I found myself waiting outside the door to the Commandant's office while Instructor Black implored him to drop me from the program. The Commandant did not waver as he directed Black on the importance of integrity.

"Did he tell you yesterday if you fought him, it wasn't over until somebody officially surrendered?" The Commandant said sternly.

"No!" Black replied in a crackling voice.

"Integrity! I was there! He told you! And now he's sticking to his guns!" The Commandant paused, and continued in a lowered voice. "I like this. What do you suppose his goal is?"

"To beat me senseless! Look sir. I've got to get some sleep."

"Oh. You'll be fine. Who's the teacher here anyhow. No, I want to see where he's goin' with this. This could get real interesting. It's pretty obvious why Casey sent him here."

"With all due respect sir. This guy's certifiable. And I know where he's goin' with this. And to be perfectly honest, I don't find it all that interesting." Black wined.

"You brought this on. Now, let's see how it's gonna end. Go on. Get back to work. Send in VesBucchi."

"Hey! Amerigo VesPucci. Get your ass in there." Black said caustically.

"Don't sit. You won't be here that long." The Commandant began. "Run with this. Realize though, you'll attend all forms of training and any sub-par performance will not be tolerated. You have a special burden to succeed here. Now get out of my office."

That 'special burden to succeed' thing reared its ugly head once again. What the hell does that mean? I wondered. Over the next day and a half, I floundered wearily through training. Luckily, my teammates supported me in every manner possible. During a stationary target shooting test, Joey even fired a few rounds into my target. This detracted from his own results, while supplying me with a sufficient number of points to receive a passing grade.

Instructor Black and I had endured two consecutive sleepless nights. As evening set in on the third day, I initiated the same harassment I'd inflicted the two previous nights. This time however, I allowed him to drift into a deep sleep only a few hours before dawn.

I gently picked the unsophisticated lock to his door with a knife given me by our trainers. When I stood over Instructor Black, who by this time was basking in deep R.E.M. sleep, I struggled with the decision that confronted me. Should I beat him into submission and, in the process, make good on my word? Should I show compassion and, in doing so, demonstrate that I was above his level of morality, and remain true to my father's credo which, in part, forbade throwing the first punch. I vacillated with my decision for about ten seconds. Then, with a barrage of punches to his slumbering face, I proceeded to beat him to a pulp. He was unable to resist. He passed directly from sleeping to a comatose state. "Whenever you look in the mirror, you'll be reminded of how you couldn't cut it." I kept repeating.

After regaining my composure, I found myself staring at his mangled face for what seemed an eternity. The odd thing was, I was never unaware of the damage I was inflicting. I suppose that's what began to frighten me the most. Was I so absorbed in the end result that I'd neglected to consider the means by which to accomplish it? I felt for a pulse.

"My God." I said aloud. I had thought that I knew my limits. Only now did I realize that there were boundaries, outside which I would travel, given the right circumstances. There were now unfamiliar circumstances to consider, and they would get increasingly more trying.

Three hours after this unfortunate incident, Instructor Black was discovered semi-conscious in his blood drenched bed. He was immediately scurried to a hospital as I lay sleeping in my cot. I was the only one who missed his departure.

I woke to find that I was the only team member left in the barracks. I glanced outdoors and noticed that the sun had almost run its course. I frantically searched until I found a set of fatigues. Grunting in frustration, I clumsily attempted to draw them over the fatigues I still wore from the night before. With combat boots in hand, I flew into the early evening grey.

I was certain that I was now through in the program.

❖ ❖ ❖

I gave a shout as I was tackled from the rear and pressed to the ground.

"What the...! Quinn! What the hell are you doin'?"

"Shhhh! Shush. Everything's cool. You're not in any trouble. We're in the middle of..." Quinn quieted sharply. "Oh shit." She looked up. Her eyes telescoped from their ports. "Damn it! Not again."

Quinn had just been electronically wasted. She was in the midst of a game called Interdiction.

Interdiction was little more than the running of a gauntlet of CIA paramilitary agents firing amplitude module weapons. Everyone wore receivers on their chest and abdomen, and partial receivers on their head. This limited the kill zones to those areas, and disregarded wounds altogether. The mission was to get at least one person to the opposite end of the pit without being extinguished. Considering the area was usually saturated with agents, this task was monumental.

Many of the structures along the street had first floors, and therefore came complete with four fake walls, furniture, and a temporary ceiling as well. Consequently, we couldn't race down the backside of the building toward the opposite end without first climbing over the scaffolding, above the first floor, and precariously traverse our way along the connecting beams of each structure. The only major flaw to this plan was the guard posted at the base of the staircase, who was located right next to the only beams leading to the top of the scaffolding on either side of the street. Eliminate the guard, I thought, and we could perch two people above the arena. This would give us a clear firing zone and enable us to triangulate any target drawn out into the open. Of course, there was now the matter of getting the enemy out in the open.

"Sorry Quinn." I said, feeling a bit stupid.

"Ahh, it's all right. They'd of won anyhow. I just hate the humiliation of the Dead Room. Downtrodden, Quinn meandered to the Dead Room, which was the name given to the place where anyone killed, from

either side, went when eliminated from play. The
dead would watch the game being played out on
several 27" screens. It was always the same, we would
watch solemnly as our comrades were obliterated,
and listen to the taunts and jeers of our battle tested
opponents.

On this day, following play, we were allowed to
accomplish our five mile jog (countless laps around
the street) and then turn in a few hours early. We
dedicated this free time to getting to know one another, as much as was allowable, and brainstorming
on ways of beating our adversary at Interdiction. I
remained on the sidelines and just enjoyed the discussion until it eventually came around to the subject of
developing strategy for Interdiction. Many ideas were
brought to the fore and later dropped. I listened in-
tensely, considering the pros and cons of each, never
adding my opinion. It became apparent that none of
us had any practical experience in military strategy.
Soon, squabbles broke out concerning who was most
qualified to lead the group. Eventually, I got pulled
into the discussion along with the rest.

"Ole pretty-boy, frat-brat over there could give us
pointers on battle field tactics. Maybe if we were
gonna drink 'em to death or somethin'. But not strategy. Please!" Jerimiah overindulged himself.

"He's Italian. He's gotta have more to offer than
you guys. So shut the fuck up an let 'em' talk." Joey
said with exaggerated hand motion.

"Was that racist you little guinea prick? I'll fuck
your gay ass up. Little guinea motha' fucka'." Jerimiah
responded. He attempted to pull Box into his enthusiasm with a combination of 'high and low-five's,' but
Box remained perfectly still.

"Yeah. Let 'em speak. And before you reign in with
any Hispanic jokes... I'll slit your African-American
throat in your sleep." Rivas stated cordially.

"Well?" Debara prompted, looking at me.

"Told ya he's full of shit." Jerimiah contended.

"He may be full of shit…" Box began. "But this entire operation was his, and only his, idea."

"Good goin', ace." I said in disbelief.

"Your idea. Give me a break. No friggin' way. Your idea? Is that true? Tell me that ain't true." Debara babbled.

"It's true." I answered.

"So? What exactly have we gotten ourselves into?" Joey spoke gingerly.

"We can't say." Box rifled a response, preempting my own.

"Well? Do you know anything that'll help us get through this war stuff?" asked Debara.

"As a matter a fact…" I got up from my cot and signaled for everyone to gather around. "The way I see it, we need to get two people up on the eye beams that run across the top of all the buildings, parallel to the street. Then…"

"Who?" Box inquired.

"Who, what?" I answered.

"Who up top?"

"It doesn't matter." I shrugged, agitated with his interruption. "Me and you. Anyhow. Where was I? Oh yeah…"

"Bullshit." Box said in monotone.

"You'll be fine. Trust me."

"Nope. Pick someone else." Box remained calm but determined. I took him aside.

"What are you doin'? I'm trying to sell this over here and you're making me pick up the prison soap."

"I'm not going up there with you. Pick someone else. That's all I'm saying on the subject. Pick someone else. How 'bout your buddy Jerimiah. You should get a big kick outa' seeing him break his stinkin' neck."

We returned to the group as I continued to lay out my plan. "Me and Box will situate ourselves on the roof. Four people. Debara, Christina, Joey and Jesus will make their way halfway down the street and form a circle. They never begin shooting until at least that point, because it's the point of no return."

"So we're decoys." Debara interjected, disappointed.

"Sort of."

"Why us? Why not you and Box?" She persisted.

"Because you're good marksmen and tough targets to hit. Small stature and all. Oh. Excuse me. Markspersons. But don't worry, because I've got a few ideas about delaying your inevitable deaths."

"I'm sure we're all comforted by that thought. But who's gonna run the gauntlet?" Debara questioned.

"The cheetah. Lourdes, of course."

"Wooo!" Lourdes shouted with jubilation. She began prancing up and down the room, assuming the runner's start position and simulating a sprint in super slow motion while humming the theme to Chariots of Fire.

Joey asked, "So what's to prevent the four of us from being instantly dissolved?"

"This." I replied, and then fell to the ground, laying on my back. Folding my legs in a Yoga-like position, I crossed my calves and laid my hands, as if gripping a gun, between my legs, atop my ankles. In this fashion, I could fire my radio-wave weapon while simultaneously protecting my kill zones.

"What's to stop them from shooting your legs and ass?" Jerimiah asked.

"Nothing. There aren't any receivers there, so don't worry."

"But if these were real guns..." Jerimiah started.

"But they're not, and that's all we need be concerned with. Don't you see? This is about winning, plain and simple. This isn't the real world. This is our only world. Let's adapt to it and win. Now. A couple things I've noticed everyone doing wrong. When a target is fleeing you, don't trail it with your fire. Shoot in advance of them and run your fire backwards. When shooting around a corner, don't expose your kill zone by using the incorrect hand. Around right corners, use your left hand. Around left corners, use your right hand. When in motion, bank on your opponent missing with his first round. Wait out his first shot as he changes direction, and steady your weapon before firing. Now. We're gonna need to take a few pre-preemptive measures. Lourdes. Tomorrow, during live fire, I want you to liberate a hand gun. I don't care what kind."

"Why..." Lourdes attempted to interject.

"Because you're the last one they'd expect." I fired off rapidly. "We'll also need some mirrors. Descent size ones."

"Mirrors?" Joey questioned, brushing back his hair with his fingers.

"Later. Just get 'em."

"Consider it done," Rivas insisted.

"Why weren't we privy to this brilliant shit before, when we needed it?" Jerimiah qualified his statement. "Not that it necessarily helps us now, mind you. But why now?"

"The way I figure it." I stopped and noticed I had a captive audience. "Whenever we beat them, or perform a task at the highest standard, we're through with it. I gotta figure it all culminates with Interdiction. If we try something new and it fails, we won't get a second chance with it. They'll be even more prepared — if that's possible — the next time. So I wanted enough time to analyze what all it was that we were doing wrong. More than that. If we hit 'em all at once with a synchronized plan, they won't know what hit 'em. There not expecting any metamorphic changes. That's why I didn't want any piece-meal adaptations. All at once. One chance. That's all we'll get, before they bring the next candidates in."

"You know this?" Lourdes wore a look of sadness.

"I don't wanta go back to where I was. I belong here, damn it. I can do this. One chance is all we'll need. I'll be ready. I'll get to the end. Just make me a path. That's all I ask."

"No. I don't know that for sure. But I sure liked your speech. Anyhow. Lourdes. You'll secure us a gun tomorrow. Without that... I'm afraid everything else is moot."

❖ ❖ ❖

The following day, Lourdes' overt nervousness drew unwanted attention. She placed far too much pressure on herself. Her strength was that she desperately wanted this job. Her weakness however, was that she desperately needed this job. Everyone deliberately avoided her on the range in an effort to defray attention from her unusual behavior. The result, of course, was that it drew critical observation her way. All the weapons were laid in shadow cases that were essentially imprints of each particular weapon. To steal one meant taking a weapon from an unused case so as not to draw attention to an open shadow case that featured an empty space. Only weapons that were fired or seen removed from their cases were inventoried on the spot. A complete inventory was only conducted prior to each live fire exercise. This would buy us enough time to use the weapon during the Interdiction exercise before it would be discovered missing. At least that was the plan.

"Freeze! Take one more step and I'll blow your fuckin' head off!" Hollered one of the security men. He placed a 12-gauge shot gun to the base of Lourdes' head.

"Instructor Jones sir?"

"Whata' ya got here." Jones responded as he approached calmly.

"She's stolen a weapon, sir!"

"She has. Tisk. Tisk. Shame on you." Jones reached

around the front of Lourdes, inserting his hand into her trousers, and removed a 22-caliber automatic pistol. Jones stared closely at the gun and said. "Hey, everybody! I've resolved the dispute! She's a natural blond!" He leaned in and said gently in her ear. "Now what in the world were you intending to do with this?" Stepping back, he said, in raised tone: "Take her away for questioning."

"Well. I guess your plan's mute." Jerimiah commented.

"You got it?" I asked softly.

"Ah huh." Steven Hall answered.

"Good. We're in business."

Steven was our resident communications expert. In his middle thirties, he was balding and overweight. He wore glasses and, almost always, a fishing hat. He had a knowledge of the direction of certain satellites but, ironically, no sense of direction otherwise. A male chauvinist, he commanded attention when he spoke. He had a good sense of humor, but used it sparingly.

As we walked back to our quarters, unescorted, the questions flurried.

"She was a decoy?" Debara talked in a concerned manner. "Did she know she was a decoy?"

"Before you go off the deep end..." I walked to the front of the group. Now directly in front of our billet, I held my hands out, palms facing forward, and hastily explained.

"I knew she'd be a wreck, so I used it to our advantage. But I also knew that she'd be the last to crack under pressure, because it means so damn much to her. Anyhow, we got the damn gun. That's what's most important here."

"You used her," Jerimiah said judgmentally. "How 'bout her? Did ya ever consider her?"

"She is us! And we're her! And if you don't see it that way then maybe you're not us. You think I liked making this decision? Why don't you try taking some risks for once. You think it's easy deciding people's fate. Well, I'm here to tell ya it ain't. It sucks! But someone better damn well do it! Sacrifices have to be made, buddy, and someone has to decide where and when! You're welcome to the position. Because I sure as hell don't want it. When she returns, I'll suffer any consequence she deems fair. So take your holier-than-thou attitude to the N double A C.P. because I personally don't give a flying fuck what's fair! I'm here to win. And anyone that isn't, can join another game. Our country isn't paying us to lose."

"Win at all cost, right?" Jerimiah persisted.

"No. No, but I'll spend every last dime to stop from losing. Then, if I still lose, I can live with myself. My father taught me that. Winning at all cost — no. But don't concede until you're spent."

I reached into my pocket. "It appears I've got a couple nickels left yet to spend. Are you in or out. That's all I'm asking."

We entered the barracks and gathered around Steven to see what he swiped. "

So what'd ya snag? And please tell me it isn't a pea shooter like Lourdes grabbed. Well?" I queried.

Steven acted coy and unsure. "Well. You said just grab a gun. Any gun. That's whatcha said. So I grabbed one that looked cool."

"What do you mean by cool exactly?" I became uneasy. "My only instructions were to grab a gun that was small and coated in bluing for concealment purposes. How in tarnation could you screw up those directions?"

"It was that bluing part that confused me."

My head bent to my hand, as I rubbed my forehead in frustration.

"Just show us what you've got. Lord. please don't make this a flare gun."

Steven reached far down into his pants and removed a nickel plated 357 Magnum revolver.

Rivas was especially impressed. "You ever been to Miami? Let's start planning our vacations together my friend."

"She's beautiful." Joey admired, pretending to cry joyfully.

"I did good?" Steven asked knowingly.

"You did real good. Real good." Box bolstered Steven's confidence. "Okay boys and girls. Let's get some rest. Tomorrow's `D-Day'."

We began the day with a little morning jog. Lourdes was back with us. She had a split lip and a blackened eye, but they in no manner deterred her. She was a resilient girl. As we passed by the structures at the far end of the pit, we surreptitiously placed mirrors at key locations. Beneath the clothing of a select few, we strategically fastened smaller mirrors to the chest. This was done to only to a few, because I knew that they would be immediately disqualified once the infraction was detected by the observers who watched on closed circuit television from outside the compound. I decided that these people would travel along the perimeter of the street and strafe the buildings as they went along in an attempt to terminate as many enemy as possible. The mirrors would refract any signal sent in their direction and, in doing so, cause the signal to be absorbed by the assailants receiver. Once turned off, units could not be turned back on without a key. The key was controlled by the Commandant outside the compound. If we were able to traverse the gauntlet prior to that, we would win.

"It's time, Box." I said, my heart racing. "They'll be calling us to the staging area in ten minutes. Remember. Don't wait for us. Scurry along and conceal our absence."

I sighed tensely. "I appreciate all the cooperation, guys. Good luck."

Box and I meandered to the side of the compound opposite the end we would attempt to gain. The guard

had grown accustom to us doing this. I'd been dragging Box to this end of the compound every morning
for weeks, under the guise that I needed privacy when
conferring with him. This is why I needed his assistance in this particular endeavor and no one else. The
guard was relaxed and nonchalant — just as I'd expected.

We neared the post and I mumbled to Box, "Get
ready with the gun."

"What gun? I thought you had the gun?"

"You better be kidding."

"You didn't think I had a sense of humor, did ya?
This thing sure is cold. My nuts are in my throat."

"I told you to put it behind you."

"You ever had a bazooka in your butt? Oh, wait.
You don't have a butt, do you? Sorry."

"You picked a peculiar time to become funny. Okay.
Let me distract 'em." We approached the staircase
where the guard stood. "Sergeant Walker! Shot anyone today?"

"No. But it's still early yet. Lot of daylight left."
Walker responded.

"There's always spotlighting." Box joined in, referring to the practice of placing a spotlight on the deer
and freezing him in his tracks.

"That would be illegal." Walker rebutted authori-
tatively.

"Yeah, Box." I said. Turning toward Walker, I added,
"You can free 'em, but you can't give 'em a sense of
humor." Walker busted out laughing and then began
to slap me in the chest like buddies often do. I signaled
Box with my eyes. He reached into his pants and
ripped out the 357 magnum. The hammer snagged his
shorts on the way out, exposing his heart laden
bloomers.

"Hey Buddy. Put your racist arms in the air." Box
demanded. The guard turned with dreaded anticipation. He immediately surrendered his weapon. His

fear turned instantly to laughter, when he noticed Boxer's shorts.

"Maybe there's hope for your sense of humor yet." I declared, grin still on my face.

"Get your hands up, too!" Box yelled without conviction. "What kinda crack was that?" He looked down at his shorts. "They're all I had left clean. They were for my birthday. My wife. You know. Damn. I didn't want to ruin 'em.

"So. You're married, huh?"

"I don't think we have time for this. The roof you know," Box reminded me.

"See ya in the victory circle, Holme."

We gagged the guard, cuffing him to the back of a building. I figured that even if he were discovered missing, we would already be on the roof and the game would be underway. I scaled the angled truss to the top and crawled, hands and knees, to the half way point of the street. I poked my head over the top to see if the game had yet begun. The four who would form the circle would go first, so I looked for them. Nothing yet. I searched for Boxer's head, but saw nothing. I didn't know it at the time, but he was unable to make the climb.

"Where the hell is he!" I whispered loudly, perturbed. I was ecstatic, however, to find that I could see at least five opponents clearly. I stole another peek. Christina, Jesus, Joey and Debara had formed a perfect circle and fallen to their posteriors. I got goose bumps. Silence hung over the arena. I knew that our opponents must have received a sinking feeling when they saw them perform this nonsensical act. I turned back to the rear of the building and fired several perfectly placed beams, sending five adversaries to the dead room. The Circle had yet to fire, as our Strafers blitzed the sides of the street. Screams of frustration resonated as a few more of our adversaries died, without being directly fired upon, and having

themselves fired directly at the chests of our runners
who veiled their mirrored apparel. One of those runners, Tina Parker, became cornered by the freshly
dead, and was physically assaulted when they discovered the hidden mirrors. I hadn't considered this possibility. Steven broke rank and started down the street
to assist her. He was immediately shot with a radio
wave. This mattered not to Steven, but weighed heavily
on the overall picture. I realized that this was a calculated move, designed as a fail-safe, under the remote
possibility that we would gain the upper hand.

The guard's M-16, I thought. That's it. Oh shit! I had
left it at the base of the beam. My mind went into
overdrive. Box had a gun. But if I called to him, I'll give
away my position. I could hear calls from the rest of
the team. They weren't going to be patient while I
considered our options.

"Box! Box!" I screamed, but couldn't be heard over
all the other yelling.

"Everyone shut up!" It became remarkably quiet.
"Only Box and me! Box!"

"Yeah!"

"The gun! You got it!"

"Roger that!"

All I could think was that I wished I was speaking
with Joey. "Joey." I said to myself. "Box!" I called out
once again.

"Yeah!" Box replied with impatience.

"Run it to Joey!" I redirected "Joey! Stay put! When
you get it, do your thing!"

"Fuckin' ay!" Joey responded with jubilation.

Box ran unobstructed to Joey, sliding head first into
the Circle. Joey took the 357, pointing it like an exten-
sion of his appendage. He fired. Deadly force was
avoided by mere inches. Tina's assailants fled in a
frenzy up the staircase. Steven, now disqualified along
with the runners, assisted Tina to safety.

"Okay! Nothing's changed! Continue the course!"

I shouted. Nothing seemed to be happening, however. They remained entrenched, waiting for us. I looked down and caught a glimpse of an aggressor. He was sheltered from view, satisfied that he could not be seen. He did not however, detect the crucial mirror located only thirty or so feet from him. I did, and could see him clearly in it. I fired several beams into the mirror as he came in and out of view. I nailed him. He became enraged, throwing what can only be described as a temper tantrum. His teammates now felt vulnerable, and began to act individually. A target rich environment suddenly appeared, and the Circle had a field day. Our battle-tried opponents were falling apart at the seams, and we were ready to rip them in half.

"Send Lourdes!" I hollered. Then, on the peripheral, I witnessed a very disconcerting image. Ten additional men entering the game from the floor of a building below me. "Wait! Don't send her! Has she gone?"

"No! Not yet!" Chavez called back. "Why! What's happenin'! What's goin' on! We should send her now! No one's around."

I would come to find out that these were the men we had illegally eliminated. They were returning to the game in likewise illicit fashion.

I could never take out ten men and expect to survive. I crawled back for the M-16. As I did, I called for everyone to hold steady and described what I'd just seen. I didn't know what, if anything, I would do with the gun once I retrieved it, but I'd decided I'd be better off with it than without it.

I made my way back and seized the weapon. Crawling once again toward the center of the street, forty feet above, I was startled by a thunderous crashing in concert with screams of distress. Box had assaulted his way through the building's adjoining, thin, plaster walls. With surprise in his favor, he was able to eliminate eight adversaries before meeting his own end. Although his gun was electronically rendered inoperative upon his demise, it didn't prevent him from physically punishing additional players into submission. The rules of the game were being radically modified as the situation evolved.

Back again on the ledge, I bore witness to the scores of walking human carnage as they made their way to the Dead Room. When I should send Lourdes to the opposite end of the compound to sound that magical horn, became paramount in my mind. The Circle reined havoc on our foes. But confirming that we had eradicated enough of them, such that the probability of success was high, was preeminent.

Suddenly, a man appeared on the horizon. He appeared to be headed for the staircase that we were attempting to gain. At that very moment, several of the dead, who were hidden from view for a time, walked expectantly to the street. We fired upon them, but our weapons indicated their systems were already inoperative. The man on the horizon placed his first foot on the staircase when I heard Joey scream out: "Key!"

"Stop 'em!" I answered. I knew that we would meet certain extermination if that key fell into the hands of these men that we killed illegally.

Joey came to his feet and took careful aim with the 357 magnum. As the man stood eerily solemn, Joey squeezed off the trigger.

"I'm spent!" he yelled.

"I'm not!" I followed, rising to my feet, M-16 pointed squarely at the man perched on the long staircase. The man took another timid step.

"Shoot 'em!" Joey advised.

"Do it!" Debara added, nervous.

I could feel all eyes upon me. It was center stage, front. "Does this man understand the risks involved here?" I wondered. I could sense my breathing, and then, stillness. I became almost dormant, cold, as I had prior to the fight with Instructor Black.

"No! Don't!" Box screamed in fear. "He'll do it, damn it. He'll really do it." He said to all those who were coaxing me on. And by now, that was everyone.

"He's right, Booch! This isn't that important!" Debara persuaded, now frightened.

"Come on down! Hey! I knew my gun was empty before I pulled the trigger!" Joey explained. I knew now that they had only been trying to scare the man back by yelling for me to shoot at him. But I also knew that Joey truly believed he had a shell remaining when he fired. He felt confident in his own ability to turn back the intruder safely, but seriously doubted my own. This was likely every one else's belief.

I fired.

The man crouched in fear as the bullet traveled to destinations unknown.

"He's not gonna do it, you stupid shit! Bring us the damned key! Hurry!" One of the undead yelled.

I knew that the key holder was not significant in the command structure and that the dead could not go to the key. Rather, the key had to come to them.

The key holder stood up and took two more steps. I re-targeted three steps below him. Anticipating a slow descent, I waited until he began to walk. When he did, I fired. The bullet missed his leg by three inches. He retreated like an extra in a Godzilla movie, stopping only momentarily to heave the key to the base of the staircase.

The dead swarmed to the key, not deterred whatsoever by my superior fire power. I delivered several carefully plotted bullets in a tight pattern where I determined the key must have fallen. I couldn't send Lourdes while live fire was present. I also felt that I lacked sufficient data concerning enemy numbers, to risk sending her through the gauntlet. The dead then took a calculated risk. They formed a solid mass and

methodically shuffled their way to the site of the key.
I couldn't fire so closely to such a large target without
running the risk of a real casualty. My options were
suddenly singular.

"Send her!" I called out.

"Now?" Lourdes responded with commitment.

"Now!"

She bolted, hitting her stride in the first ten yards or
so. Her feet struck the dirt in a rhythmic beat, like
Secretariat on the home stretch of Churchill Downs.
Her determination brought a lump to my throat, as
she bobbed and weaved her way down the street,
avoiding the few enemy that remained. She was alone.
We simply couldn't risk hitting her with a stray beam.
Our final bullet had been fired, and we were armed
now only with cheers of support.

"Go! Go! Go!" I belted out, then internalized. "Go,
Lourdes. Do it for us."

Everyone chimed in with their own words of encouragement, and then, as if orchestrated, silence. We
watched helplessly as she expended all her strength
and energy running serpentine through the street.

They found the key. One by one they unlocked their
frozen potential and stepped to the fore. Realizing
that we would not come to her defense, they briskly
moved into plain view, attempting to face Lourdes
squarely as she neared the horn. Lourdes un-har-
nessed a hidden reserve of energy and split her attackers before they could converge on her. I watched in
amazement, never really believing she would succeed. I leaped from my crouched position, threw my
arms into the air, gun in hand, and mimed screams of
elation. The horn resounded throughout the desert.

I reflected on our struggle here as I watched the
other team members, excepting Box, charge toward
Lourdes. My attention slowly fell to where Box was
standing at the base of a building across the street
from me. He looked up, then toward the jubilation at

the end of the street, returning once again to me. He held his hand high in the air, thumb extended, and then relaxed it to his side as he stared transfixed at the enthusiastic trainees. Lourdes took her victory climb to the top of the staircase, humming loudly the music to Rocky. Debara stepped back from the gathering and waved gently in my direction. I held my palm to her in acknowledgment, not quite sure what I was feeling. It was over.

When the final tallies were made, there were sixteen trainees left. Two of our teammates were spies for the opposition. Apparently not very good ones. Our unit became known as 4PM, due to the number of its members. Simply put, sixteen-hundred hours is the military equivalent of four o'clock in the afternoon. Conveniently, Pseudo Miranda shared the same abbreviation as Post Meridian, hence 4PM.

During our final days in Tonopah, we were given detailed instruction on our first mission. We were to intercept Colombian cocaine coming into America while posing as Coast Guardsmen. Once we secured the vessel, we were to send the crew back to its origin with a message for the drug lord to send a representative to Zurich, Switzerland, to discuss an operation of mutual benefit to themselves and the United States Government. At least that was the plan.

I was proud of what we'd accomplished here in training, but was concerned whether I had the ability to carry it over into the real world. For now, I just wanted to tell someone of my accomplishment. That, of course, was impossible. I settled instead for a telephone call to my parents to tell them that I'd finally graduated from college. They were quite complimentary, so I pretended they were congratulating me on what I'd really just completed. This worked well, and was the means by which I sought comfort through the years, by calling my parents, my best friend Mark Rizzo, or my friends in Kentucky, the Gevedens, and talking about the mainstream equivalent of what I was doing.

I would look back on these days in fond remembrance. They seemed safe, there were boundaries.

Chapter 6

When the training in Nevada was complete, I returned to Murray to attend a few summer classes in which I had enrolled prior to going to Tonopah.

It was the latter part of the summer before Boxer paid me a visit.

"You alone?" he muttered, as he poked his head over the threshold.

"Not any more. How you doin' partner! You look good. Wife must be treatin' ya well. Come on in!"

"No. I'm not asking for myself. I brought a few people with me. Are you expecting anyone soon?"

"Why?"

"We're gonna install a STU III (pronounced Stew Three) Secure Phone in your bedroom."

"Oh. Oh shit. My girlfriend. Umm. Yeah. I'll call her and tell her that we're goin' to the lake together or something."

Andy (short for Andrea) had been my girlfriend for a couple of years. She was also attending classes and was under the impression that I had been in Massachusetts visiting my parents for the past month or so.

"Good. Do that." Box removed a brick (hand radio) from his breeze jacket. "This won't take long, believe me. These guys installed one at my place in a snap." Box walked into my bedroom, and upon looking at its condition, he added: "Well, maybe `a snap' was a poor choice of words."

"You're just not used to seeing a bedroom that gets a lot of use."

"Right. Hey! I'm gonna need to demonstrate the proper use of this puppy."

Before I departed for the lake, Box told me that we would be flying to the Florida Keys in a week. Specifically, a tiny island called Islamorada. We would depart out of Paducah, Kentucky and arrive that same day in Homestead Air Force Base, Florida. From there, we would go directly to the Drop Anchor Hotel in Islamorada, where the 4PM team would receive a detailed briefing on its initial interception of a drug shipment originating in Colombia.

"What do you think about driving instead of flying?" Box suggested tentatively.

"Excuse me?"

"It's a simple suggestion! I thought it was something you'd prefer to do. But if it isn't, then fine. We'll fly."

"Chill out. We'll drive. But tell me the real reason."

"They've got me in charge of the mission. I really thought they'd give us someone who'd done this sort of stuff before. I thought we'd talk about it for a couple days before we get there. I don't know why they didn't just give the damn job to you."

"Yeah, right. They're gonna have me lead us. Take your head outa your ass. I'm an impromptu kind of guy. I don't much go in for this planning stuff."

"Impromptu is what we need! At least that's the way I see it. Look what you did in training."

"That was training. Anyhow. Don't worry. I'll be right with you. Shoulder to shoulder. We're a team, right?"

We drove my 1982 Corvette to Florida, stopping along the way for the essentials: gas, food, and beer. It was almost midnight on our first day on the road, and we were passing through Georgia.

Box was fast asleep when I spotted them. I slammed

on the breaks, bringing the car from seventy-five miles
per hour to a screeching halt. Box jettisoned from the
automobile, gun in hand, and took cover along side
the vehicle.

"Stop playing around Box," I teased.

"What the hell's goin' on! Where the hell are we!
Why did you slam on the brakes!"

"The beef's prime for tipping."

"What?"

"You ever tipped a cow?"

"That's why you almost killed us? Cows? First
chance we get, we're getting you some help."

"Come on. It'll be an adventure."

Box holstered his weapon and reluctantly followed
me. I had never done this before, so I wasn't quite sure
what to expect. I did know, however, that Box needed
something to distract him from his anxiety. He also
needed to know that we were of one accord.

Most of the cows were sprawled on the ground,
something I hadn't anticipated.

"It appears that someone has already tipped these
cows. Now can we get the hell out of here?"

"Over here." I said eagerly. I found one cow that
was sleeping upright. I had Box line up on my shoulder and explained the importance of slamming into
the cow simultaneously.

"This cow has horns," Boxer commented.

"Cows have horns," I assured him.

"They do?"

"City boy?" I joked.

We slammed our bodies into the side of the bull and
fell immediately backwards. The bull delayed before
losing its balance and crashing to the ground. It batted
its head into the dirt numerous times psychotically
before regaining its feet. As it looked around, confused, it was attracted by the sound of our gut-wrench-
ing laughter. It charged with malice.

I headed directly for the barbed wire fence that we

had crossed earlier, launching across it like a football player diving for the end zone. Box played ring-around-the-cows with the bull, before heading for the fence. He leaped, clearing none of it, hanging his leather coat on the wire. The bull collided with the fence. Box separated from his coat, finally escaping the wrath of the bull.

After his ritualistic complaining, Box admitted that the experience was worth a leather jacket.

"If I'd remained sleeping, the day wouldn't be remembered. But I promise, I'll never forget this one."

The following afternoon, we stopped for lunch at a Burger King restaurant in northern Florida. Box confided that he was quite scared of the mission at hand. He was visibly wrought with tension. "It's all you can drink, you know." I explained.

"Huh."

"The soda." I pointed to the self service fountain. "Free refills."

"I know that! I'm talking about something real important here." Curiosity finally got to him. "Okay. So, it's free refills. What's your point."

"You bought a large?"

"I didn't feel like running back and forth for refills."

"So you pay a buck more. The ultimate in lazy."

"Is there a point to all this?"

"You're settled. Only a married, settled person, would do that. Look around. Do you see any young people with large drinks? You've gotten to the place in life where you're willing to pay a higher price for convenience. You're settled."

"Because I purchased a large? You're serious?"

"An unsettled person wouldn't worry so much about the possibility of dying."

"Maybe I have reason to stay alive. Maybe I have

people who would be just a bit concerned that I tipped cows at the stroke of midnight. Yeah. Maybe I'm a bit conservative and a touch cautious, but I have more than myself to think of here."

"Exactly."

As we began the last leg of our trip, I slurped down the final drops of my drink and we left.

Box was never a one to pass up an opportunity to gloat. "Nothing so quenching as a big Pepsi on a hot day. Yup! This puppy oughta last until next stop. Aren't you glad we got... Oh no, I'm sorry. I forgot. You got a small soda, didn't cha'? Oh well" Box sat back in his seat, full of himself.

The Drop Anchor Hotel sat on the ocean, separated from the water by a narrow dock. An in-ground swimming pool and a few shuffle boards occupied the center of the U-shaped structure. Coconut trees were plentiful, and added a sense of serenity. The elderly couple who ran the facility were also the owners, and they treated us like family.

On this first mission, as with all future endeavors, the entire team was not present. Christina, Jerimiah, Rivas, Joey, Rick, Steven, Lourdes, Quinn and Debara completed the eleven of us who would form the backbone of 4PM.

The mission would take place the next day. A boat, a Hatteras, would anchor a few hundred yards from the hotel's dock, and we would be taken on board by a smaller boat. Once we were aboard, the men who provided the ship would depart and we would be on our own.

Box took us through the detailed list of instructions, assigning specific responsibilities to each of us.

Steven would provide constant updates on the exact location of the target ship, and warn of any impending United States drug interdiction craft. Debara was in charge of piloting the 1984 Hatteras. Joey was in charge of explosives. Christina would handle any Spanish interpretation, but, like all the others, she was also expected to hold her own with a weapon. Jerimiah and Rick supplied the muscle for lifting the large amounts of drugs. Lourdes' marksmanship made her a must, but her devotion to Pseudo Miranda was sufficient reason to have her accompany all missions. Rivas and Quinn were expert divers, and would be called upon if we had to go below the craft for the hidden drug shipment.

As for me, Box's instructions were simple.

"If there's trouble of any sort — Or if they refuse to cooperate — make it happen."

I suggested we all have a couple drinks at pool side somewhere around 9:00 p.m. Box diffidently agreed to the proposal, but kept a vigilant eye on us. He had serious reservations about the possibility of being hung-over on our first mission. The atmosphere soon became relaxed, and Box, having himself consumed a Screwdriver, seemed less guarded. I took advantage of the changing mood and introduced a few more fifths of Vodka. Soon thereafter, Rick challenged everyone to a contest to see who could consume the most alcohol under water.

When I awoke, I was stark naked. In fact, everyone was. The pool cleaner was busy removing bottles and cans from the water. "So. What the hell happened here last night?" I asked him innocently.

"Oh, some young men and women got drunk and stupid last night. Kept up a lot of folks. Retired people you know. We cater to the retired. Anyhow. Before I was gonna throw 'em out, I went around to our guests to apologize for the disturbance." The old man pulled a bottle from the pool and poured the water at my feet.

"Everyone said the same thing. Said it was the most

fun they'd had in years. So I guess I'll let 'em stay."

The old man owned the place.

❖ ❖ ❖

The Hatteras arrived. I watched silently as it bobbed on the vast sea. The smaller craft came into view and my head immediately cleared.

We're really going through with this, I thought. We were all dressed as tourists, attempting to remain inconspicuous.

We boarded the transfer craft and eventually transferred to the Hatteras. Debara took the helm and was directed by Steven to set a course bearing of 71 degrees Longitude by 22 degrees Latitude, in the direction of the Southern tip of Andros Island. Steven was hooked up directly with Mena, Arkansas, which, in turn, had a direct link to Air Force Reconnaissance aircraft. All courtesy of Equatorial Communications.

If everything went as planned, we would intersect the drug vessel approximately seventy-five miles off shore. This left a substantial amount of time to prepare ourselves mentally for the interception.

We had been at sea for three hours and still had no visual contact with our target. Box was feeling the pressure.

"Steven, I don't wanta' end up in the Bay of Pigs. Where the hell are they?"

"Oh, don't worry about that. The Bay of Pigs is on the Southern border of Cuba. We should hit Havana long before that," Steven responded sincerely.

"God, tell me he's kidding. Just tell me where the hell they are."

"Apparently we're headed right or I'd have received an update."

Box became a bit agitated, "Could ya please check."

Steven radioed Mena and got a prompt response. "We're right on course. Should see 'em within the next twenty minutes or so."

"It's a pretty big ocean. Are you sure?"

"Neither of us have altered our course one iota."

As we neared the intersect, course changes came in rapid succession, Debara and Steven worked together as if they had been doing it for years. We skipped along the placid ocean at a rapid rate of speed, closing the gap. Our hearts quickened as we listened acutely to our ever changing course. We huddled closer, legs and shoulders filed tightly, secure. I began to yawn repeatedly, something I did whenever I sensed my nervousness. Jerimiah pounded his elbows against the side of the boat as a way of psyching himself up. I remained quiet, never a one to use artificial means to prepare myself. Joey, sitting to my right, vomited, short and projectile, over his rifle.

"Nerves?" I asked

"No," He answered, bouncing his head back and forth.

"Something you ate?" Box inquired further.

"No, just something I do," Joey replied, never acknowledging us with eye contact.

"So. How do you feel?" Box asked me.

"Nervous. But I'm always nervous. I think I do better that way." I responded.

"I'm countin' on ya." Box grabbed my knee, cracking a tense smile.

We became distracted by the sudden change in cadence between Debara and Steven. Up till now, Debara had echoed Steven's calls for course changes. The only voice heard now however, was Debara's call for answers.

"We should have seen the damn thing by now! Where are they! Where the hell are they!"

"They should be right in front of us." Steven said.

"Well, they're not! Whata' we do now? Wait! There! Hold on everyone!" Debara said as she tossed the craft into a hard left bank, pulling us forward once again. She was a predator closing in on the kill.

Our boat throttled back abruptly.

Debara called out, "They're stopping! Is everybody ready?"

It was time. With bullet proof vests about our torsos, we readied our weapons. Two magnetic signs were placed on either side of the ship, signifying that we were the United States Coast Guard. Everyone except Box, Debara, and Rick, all dressed in appropriate Coast Guard Attire, hid from view. As we pulled within a short distance of the vessel, Rick, with the assistance of an intercom, directed them in fluent Spanish to chop their motors. They did, and offered no resistance.

I knew the next thing I did would change my life forever. Once I boarded this ship with a gun, there would be no turning back. I was bombarded with thoughts, but only one stood out from all the others. What would it feel like if these people actually fired bullets at me?

As our Hatteras pulled alongside the drug craft, a large Bayliner, we snapped from our prone positions, pointing eight assault rifles at its occupants. The apparent leader of the vessel yelled.

"No Coast Guard! Coast Guard Marauders!"

The crew became extraordinarily relaxed, welcoming us aboard. Box looked confused, doubtful of the Hispanic man's veracity. I didn't wait for Boxer's directive, fearing that it would allow him time to appear indecisive. I knew he was frightened at the possibility of one of us getting killed under his command.

"I'll go first. Turn this tub into Swiss cheese if they try anything. Oh Yeah. Jesus, I'm gonna need you as a translator."

"I'm there! Do you want me to tell him about this 'Swiss cheese' thing?"

"As a matter of fact, yeah." I climbed aboard with Rivas, and immediately placed the barrel of my gun to the man's skull.

"The cocaine. Where is it? And don't waste my time or I'll splatter your brains across this deck!"

With translation, he responded, "No need for threats. We got your coca."

He then cautiously reached into the false bottom of a seat, assuring me that he was getting the drugs, and only the drugs. I stood at his back, holding his right hand twisted with my left. He gently removed a kilogram of pure Colombian cocaine, and handed it to me.

"This is for you."

"What's goin' on Ves!" Box called out.

"I think you need to come over here Box! Everything's fine! But you need to come here now! Tell Steven we need updates every minute. Or sooner if things change. I don't want the real Coast Guard to show up!"

Box boarded with Joey, Jerimiah, and Rick.

"What's wrong?" Box asked.

"This is what's wrong." I showed him the bag of cocaine.

"So? This is what we came for, right?"

"We came for several hundred pounds of the stuff, not a key." I shook the bag of cocaine in the man's face.

"This is a fuckin' pay-off! These assholes have been paying off the Coast Guard. Shit! Why didn't our people know about this?" I hurled the bag into the ocean and then grabbed the Spanish man by the back of the neck.

"Where's the shipment?"

He became frantic, throwing his eyes toward his men. Joey held out a grenade, deterring them from action. Not that it was necessary. We still had several guns pointed at them, and they were disarmed.

"You can't do this! We have a deal!" The man proclaimed.

"Not with us you don't," I assured him. "Now where's the real shipment?"

"We don't have any. Not on board."

"You ever heard the saying, `If it ain't broke, don't fix it'? Well. There's gonna be a lot of fixin' going on around here if I don't see some snow real quick like."

I signaled for Rick to toss me his shot gun. I pumped it. The man cringed.

"Nice stereo. I'd hate to be you sailing all the way to the George Town (a reference to the Cayman Islands) without this." I said sarcastically, and then blew it apart.

There was no reaction.

I conferred with Joey and Box, just outside of hearing range of the drug trafficker. I asked Joey if it were possible to attach a timer to a C-4 explosive and have it remain inert. He responded in the affirmative. Composed, and in an audible voice, Box then directed the sinking of the vessel. Joey affixed the plastique to the engine bay, in plain view of our captives. As the timer wound down to thirty seconds, the Hispanic man reconsidered.

"Sub. Subbb… Submarine."

"Turn it off," Box directed Joey. "The cocaine?" He demanded of the trafficker.

The man walked below deck with Box and I trailing. He handed me what appeared to be a video joy-stick.

"Remote. Thirty kilometers." He waved his arm in a swatting motion to the rear of the ship.

"Steven! Someone get Steven here ASAP! Debara! Tell Debara to do her best and work the SATCOM (Satellite Communications)!" I settled the man by placing my hands on his shoulders and repeating the words `It's okay' a few times.

"I think they've got some sort of submarine and they're somehow able to control it with this doohickey here," I said to Box.

Steven entered.

"What's up?"

I explained to him what had transpired. Meanwhile, Box called Rivas down for translation. After a short discussion with the drug trafficker, Steven explained what was going on. They had been towing a small submarine full of cocaine. They'd released it as we were about to come upon them. The drop location was plotted on a map, and the sub was hovering just below the water's surface. After our departure, they would remote control it back to the vessel.

Steven guided the mini-submarine back to the boat and we emptied half of its contents into our own ship. Box then gave the man a sealed letter and instructed him to give it to his boss. Box told him that if he had a representative meet with us, and other drug lord representatives, in Zurich, Switzerland, we would return the remainder of his shipment to him. The man knew that he would surely be killed if he didn't return with the money or the entire shipment of cocaine, which assured us that he would deliver the letter as an explanation for not having either.

(We would later discover that Juan David Ochoa, eldest son to Don Fabio Ochoa, had purchased several Jacques Cousteau-type submarines for the expressed purpose of drug smuggling. The letter would be delivered to Don Fabio.)

We stowed the 300 pounds of pure cocaine in the center of a specially designed, two layered fuel tank that allowed fuel to flow around a concealed compartment, then transferred fuel from the other tank to insulate the cocaine from possible detection.

We cast our weapons into the ocean as we neared some Coast Guard patrol ships. With fishing poles dangling overboard, we motored back to Islamorada and returned home.

All in all, it was a smooth operation.

The same could not be said of the mission that followed.

Chapter 7

Our next intercept was scheduled near the end of the
summer. Box had received an intelligence report on
the likely route of a cocaine shipment originating in
Cuba. René Cruz, who ran the Cuban drug smuggling
operation for Fidel Castro, had masterminded the
maiden voyage of the Lazy Lady II.

The Lazy Lady II had traversed three thousand
miles to our western seaboard by way of the Panama
Canal. A new Hinckley Downeaster, it was not designed for speed. This was our inherent advantage.
Fuel and subsistence requirements made the Hinckley
a cumbersome, less expedient craft, than a Hatteras.

We would attempt to cross its path approximately
three-hundred miles north of the Tropic of Cancer in
neutral waters. As with the prior intercept, the overall
mission was to draw Cuba into Pseudo Miranda.

Time was in our favor. Box and I used the time to
cross the country, discussing what was right and wrong
with our first seizure. Our final destination was Imperial Beach, California.

Driving through the night, I could feel the winds of
change streaming across my face. Although Box and I
enjoyed our normal diet of ridiculous conversation,
we left room for large doses of more substantial
thoughts.

"Box, what do you think about what we're doing?
The ethics of it and all?"

Still half asleep, Box answered. "I guess I focus on
the intended results. I'd certainly rather do this than
nothing at all. You can't bog yourself down with

ethical questions. If they'd wallowed around contemplating the ethics of the atomic bomb, we'd all be
speaking Japanese. I'm fine with it. And so are you,
damn it!"

I continued to dwell on it, but kept my thoughts to
myself. I knew that Box was troubled by it also, but
chose not to deal with it openly. I respected that.

The team gathered at the Del Coronado Hotel in San
Diego on the edge of the Pacific Ocean. Having arrived in pairs gradually throughout the evening, we
finally gathered together on a large outdoor deck
overlooking the beach. We relaxed and sipped frozen
Margaritas.

Box briefed us openly in the midst of the public
surroundings about our impending mission.

"Debara. The Lazy Lady II is a large sport fishing
vessel, and should pose no threat for escape once
you've got a visual. Intel shows four on board, as we
expected. Again, nothing we can't handle. We show
force like last time, and everything should go smooth.
The key is communication. Steven? Where the fuck is
Steven?"

"He's over there rapping with that chick."
Jerimiah directed our attention to a table at the opposite end of the deck.

"For God's sake will someone drag his butt over
here. Where the hell is his mind anyhow?"

"I think the answer's self evident." Debara said,
impressed with Steven's savoir-faire.

"I don't get it. I'll go to my grave never understanding women. Look at 'em. All he's missing are the pens
in the shirt pocket and he's rubbing up against that."
I said.

"Shit, it ain't right, man. You and I should be all
over that." Rivas added as he pointed to several other
women, "And that. And that. And that."

"I'll tell you one thing he doesn't have that you both have." Debara said.

"What?" I asked her.

"He doesn't have an over inflated ego."

"Or good looks and a personality." Rivas added.

"Maybe he's well hung. Did ya ever consider that possibility." Quinn added.

"If that's all it took, Quinn, you'd be over there talking to her instead of Steven." Rivas retaliated in jest.

"Oh, boy. You're dead." I said while laughing and ducking my head below the table.

"What's that supposed to mean? Huh Jesus? (pronounced in English) Why don't we see what you've got down there." Quinn proceeded to flip Rivas to the deck, even though he legitimately resisted. We were pulling her off of him when Steven arrived back at the table.

"Looks like I missed all the excitement."

"Glad you could join us. We're not taking you from anything more important I hope." Box said sarcastically.

"No. I'm gonna get together with her later on."

"No. If we've interrupted you. Please feel free." Box motioned in direction of the beautiful women.

Steven, now realizing Box was genuinely upset, pulled up a chair.

"Maybe I'm not running a tight enough ship..." Box started to preach when Joey interrupted.

"Great. Now his ship's getting tighter."

Box giggled, changing gears a bit. "Who am I kidding. I never could keep a ship tight. If I could, I certainly wouldn't be sailing around with this character, now would I." He pinched the back of my neck and finished by saying: "Let's just do our jobs the best way we know how. I don't have to tell you how important this is. Half the drugs." He now spoke solemnly, looking over the ocean. "Half the drugs. Gone. Who

knows. Maybe thousands of kids don't grow up to
become addicts and criminals. I mean, who knows.
Maybe."

Everyone, except Box and I, traveled to the rendezvous in rented vehicles. Each car carried a hand radio,
in the event of a mechanical problem, or worse, an
accident. No classified information was ever discussed
on these bands. Throughout the short trip, singing and
perverse humor ruled the brick. I kept thinking that
we were becoming a real team. I felt they would
always be there for me. These were certainly the good
times.

Two large rubberized boats took us to the Hatteras
craft. Debara and Steven took the helm and headed us
into the open sea. The water was rougher than it had
been on the east coast. About ten miles out, I found
Christina leaning over the edge of the ship.

"Morning sickness?" I asked.

She twisted her head slowly upwards before dropping it suddenly overboard once again.

"I'm just kidding. You all right?"

She began to turn her head up once more, deciding
instead to shake it from side to side.

"Right. Stupid question. Try looking straight out
over the bow... or stern... or whatever. Just look
straight out, instead of down at the water. That's what
Debara told me to do."

"I'm fine. You got sick, too?"

"Hell, no! What kind of a wimp do you think I am?
I'm playing. I'm just playing. You'll be fine. Just stay
up here and look far out over the ocean until you feel
better."

I laid down on deck and fell asleep. Over the next
several hours, we would refuel at sea twice. I slum-
bered just below the surface, and was completely
cognizant of anything important that went on around

me. When I awakened there was a rifle barrel facing me square in the face.

"Very funny Joey. I hope that shit ain't loaded."

"We're closing in. Box said to wake your ass."

"You haven't puked on that gun yet, have you?"

"No. Not yet."

"Thank God."

Everyone was busy, checking their weapons and protective clothing. Box asked Steven for an estimate on time.

"It'll be about an hour."

The hour passed quickly. The Hatteras slammed into high gear, and the chase was on.

"Slow it down! Tell her to throttle back!" Lourdes called out. "We forgot the signs! We've got to put the Coast Guard signs on!"

Debara got the word and pulled back on the power. We hastily slapped the signs to the side of the boat and pushed forward. Nothing lost, we thought, as we neared our target. The Hatteras impacted the water, as it sprang from the surface like an air foil, revisiting the ocean each time with force. Almost everyone cheered in support of Debara, mocking our foe's underpowered craft.

I remained mute, never a one to underestimate the opposition. I was sure that I could never do what Debara was doing at this very moment. I was petrified of the ocean's power, and could not imagine myself attacking its fury in this manner. I was filled with pride for her.

"I'm gonna ease it in! They're not trying to go anywhere! Get ready!" Debara yelled over the sound of the engine.

Everyone immediately turned their focus to Joey.

"What? I can't prepare with you looking at me like that." Joey reacted.

I grabbed Boxer's arm as he sat next to me, and watched emotionally as everyone reached out with their right arm, grasping the left arm of the person beside them. Joey vomited, making it all complete.

We closed in on our target, and Debara passed the baton to Rick. The craft looked so much like the boat that Box and I spent time on in Chicago that I almost forgot what I was doing here. Their engines gurgled as they sputtered along. Four men stood on deck, appearing more bewildered than frightened. They probably noticed our Coast Guard emblems, and wondered why we were outside national waters. This was exactly what we intended them to dwell on while we tightened the gap.

I looked at Rick, trying to get a sense of our present status. I gripped my weapon, a Browning 2000, 12 gauge shotgun, tightly. Strapped to my side was a Colt 45 automatic. Box stood up, making his presence known, just as he had in the previous interception. We were close. I could hear murmuring from the ship's crew.

"Halt your vessel! This is the United States Coast Guard! We want to board! Repeat! Halt your vessel!" Rick was speaking in Spanish over the intercom.

The Lazy Lady Two followed Rick's orders, and ceased any forward progression.

"Cut your engines!"

Box, standing only a couple of feet from where I was hidden, from plain view, glanced down and smiled.

Bap! Bap! Bap! Bap! Bap!

Box collapsed at my feet.

Machine gun fire! I thought. A barrage of automatic weapon fire saturated the side of our metal reinforced ship. Then, silence.

"Now!" I screamed. Everyone spun up toward the left, turning ten weapons on the Lazy Lady II, riddling it with an assortment of bullets and buckshot. Erratically the fire was returned at close range. We paused, almost as one, for a split second, and meticulously aimed our weapons. Our return volley of fire blanketed them with lead. One assailant dashed across the deck, as several weapon's fire tracked backwards into his path.

All became deafeningly still. I looked out over a smoke filled cloud hovering at water level. The smell was intoxicating, thick and oily. Their motors were still idling, but their craft was splintered about. We held our weapons firmly on the wounded ship, not yet convinced that all was safe. We had already made the mistake of underestimating their resolve. I knelt down, balancing my attention between the ship and Box.

"How you doing buddy?" I could hardly hear my voice for the buzzing in my ears.

"I'm fine. It's just my shoulder." Box replied with a cringe in his voice.

"I think we got 'em all? Why don't you stand up again and check?" I quipped.

Bap! Bap! Bap! Bap! Bap! Bap!... More continuous fire.

"Joey! Joey!" I screamed at the top of my lungs. "Toss me a grenade!" He had one in his hand already. I was unaware that he had already pulled the pin.

"Throw me the grenade! Now!"

He threw it. Everything seemed to freeze. I saw the handle separate from the grenade. In a moment, I straddled Box, caught the grenade, twisted and threw it, all in one continual motion, to the center of the Lazy Lady II's deck. The result, however, was not so magnificent.

Not a crevice of protection existed within twenty feet of the explosion. Metal shrapnel from the grenade reeked havoc; the erratic projectiles of wood and glass butchered everything in their paths. Moments later, smoke swayed gently over the Lazy Lady II. Our team rose tentatively from hunkered positions, listening cautiously to the crackling sounds of a splintered ship seeking equilibrium. We could feel the oscillating, dull noise of the engine as the craft wobbled lifeless in front of us.

When we were convinced that all was calm, we boarded the ship. There were more passengers than intelligence estimates had accounted for. Instead of four, there were eight. No one was prepared for what we saw next. Bodies were dismembered and arbitrarily strewn about. Blood still dripped from the sides of the deck, pooling to the rear of the vessel. Chunks of flesh stuck to the cabin walls, held there by blood. A torso, head and legs displaced, functioned as a form of protection for an assailant who lie dead beneath it.

"Over here!" Christina called out.

We gathered around Christina as she leaned over the mouth of a bullet ridden assailant.

"He's alive," she said.

"So what." Joey said callously.

"So what? How can you say that? We're responsible for this? We've gotta do somethin'." Lourdes pleaded despondently.

"Yeah. I agree with Joey. So the fuck what. This guy wouldn't waste ten seconds worrying about you. He's shark bait if you ask me." Quinn said callously.

"I know CPR." Jerimiah said eagerly.

"Well, Box?" Christina asked.

"Of course. Do what you can. But, please hurry." Box answered. He knew, as did I, that it was an act in futility. But it would help them keep their sanity, and that made it necessary. "Steven! Keep us abreast!"

"Yes, sir!"

"What's the holdup!" Debara hollered from the Hatteras. She had to remain aboard in the event of a hasty departure.

"We're pumping air into a sieve." I responded under my breath. "Shit. Would you look at that." I directed Boxer's attention to the Hatteras' side. As the smoke dissipated, Box looked in disbelief at the Coast Guard sign, hung upside down and backwards. It was dimpled and mangled, but it was clear to see that we had screwed up royally, and eight people were dead because of it.

"He's opening his eyes." Lourdes shouted.

"Great. What are we gonna do if he lives? It's not like we can take him to a hospital or anything."

Box, still speaking quietly to me, pretended to be talking to a doctor. "Excuse me Mr. Doctor, we're with the CIA, and we seemed to have caused this man serious injury when we intercepted his drug shipment as part of a clandestine operation. Here's our insurance card."

I dropped the safety off of my Colt 45, and said: "Don't worry. He won't be leaving this boat."

Box gasped mildly and turned his head away, "My God."

At that moment, Rick informed us that the man had died. Box sighed openly, sending chills down my spine. He then turned back to me and asked what he should do next. I told him to sink the vessel.

"What about the drugs? And what do we do if these bodies wash ashore?"

"Screw the Coke! As for the bodies..." I pondered it. "Everyone! Listen up! Quinn! You and Jesus get with Joey and sink this tug in the most efficient manner possible. No big explosions, Joey! The rest of us will strap the bodies to the ship. Use the extra sheet metal screws that are kept below deck." The screws were long and sharp, and were used to fasten the half inch metal reinforcement to the sides of the Hatteras. "We'll have to use the butts of our handguns to hammer them down. Okay. Let's get it done."

We gathered the wood fragments that had been torn from the ships structure and laid them across the bodies, nailing them to the ship's floor. I wanted to vomit, but didn't. A lump filled my throat and pressure engulfed my neck and jaw. I nailed frantically, swearing each time I struck my hand with the butt of

my gun. I completed the vulgar task, and was making
my way to fresh air when I heard Box cry out.

"What the hell happened to you?"

Lourdes was crying hysterically and speaking inco-
herently. She was spattered with blood. Her face had
streaks of blood where she had apparently rubbed it to
keep it from her eyes.

"Are you hurt?" I asked. "Did you cut yourself or
something?"

"In here!" Rick called.

I walked into the shredded cabin area, and saw
what it was that had Lourdes so shaken. The man that
they had attempted to revive was nailed directly to
the floor. In a state of shock, Lourdes did not comprehend that she was supposed to lay the wood across
the body and nail the wood directly to the ship.
Lourdes had driven the screws through the flesh and
bone of the man she so desperately wanted to save.
She was taken off the ship and given a sedative from
the first aid kit.

Quinn, now in snorkel gear, popped up from below
the water. "Jesus is placing the final explosive below
the engine bay. We'll have five minutes to depart. Are
we ready?"

"Yeah." I answered.

"Good. I'll give 'em the go ahead."

We moved our ship away from the crippled drug
vessel and awaited the explosion. A muffled, dull
thump, and then another, could be heard and felt. The
ship slipped beneath the water without fanfare, almost anticlimactic.

"We should say something. They were people, you
know." Lourdes said in tears. "We should say something."

Christina bowed her head, glancing up to ensure
we did the same. With a crackling voice, she led us in
the Lord's Prayer. We were of one voice, excepting the
part where we asked for forgiveness; half said 'tres-

passes' and half said 'debts.' When we had finished, Joey commented sharply,

"This doesn't mean that I want forgiveness. We did what was right. What was necessary. They fired first; we just defended ourselves." No one rebutted his words, not because we agreed with them, but because we were too mentally and emotionally exhausted to argue.

Box and I leaned over the deck as Debara throttled up the engines.

"What's that in your hand?" Box asked.

I held up the submarine-controlling joy stick that I had removed from the *Lazy Lady II*.

"It's worth eight men dying for." I tossed it over the side of the ship.

"Washington may have wanted that Coke for somethin'."

"It's my ball, and Cuba can't play."

"Would you have done it?" Box asked, seemingly unable to free his mind of the thought of me almost shooting the man our team members so unselfishly attempted to revive.

"I guess we'll never know." I said, unwilling to face the dilemma this philosophical question raised.

The mood on board became sedate, only Debara and Steven spoke, and only as their work necessitated. A few hours into our voyage home, Box informed us that we would rest at sea for the evening. Most of us piled into the cabin, sleeping anywhere we could find room. Box and I opted for the stars. I hoped to find solace there, but found instead a frightened young man who wanted nothing more than to be a little boy again.

The Hatteras' pitted exterior made it too risky to chance taking it through patrolled waters, so Steven radioed for a swap. A similar craft launched out of Ensenada, Baja California, and met us half-way up the coast. The two member crew acquired a technical status of our ship from Debara, and we made the exchange in a matter of minutes. Their Hispanic heritage led me to believe that they were contract agents, doing what they were paid to do, without question. We never even traded greetings.

Twenty four hours had passed before we neared Imperial Beach. Debara cut the engines when we came within a mile of the coast. As we awaited the arrival of the rubberized crafts that would take us to shore, Box tried his best to ease our consciences.

"If they were willing to kill us, don't you think they would have killed anyone who got in their way! You have no right to hang your heads! You risked your asses out there. You didn't do it for yourselves. You did it for people you'll never even meet. People who would otherwise spit in your face. Now we have a job to do, damn it! Who wants to see this through to the end?"

"When's our next mission. Holme boy?" I asked in an effort to convince the others of my unwavering certitude. "Hey, look, guys." I continued as I stepped to the fore and placed my hand on Boxer's shoulder. "We can mope around for the rest of our lives mourning the deaths of these people if we somehow feel it'll ease our guilt, but it won't change one simple fact."

I walked to the edge of the boat and placed my arms on its side, dropping my head in frustration. I looked out over the infinite sea and said harshly, while pointing firmly out to sea, and then back to land, "Those people are killing people, and we're the only buffer in-between! So if you want to feel pity for those bastards, go right ahead! But some day, when you're crying in you're corn puffs about how the neighborhood's gone to shit, just remember you had an opportunity to do something about it. But like so many apathetic, belly aching..."

"Okay, Gipper. Enough already." Lourdes interrupted with a surprisingly flippant tone. "Count me in."

"If you promise not to finish the speech, I'm in too."
Christina followed.

Everyone formed a huddle of solidarity as Box
looked on in relief. "I thought it had the makings of an
`I have a dream,' `Ask not what your country can do
for you,' `I'm the luckiest man on the face of the Earth,'
`I am not a crook,' kind of speech." I said facetiously.

"When the breaks are beaten' the boys, you gotta
give it all you got and win just one for the Zipper."
Lourdes quoted an appropriate phrase from the movie
Airplane, and immediately led everyone in a hum-a-
long of the Notre Dame fight song, vintage Lourdes.

We were hugging one another when our escorts
arrived. The transition back to land was made easier
knowing that we were a fully functioning unit, tested
under fire. The horror of that day would never fully
escape us, and any innocence we may have had was
now gone forever.

Over the next couple of weeks, we made two more
interceptions off the coast of Florida, bringing Pablo
Escobar and José Ocampo to the bargaining table in
Zurich, Switzerland. The game had finally begun.

Chapter 8

The meeting in Zurich, Switzerland was scheduled for
the end of August. Accompanying Boxer and myself
were Christina, Joey and Debara. The five of us were the
sole negotiators representing United States interests in
this unorthodox and politically sensitive meeting. We
would be staying at the Hotel Zurich, and the drug lord
representatives would assemble at the Europa.

I met up with Box at Paducah Airport, where we
boarded a T-39 aircraft bound for Andrews Air Force
Base in Washington, where an Air Force C-5 Trans-

port picked us up and flew us to Ramstein Air Force Base in Frankfurt, West Germany.

Even more than in our previous trips, Box insisted that we not enter into any revealing conversations with the other passengers on board during the hop. He explained that 'hop' was the military lingo for bumming a ride. I was surprised at the number of people in civilian attire until Box told me that military personnel and their families travel cheaply by waiting for available space on such aircraft.

We passed through customs by way of the United States military check point. Box flashed an identification and an Official Passport as he touched each of us to signify that we were accompanying him in-country. I grabbed the ID and passport from his clutches as we made our way to the C-5 Transport. The identification was authentic CIA; I was quite impressed. The inscription at the rear of the passport read, "THE BEARER IS ABROAD ON AN OFFICIAL ASSIGNMENT FOR THE GOVERNMENT OF THE UNITED STATES OF AMERICA."

"Why don't I get a CIA ID?"

"Keep it down! You don't know who might be listening." Box, now worried, insisted.

"Yeah. We wouldn't want anyone thinking you're a real secret agent. Actually, maybe we would. It might give 'em a false sense of security."

"Funny. Very funny. You wanta' know why they don't give you an ID? Because you'd be whipping it out every time you saw a pretty woman. Who would be safe?"

"Your wife?"

Box stared at me, resisting a smile. "Give me that." He said with a snicker, grabbing the identifications from my hand.

For the first time, I realized I'd be left flapping in the wind if this operation blew up in our faces. Box, on the other hand, was a card carrying member.

Box instructed me that, if anyone were to inquire, I was to say that my father was an active duty Colonel in the United States Army. With my hair long and un-military like, people would expect my knowledge of military matters to be somewhat lacking.

❖ ❖ ❖

After about ten minutes in the air, I became bored. Box was to my right, and I already knew him. Joey was on my left. His questionable sexual persuasion, and my insatiable curiosity, inevitably led to some direct questions.

"So Joey. Are you gay?" I asked bluntly.

"What kind of question is that? What the hell business is it of yours anyhow?"

"Oh, it's not a business question. I wanta' know for personal reasons."

"You're gay?" Christina, sitting directly behind me, joined in with humor. She had been listening to our conversation.

"No. Mind your own business."

"Let's say," Joey agreed, "for argument sake, that I am gay. What of it? Would you be bothered by that?"

"No. But I have to admit, it's hard to respect a man when you envision him down on another guy. It's definitely unnatural. Not to mention gross."

"Okay. Try picturing Steven and Quinn getting it on and tell me that ain't gross?"

I shivered like an epileptic seizure. "I think I'm gonna throw up."

"Why? What's wrong with Quinn?" Box came to her defense, oblivious to the possibility that anyone might find her physically unpleasant.

"Hey, man, I'm not judging you or anything. I'm the last guy that should do that. But I don't think there's anything wrong with passing judgment on the act itself," I reasoned.

"You can't judge the action either." Christina commented.

"Tell 'em, Seedy." Debara agreed.

"Yeah. God already passed judgment on homosexuality. I suppose you have the right to quote him, though." Christina finished.

"Tell her, Seedy." I said.

"Well. If you need to know the truth. I've tried it a few times, but I don't consider myself gay." Joey said candidly.

"If you asked me, you suck one dick, you're gay." Box said with absoluteness.

"Personally, I can't imagine looking down on a naked man and saying, `I'm just gonna try this to see if I like it.' You rob a bank, you're a bank robber. You kill a person, you're a murderer. You suck another man, you're a..."

"A sucker. Look. You can't ride the back of a sheep and then ask yourself later if you're a Bestialiter." Box said frankly, creating his own prefix.

"Oh, sick! That's almost as gross as picturing Steven and Quinn having sex." I said.

"What the hell is wrong with Quinn?" Box asked genuinely once again.

"So what would you and Box have gay men do? It's not like they decided one day to become gay. It's natural for them to want men instead of women." Debara explained.

"I'm certain if you asked the guy riding the back of a sheep he'd tell you the same thing." I reasoned in a glib tone.

"A sheep can't consent." Debara returned.

"The infamous `consenting adults' defense. Sounds like the argument for legalizing drugs. You're not for that too, are you?" I said, hoping to entrap her.

"Please. Not the legalizing drug argument again." Debara threw up her arms in frustration.

"If being gay means throwing a grenade to one of us

with the pin removed, then stop it. If it means handling a weapon like you did in training, then by all means… Whatever it is you guys do. But until you decide what exactly it is that you are, I don't want you seeing me naked." Box said.

"Shit. If it means never seeing you naked again, I'll go down on the next man that walks by." I said, attempting to keep the conversation light.

The conversation was absurd, but it helped pass the time. We fell asleep four hours into the flight and remained that way until we made our descent into Ramstein. The base shared a runway with the international airport, making it convenient for our short excursion into Switzerland.

Passage through West German customs was like crossing into California with Fruit Fly infested vegetation in the trunk of your car. You simply lie, and cross on through. We flashed our phony private passports, with fictitious names and ten year expiration dates. I was asked a single question.

"What is the nature of your visit to Germany?"

The answer was simple, I was abroad on a sight seeing tour with friends.

Upon our exit from Zurich International Airport, we were met by what seemed like a United States military man in civilian clothing. In his early forties, he was tightly groomed and regimental. He recognized Box, triggering thoughts in my mind of clandestine meetings between Box and faceless agents throughout the world. The man gave us a grand tour of the city, hub to the international banking system. We finally traveled the N1 to University Street, crossing over the Limmat Quai (named for the River Limmat), where, just a few blocks to our left, in the Theater District, was the Hotel Europe, temporary home to our drug lord representatives. We continued on, passing over the north end of Lake Zurich, where we turned on to the Bahnhostrasse, or shopping street. We then crossed through the main banking district, on route to the Union Bank of Switzerland. Located at the southern end of the Bahnhostrasse, the Union Bank is built under ground, just below the main railway station, in a place called "Shopville." Box made a large cash withdrawal while the rest of us found relief in the public restrooms. Having already parked the vehicle on Lowen Street, we made our way back to the Bahnhostrasse, which happened to be only ten minutes from Hotel Zurich. With the railway station at our backs, we strolled the Bahnhostrasse on foot.

Although the temperature was brisk, it certainly didn't deter the number of tourists shopping. I noticed immediately the elegance and the cleanliness of the area. Most of the people on the street were window shoppers, not unlike the tourists of Rodeo Drive. After salivating over those luxurious items we could never afford, Box led us into a store that featured expensive suits, leathers and furs.

"Joey. Ves. You two pick suits of a conservative nature and get 'em fitted." Box said.

"How 'bout you?" Joey asked Box.

"How 'bout us?" Debara followed quickly.

"Just these two." Box began. "I guarantee it. We open Joey's suitcase right now and we get retina damage from the silk suits and paten leather shoes."

"What's wrong with what I brought?" I said, somewhat embarrassed.

"Oh please, don't get me started. What is it this time, Big Daddy Cane or *Scar Face*?"

"Neither. And you're not gonna turn me into a Boxito." I added the "ito" to Boxer's name as a satirical means to demonstrate that he was treating me like a child. He understood the reference, having only weeks earlier been thoroughly briefed on Fabito "Young Fabio" Ochoa.

"What's wrong with the way I dress?" Box felt the tables turning.

"I'm a now, eighties kinda' guy. You're a then, seventies kinda' guy. I'm flash. You're listless. I'm outgoing. You're... you're... catatonic. I'm funny. You're not. I'm..."

Box stopped me. "I get it. I get it." He stared at me, and then through me. "Catatonic? Where the hell did you come up with that?"

❖ ❖ ❖

The Hotel Zurich, situated at the intersection of the Limmat and Sihl rivers was rated five stars and was one of the most contemporary in Zurich. From the street, I could see the wavy reflections of the water and lights dancing off the windows. It was evening and it had been more than twenty four hours since my departure from Paducah.

We ate at the hotel, which served fine cuisine, Swiss style. I had the veal and mushrooms, smothered in a creamy white wine sauce. Although this had been the best meal I'd eaten in a couple days, my stomach disagreed. I vomited immediately afterward, but the meal was well worth it.

A conference room had been reserved at the Hotel Zurich for our anticipated guests. To determine the authenticity of all the participants, they were made to surrender their organization's shipping code symbols for a prescribed time period. These symbols were used when large traffickers allowed smaller organizations to *piggy-back* on a given shipment. The symbols were controlled by a cache of high level officers within the organization, and were secured like nuclear launch codes.

Box was scheduled to lay out the technical details of the proposed operation, and I would intercede on any disputes, attempting to resolve them in favor of United States interests. Christina would handle all translations. We brought only one translator so as to avoid any attempts on the part of the cocaine traffickers to divide us on any issue. Joey would discuss sideline matters with Sicilian representatives that would work as a buffer for many of the drugs that would be allowed into the country. Debara's role could best be described as feminine persuasion. The southern hemisphere drug lord is not partial to the modern woman. If her beauty, and not her mind, could be used to swing the pendulum in our favor when a representative teetered on the brink of assuagement, then Debara's presence was vital. This was not a game of political correctness.

At precisely eight the following morning, we entered the meeting room, fully expecting to be the only ones present. To our surprise, the room was filled with people helping themselves to a breakfast buffet. If I hadn't known better, I would have thought it was the gathering of a bowling league. A number of the group were American. Obviously, the influence of a pretty woman was considered a prudent addition to a drug entourage as well. There were no suits visible. The diversity of colors worn ranged from brown to light tan, with an occasional yellow for contrast. The women, exactly one per representative group, leaped from the page with colors galore. I felt like a character in *The Far Side* comic strip, who suddenly realizes he has just committed a grievous faux pas by overdressing for a meeting of drug barons.

The room gradually quieted as our guests began to take notice of us standing in the doorway. As I gazed out over our captive audience, I turned my head momentarily toward Box.

"You must get this a lot when you enter a room." A comical allusion to the fact that there were no black people among our counterparts.

"I can handle it." Box asserted. He then glanced at me.

"You're in charge."

"What!" I blurted out.

"We can't take the chance that these people don't deal with black men. You're in charge. I'll advise you if it gets too sticky.".

"I would consider now to be too sticky." I said anxiously, as Box charged off across the room, weaving his way through the crowd with arms stretched upward to thin himself as he slipped sideways passed the final group.

"Where the hell do you think you're goin'? Hey! Get back here! I'm in charge!"

"Come here! I want you to meet someone!" Box called out from across the room. As I approached, I was taken back by the familiarity Box demonstrated toward this sophisticated looking, grey haired gentleman. He was equal in stature to Box, and quite svelte for a man of his age.

"John Hull, this is Anthony VesBucchi. Ves, this guy and I go way back. He's here because he's mutually trusted by both sides. It's the Campasino's (Coca Farmers) way of ensuring we're who we say we are."

John Hull ran a small cocaine operation out of Northern Costa Rica. His plantation included a sizable runway, capable of accommodating large military aircraft. The United States Government, although fully cognizant of Hull's involvement with the cocaine trade, had helped in the construction of the runway. Costa Rica's northern neighbor evidently proved more threatening to our government than the cocaine trade. The United States government utilized this runway to fly in supplies for the Nicaraguan Contras, and to insert Contra troops back into the field after they completed para-military training in the Costa Rican jungles. John Hull was a man who knew how to appease all camps.

"So. Whata' ya think of our little get together here?" I asked.

"I'm not sure what to think yet. It all sounds a bit rogue to me. Of course, it mustn't be any more off-

black [grey] than the little matter on my coca plantation. Huh, boys?"

"I'm sorry, did you say coca…" I started, before Box
interrupted.

"We should probably get this thing rolling. If you'll
excuse us, Mr. Hull."

As we made our way to the front of the room, Box
explained himself.

"Take a good look around you, these people are all
connected to the drug trade in one form or another.
Maybe you forgot that somewhere between the caviar
and the crumpets…"

"They have crumpets?"

"No! I don't know. The point is, what the heck were
you acting so shocked about back there. Of course, he
has a drug farm."

"Plantation." I corrected. "But you aren't friends
with all the other farmers?"

"Well. Someday you're gonna be explaining to some
young agent why you're friends with *Don* Fabio
Ochoa."

"I suppose. But I still want an explanation sometime."

"Fine. Get your mind on this now. It's time," advised Box.

Box distributed bound folders to each of the camps,
and then made his way back to the front of the room
where he pulled down a large projector screen. Although I was supposed to be the one doing all this, I
stood in place, awaiting some indication from Box as
to what I was supposed to do. Box dimmed the room's
lights and turned on the over-head projector. The
room became silent.

"What are you waiting for." Box whispered.

"A clue." I whispered back.

"Read the slide and wing it."

I knew that once I got the ball rolling, I could improvise my way through the briefing and negotiations. I walked over and turned the lights back up. Box remained calm, but concern was drawn on his face. I wanted to get a quick gander at the folders Box had passed out, but did not want our guests to become alarmed at my lack of insight. I removed the folder from the camp of Louis Porto, the Peruvian drug baron, and brought it with me to the podium at the front of the room. With a glance of its contents, a matter of critical importance occurred to me. The folder included several sheets of ordinary note-book paper, and a cheap fountain pen.

"Ladies and Gentlemen." I read as much of the folder as I could while I spoke. "The contents of this binder are classified."

Christina translated for our non-English speaking guests, even though each camp came prepared with its own American negotiator.

"If you need to take notes, paper and a writing instrument have been provided. You will not be allowed to take this document, or any part of it, with you when you leave."

Under normal circumstances, notes taken during a classified meeting would fall under the same classification as the meeting itself. However, in this particular instance, we would not be concerned if the representatives lost their notes. We only worried about the possibility of a trail of evidence leading back to the CIA. Everyone felt that mere notes could never form a credible foundation for such an accusation.

"I want you to study the aircraft modification schedule included in your package. We would prefer you not fly any aircraft in from outside our borders at this point."

The package did not address the issue of where the craft should emanate from, I just thought it would cut down on the logistical problems. "So, I would suggest a little capital investment at this point if you don't already have a few aircraft in the United States already."

Everyone laughed, men first, except for us. I figured that this meant they already had lots of drug planes in our country. "I guess we won't have to worry about the 'Filing Flight Plans' section then." They laughed once again. "So, we'll equip your aircraft with transponders in Mena, Arkansas." A repetition of the name Mena coupled with chuckling could be heard throughout the room.

"Stop me if I hit a subject you know nothing about." I said sarcastically. I was amazed at how smoothly it seemed to be going. "We'll equip any special craft you may possess, which is presently in your own country, on a case by case basis. This means sending trained personnel to Costa Rica to join with your aircraft at Mr. Hull's plantation." I had just committed John Hull to the operation more than he had been prior to this meeting. I wasn't quite sure why I felt it necessary to do so, other than the fact that we could more closely monitor his operation if we periodically had CIA personnel on the ground there. Many heads turned toward Hull for acknowledgment. Hull stared at me with a mild face, gently tipping the brim of a hat he did not wear.

Each camp huddled in discussion as they carefully considered every nuance of this sixty-two page rule book. The drafter of this document simplified the technical details to the degree that I almost forgot what it was we were forming an alliance for. Schedules were drawn not only for aircraft modifications, but also for weapons shipments, satellite computer hook-ups, and intelligence transfers.

When disputes or questions arose, a representative from each camp would approach the table at which we were sitting and request our assistance at their table. Invariably, the female representative would do the approaching. She would then escort us to her table where I would negotiate with the English speaking representative. If a question came up that involved everyone, and not just a single camp, then the woman from a given camp would stand and wait for us to recognize her. Once we did, the English speaking representative would ask the question in an open forum. For the most part, their ability to work within the parameters of our extremely tight and condensed schedule was remarkably good.

The organizations of Louis Porto and Roberto Suarez (Bolivia) were elated with the new arrangement. They would produce most of the coca paste in South America, and would do so predominantly with their own crops. The Peruvian and Bolivian coca bush was the richest plant in the world due to the climate, rain fall, and altitude of the regions. For this reason, the Colombians were pleased to receive their paste. The fact that the Peruvians and Bolivians would no longer pose a threat to business also pleased the Colombians. The Porto and Suarez camps were likewise content not to face the possibility of arrest attempting to fly drugs into America, or the threat of extradition for their involvement with drug trafficking.

With the prevailing mood of cooperation, there were still a few hurdles yet to cross, but none rivaled the level of intensity developed over the issue concerning the amount of drugs to be seized.

A short, somewhat pudgy, Hispanic woman stood, clearing her throat lightly. She was mild and polite in a puppy dog sense. I surmised that she must be the sister of someone important.

"Yes. We recognize our distinguished emissaries from Puerto Triunfo." I said. Pablo Escobar kept a palatial estate on Puerto Triunfo some one hundred miles East of Medellin, Colombia, on the Magdalena River.

A man with a southern accent rose to his feet, and,

CIA: COCAINE IN AMERICA

with his hands bracing him as he leaned over the table, he said in a cocky manner: "You expect us to just hand you half of our drugs. You must be crazy. Do you have any comprehension as to how much that is? We figure you're getting about two percent now, so we'll give you fifteen."

"If the fifty percent that we take of what you stand to make is a large amount of money, then the fifty percent you get to keep is a lot also. Except now Mr. Escobar won't have to live looking over his shoulder all the time." I countered.

"We see what's gonna happen. You will take the fifty, and tip the DEA off to another twenty-five or so more."

"If the DEA, or anyone else, intercepts a shipment coming through our safe corridors, then we will count that toward the fifty percent. But if you get caught running a shipment outside the guidelines of *PM*, then you're on your own." I answered.

"We still think we're getting the short end of the stick. You'll have to do better or count us out. And if we go, you can bet so will the others"

"Where are you from!" Debara demanded.

"Excuse me? You don't speak to me unless I speak to you first. Do you understand me." The southerner said pompously.

Debara climbed over our table, walked briskly across the room, and leaned over the southerner's table, matching her face to his. Box tore from his seat, but was slowed by the grip I had on his suit coat. Debara said firmly, "I'll beat you like a red-headed step daughter. Now sit!" She stepped back and continued. "It's simple, people! We can fill this room with organizations who would gladly hunt you down for a much smaller chunk of the market share. Now, the way we see it, as *Don* Fabio goes, so goes everyone else. Not Escobar! So if anyone here is not pleased with our offer, leave now! But realize, we'll be giving everyone

that stays the necessary information to destroy your
bosses' empires. If you doubt the Company's resolve,
or its ability to create havoc in your lives, just take a
close look at what we did in Vietnam. We'll work with
you on all the logistical matters, but not the end result.
Now? Any more questions?"

"We're leaving. I won't have this *woman* speak to
me in this manner." The southerner looked down his
nose at Debara.

"Maybe you don't treat your women as equals in
Colombia, but we sure as hell don't have them around
as window dressing in the CIA. You want in on this?
You have to make her happy first. We're not begging
your participation in this! We're offering it. Now get
your country's Benedict Arnold ass outa here, before
I throw you out." I said in support of Debara, not quite
convinced that she had made the right call.

"Fine! Good luck tryin' to make this work without
us." The man stood to leave, but it was obvious that he
had no support among his colleagues. The Colombian
that accompanied him made a hasty appraisal of the
other participants, and performed a face saving action.

"Sit!" The Colombian said sharply in English.

"Seedy. Translate." I said anxiously.

"My American friend does not speak for 'El Padrino'
(The Godfather)." The Colombian began.

"The Godfather?" I inadvertently blurted out.

"Yes." He responded, still being translated. "The
numbers look real good to me. You must excuse my
friends ignorance. He doesn't know much about our
culture. We respect our women."

Turning to face Debara, he continued.

"Please excuse his rude behavior. You are a very
strong and noble woman. Very intuitive. My apol-
ogy." He then re-addressed me. "Come through with
the weapons and reports, and we will do whatever's
necessary to make good on our bargain." He walked

forward and shook my hand, gripping my elbow with his free hand.

❖ ❖ ❖

It took only a single meeting to set the deal. Peru and Bolivia were virtually neutralized, and Carlos Lehder would offset the effects of the Cuban drug trade. The Colombian cocaine market was now centralized and shrunk in half.

After the customary departure well-wishing, we finally had an opportunity to step back from the events of the day and assess our performance.

"Where the hell is Joey?" I inquired.

"He's off wining and dining his La Cosa Nostra buddies." Box responded.

"Amazing. We're in Switzerland, saying `Cosa Nostra' and `CIA' like others say `Moose Lodge' and `PTA'. Something' doesn't seem quite right about that. Not sure what it is, but it doesn't sound quite right."

"I keep pinching myself." Debara remarked. "It's mind boggling what we're doing here."

"Speaking of doing. Damn good job in there today. You brought us over the top you know." I said.

"Not that I need your approval. But, thanks."

"You know. One of these days that chip's gonna fall and break your foot." Box said.

"I'm sorry." Debara conceded. "You're right. I just don't want you to think I did all that to prove I was equal or something."

"Why? Do you think men don't have to prove themselves. Not a day goes by that I don't feel I have to prove myself. Being female doesn't give you sole claim to that insecurity." I reacted.

"Who do you have to prove yourself to?" she asked.

"You, for one. And Box. He won't ever feel comfortable around me."

"I'll settle for safe," Box said.

"That stuff about women not bein' window dressing. Were you serious?" Debara asked me.

"Hey. I don't particularly care about roles. I'd run naked through the Mormon Tabernacle Choir if I thought it would help the drug problem." I replied.

"That would just increase drug use." Christina joked.

" You know. With all our differences, we sure don't differ on this. I want *Pseudo Miranda* to work so bad... so damned bad." Debara said. "Why you smiling?"

"Nothing. It's just that whenever someone says *Pseudo Miranda*, it blows my mind. I came up with that name, you know?" I said.

"Oh, come on! Now you're gonna claim you named the operation too. Box?" Debara said, flabbergasted, but still pleasant.

"Yeah. The shithead did." Box answered, then qualified his remark. "He was screwing around at the time. *Pseudo Miranda* just came out with all the other spew. It's a stupid name, I think."

"How did you come up with it?" Christina asked.

"I thought `pseudo' was the ultimate in fake. People who use words like `pseudo' instead of fake, are really phony themselves. So `pseudo' is the phoniest of fake words. I came up with `Miranda' because that United States Supreme Court decision is most associated with our Constitutional protection against legal persecution. Also, `Miranda' himself was Spanish, which I thought was appropriate." I explained.

"You are so full of shit! I was standing right next to you the whole time! He just blurted it out without thought. He makes it sound like he was sitting in a think-tank or something. Boy, I'll tell ya. You're gonna talk your way right into the presidency some day. `Legal Persecution.' Give me a break." Box corrected.

"Don't listen to him." I said aloud. I then leaned in toward Christina and Debara and whispered, "He has this major jealous thing goin'. You have to feed his ego."

"You two crack me up." Debara said, as she looked out over the Limmat River.

I looked silently at the faces of my new friends as they gazed quietly at the running water. I knew their faces would not remain young for very long. Time was passing. I studied their features, not wanting ever to forget their faces as youth was yet about them. I valued this moment more with the passage of time.

On the way back to the hotel, Debara asked Box if any thought had been given to the heroin problem. She was concerned that a deficiency in the cocaine supply would somehow give impetus to a sullen opiate market.

"As we speak, Lance Motley is meeting with Khun Sa somewhere in this city." Box said.

"Lance..." I fished for his last name.

"Motley." Box filled in the blank in a manner that inferred I should know the gentleman.

"Is meeting with..?"

"Khun Sa. Oh, maybe I forgot to tell you about this. Lance Motley — who I can't stand, by the way — is sort of a Soldier of Fortune. He's been a hired gun in South-East Asia since Vietnam. Khun Sa and he have had a business relationship for years. Hence, his being hired for this operation."

"Who the hell is Khun Sa?" I asked.

"How the hell did you ever get chosen for a drug operation? You mean to tell me you don't know who Khun Sa is?" Box asked in disbelief.

"Why would a guy who grew up in Hopunk, Taxachusetts and schooled in Possum Creek, Kentucky know an Asian farmer from... where the hell's he from?"

"Asia." Box said without emotion.

"What part of Asia?" I asked impatiently.

"Burma." His speech was numb. Bringing his hand

to his scalp, he began to scratch. "Every time I begin to feel comfortable in your presence, something like this comes up." Box then smiled and shook his head, as we continued walking.

"So. Why do you hate this guy Motley?" Christina inquired
of Box.

"Sure as we're standing here, he'll be making money hand over foot on the heroin trade. He has no particular allegiance to America. He's in it for the money. And he'd slit his mother's throat for a few more pounds of it. The problem is, the CIA needed someone who was trusted by Khun Sa."

"Why didn't they hire someone who was trusted by Ochoa or Escobar if that was so damned important?" asked Debara.

"Are you kidding. We'll never meet any of those people. We'll never even get close to them. No, I'm afraid this is as close as we get." Box stated.

It didn't matter, I thought. If we could get close to fifty percent of their drugs, that would be close enough for me. It didn't seem possible that we had accomplished all that we needed to in such a short period. I was sure that as we moved through the operation, it would be necessary to continually modify the logistics. If only I knew how much modifying was needed.

Chapter 9

Awaiting word on the maiden voyage of a drug craft flying through *Pseudo Miranda* corridors, I assimilated back into mainstream life in Murray. It was clear that my life was no longer a continuum, but rather a collage of snap shots in a picture album, with each page came a new event, a profound change.

It was a beautiful September afternoon. I was sitting on the grass staircase overlooking the Murray

State University baseball field, dreaming of what could have been had I traveled a different path when Box appeared. "What in the world are you doin' here? What if someone sees you?"

"What if? Who cares. As far as anyone's concerned, I'm a friend."

"Are you?" I capitalized on his reference to friendship.

"What? A friend?" He paused as I nodded. "Yeah, I am." He said softly. "So why are you here? And why alone?"

"I was a pretty good pitcher, you know. My father taught me." I tossed some grass into the blowing air. "Boy could I throw a baseball."

"Ninety-something miles an hour, the way I hear it."

"How the hell? Oh, yeah. How stupid of me." I almost forgot who it was I was talking to. "It's funny how people's lives take such turns. I just don't ever wanta' be a coulda' been. No regrets. You know?"

"You'll always have regrets. Be content to look back and know you did your best. In fact, be content to be able to look back at all." Box attempted to place things into proper perspective.

"You sound like you know something I don't?"

"You know all right. You just chose to ignore the warning. You and I already had knowledge of *Pseudo Miranda* when we went into training. If we had failed, they couldn't have afford to have us running around with that information. Damn lucky we made it through."

"Come on, Box. No fuckin' way they would have killed us." My eyes fell upon his down trodden face, finally acknowledging what I had often attempted to suppress.

"Sonofabitch," I picked myself up from the grass. "You hungry?"

"Enough to eat a horned cow."

"Cows do have horns," I insisted. "It just so happens that bulls do too. Which, I might add, segues nicely into where we're going for lunch."

"That means steak, right?"

"Sort of."

I took Box to my favorite restaurant, McDonalds. As we pulled into the parking lot, he bowed his head in disappointment.

"I should have known." He drew his head up and shook his hands in front of him. "What does this have to do with beef?"

"It doesn't. But a lot of cute college girls come here. And the food ain't bad either."

We were about to enter the restaurant when I noticed them: two women on horse back. Even in Murray, this was a bit unusual. I tapped Box on the shoulder and told him to follow me. After some sensitive negotiations, I was calling for Box to join me on horse back.

"Why?" He questioned. "Just tell me what in the world would possess you to get on that thing? We're in a parking lot, for God's sake." Box spun around toward my Corvette. "They're taking your car, by the way. But, of course you probably knew that. I'm sure it has something to do with your sitting on the back of that damned thing."

"It's a horse. Not a thing. Climb aboard. They said we could take 'em through the drive-through and no further."

"The drive-through? We're going through the…" Box pointed to the drive-through. "On these. Have you ever ridden one of these things?" Box said as he mounted the horse.

"No. I told her I had. But, no, I never have. It's not like we can break 'em or anything. I've watched *Bonanza*. You steer 'em with this."

"That's called a rein. Even I know that."

I gave the horse a little nudge with my feet and he

CIA: COCAINE IN AMERICA 123

miraculously began to move. "Oh, my God, he's movin'! Look, Box! I'm riding a horse! Yee! Ha!"

I'm not sure what it is about a horse that makes people scream these two words in this particular order, but I was overwhelmed with the urge to do so. Boxer's horse began to move at much the same languished pace as my own, bringing creases of joy to his face.

"Giddy-up! Giddy-up! This is great!" Even though our horses never moved faster than the average person could walk, we were ecstatic to have them move in the direction we wanted them to. We pulled our horses to the drive-through speaker and ordered our food like we imagined a Texan would have. I was first.

"Howdy maam. I would be a might pleasin' if you would be kind enough to get me some of them there fries you be a serving up at this here fine diner of yours. It'd be mighty hospitable of ya to fire me up a couple burgers on the griddle, too, and toss a hunk a cheese on 'em while you're at it." The girl at the drive-through window could see us clearly.

"Would ya like any thing to drink with that, Little Joe?"

Box leaned over his mount.

"You're darn tooten we want some beverage with ar' slop. But first burn the moo outa' a couple more burgers. And throw in one of those cute little apple fritters of yours. We'll be washin' ar' chow down with a couple large Diet Cokes." Box leaned over and hugged his horse, kissing him on the neck. "I need to get me a cowboy hat." He said ardently.

Under my breath, I said, "Two minutes on a horse, and he's John Wayne."

"What?"

"You should. You'd look good in a hat." I answered.

"I would, wouldn't I."

❖ ❖ ❖

After we ate, returned the horses and got my car back, Box told me to drive directly to Paducah Airport. With just the clothes on my body, he expected me to fly with him to Southern Texas for the virgin mission of *Pseudo Miranda*.

"What about my gun and stuff?

"What about 'em?" Box answered.

"I don't have them. They're at home."

"Don't worry. Everything you'll need will be given to you in Mena, Arkansas, or Hondo, Texas."

"Well, which is it? Mena or Hondo?"

"I'm not sure."

"Oh, that's real comforting."

"Don't panic." Box laughed. "It's just an in-country intercept. You won't even need a weapon. Only Joey will be armed. That way, if for some bazaar reason another police force catches us, we won't have a lot of weapons to stash."

"Why have any weapons at all then?"

"In case the people that catch us aren't the police."

"You mean we kill some poor bastard who has the terrible misfortune of happening upon us."

"Where we're goin', no one's gonna just happen upon us."

"Fine. But, in the future, let me know in advance when we're gonna be up all night so I can plan my sleep around it."

"Don't worry about that. We've got pills."

"Fantastic. You've got pills. I thought we were in the business of stemming drug use."

"These are prescription."

"Good. I'm sure my body'll know the difference."

We flew out of Paducah shortly before dusk, refueling in Mena, Arkansas, before continuing on to Hondo, Texas. Darkness prevented me from getting a good look at either airport. Inside a small aircraft hanger at Hondo, we met the other team members. Of the eleven agents that worked the pre-*Pseudo Miranda* interceptions, only Christina and Chavez were absent. Those of us that were here, suited up in camouflage fatigues and flack vests. Steven carried a miniature satellite dish and connecting phone, linked by several feet of cord. Joey was armed with a 30/30 hunting rifle, but no grenades. We were all given a pair of ice hooks to facilitate the lifting and handling of the cocaine.

A pair of Huey Helicopters transported the nine of us to a location some eighty miles north by north-east of Laredo near the Nueces River. When we arrived, complete darkness enveloped us. The choppers departed.

I wondered if anyone knew what we were supposed to be doing. I knew that an aircraft was to be intercepted, and led over our general locale to release its cargo, but how it would happen was beyond me.

"Where the hell are we?" I asked.

Steven unstrapped a large square flash-light and pointed it directly in front of him. "The ILS Tower should be right...there!" He turned slightly to his left. "There she is. We're fine. The aircraft should pass directly over her and drop its cargo." With the light still shining upon it, I gazed in reverence at this twelve foot pole as it stood juxtaposed to the wide open Texan desert. With its vertical and horizontal moving arms, it appeared as an alien droid in search of life. I wondered who had come before us to set it up, and who would follow to tear it down. Did they know its ultimate purpose? Could they comprehend the importance of their endeavor? Only Steven was unimpressed with the modern technological genius of making this system completely mobile.

"Where should we wait?" Box asked Steven.

"Heck, right here's fine." Steven said with assurance.

We huddled snugly between several Yucca plants, careful not to sit on any fire ant mounds. We sat facing the ILS tower and spoke of the universe and all its wonder. As the talk became more scientific than poetic, I asked Steven which star was actually considered to be the North Star that the prophets followed in search of Jesus Christ. Steven roamed the brightly lit sky in front of him expecting to find what he was looking for.

"That's strange?"

"What's that?" Box asked.

"That constellation should be in the south," Steven seemed confused.

"Maybe that is the south, you moron," teased Quinn.

Steven spun around, and breathed a sigh of relief when he spotted the star he was looking for. "There it is. That's the star of Bethlehem. At least that's what most people think was the star that guided them."

"So that's north then?" I asked.

"Sure is." Steven responded.

"Then we're north of the ILS thing-a-ma-jig. Correct?" I continued.

"Shit. You're a regular Magellan." Quinn prodded.

"No. The reason I'm asking…" I looked back and forth, attempting to get straight in my head what the inevitable course of the drug shipment would be. "Am I wrong, or are we in the direct path of the drop?"

Now everyone was doing what I had done. Only now, there were eight people twirling into one another, and mumbling aloud.

"What is everyone so worried about. The plane's flying south. You know, Mexico. South. We're north. He just said it. We're north." Steven muddied the waters with directional mumbo-jumbo.

"Yeah. Everyone calm down. Steven navigated us on the high seas several times, so I'm quite sure he can handle this child's play here." Lourdes assured.

"Wait." I interjected. "Everyone please bear with

me for a moment. I know I'm probably just in a panic mode. But—for me, please—one more time about that `Mexico being in the south' stuff. See. Because, the way I understand this, he's in the south now, but he's flying north, right? And we're north of that ILS thing. So doesn't it stand to reason that he'll fly directly over our heads?" I was feeling a bit embarrassed, collectively, as well as for myself. After all, here we were carrying out a complicated and dangerous clandestine operation for the United States government, and none of us could readily comprehend this most basic question.

Box became impatient. "Wait. Steven. Look at me! What side of an ILS tracking beam does an aircraft land?"

"This side." Debara said, sounding discouraged.

"Fine. Now where should we be sitting?" Box said, annoyed. Steven was reluctant to answer, baffled somewhat by his inability to perceive directions.

"I would think on the other side of the pole." I said, as if stating the obvious.

"Let's just do something for God's sakes!" Jerimiah declared.

"Yeah. Let's go. He's right, we should be over there." Debara took control.

We moved, feeling more stupid than afraid. Steven moped along, pointing his flashlight out in front of us as we zigzagged our way around the pointed plants and ant mounds to the other side of the pole. Jesus injected a few rattle snake sound effects to keep our blood pumping. Then, a resounding noise split the evening sky. "What the hell was that!" Jesus said loudly.

"The chase plane. Take cover!" Debara warned.

We scattered in all directions, not knowing which route would provide the most security. I sprinted on a track perpendicular to our present line of travel, making a sudden stop as a yucca thorn pierced my thigh.

I withdrew my leg from its menacing tentacle, cringing in pain, resisting a shriek. Steven became the brunt of profane screams as everyone found an enemy in the Texan landscape. The shouting ceased abruptly when the sputtering of a twin engine, propeller driven aircraft was heard in close proximity.

"What the hell do we do now!" Quinn called out.

"Listen for the percussion of cocaine satchels. If they continue to get louder, run for your life!" Box advised.

"Which way!" Joey screamed in panic.

"Any way!" Debara yelled insistently.

Because the plane flew at an extremely low level, the 200 pound, cocaine filled duffel bags began to burst at our feet at the instant the craft passed over head. This provided no opportunity to anticipate the drop pattern of its cargo.

"Fuuuuck!" Joey screamed, as the trail of bags poured in directly behind him. He sprinted past, within three feet of where I was standing. I stood perfectly still, waiting for the storm to pass. The impacting thumps grew louder as the drugs neared. A breath, then a thump, another breath, another thump. With each inhalation came the thought that they were somehow linked. I waited tensely for these otherwise unrelated events to converge.

I heard what sounded like a vehicle skidding on dirt, as a duffel bag plummeted from the sky, landing no more than ten feet in front of me. I stood motionless, with dust flowing across my body. The plane sputtered away. When I could no longer hear the engines, I dropped my head forward, exhaling a breath of air.

Box conducted a roll call. As each person responded to their name, Steven shined his light upon them to determine their condition. The light traveled along the ground, following a tightly grouped chain of brown duffel bags, as Steven attempted to illuminate me. I stood near the end of a snaking trail of narcotics, having missed certain death only ten feet to the front and fifty feet to the rear. Box stepped in front of me.

"You okay?"

"Yeah." I said, not able to express the full depth of my fear The Lazy Lady II incident had been frightening, but not in the same manner as this. I could define the enemy at sea; it didn't attack capriciously in the dark, without fear, or emotion. Here, in the middle of the Texan desert, there was only faith and luck. I was never very lucky, and I didn't feel that God owed me any favors.

"Well. We best grab this shit before our limo returns." Box referred to the helicopters that would soon return to take us and the cocaine to Mena, Arkansas.

We formed units of three. The middle person gaffed a bag on either side with each of his hooks, while the other two gaffed the ends. First, we had to gather up as much of the spilled cocaine as possible and resecure the ends of the duffel bags.

"Holy shit. I'm losing feeling to the side of my face. I think I'm having a stroke!" Steven said anxiously.

"Did you rub your eyes and mouth with your hands?" Quinn asked.

"Yeah, I think so."

"It's the coke, you moron." Quinn said, shaking her head.

We piled the eight duffel bags full of pure cocaine at the point of our arrival. The chase aircraft by now had radioed back to Hondo, alerting them to the drug craft's rendezvous with the ILS tower. Steven struggled to reach our friends in Hondo, but couldn't make any progress.

"Carry it over there." Steven directed Jerimiah, pointing to his left, as he sat listening for the reception of his signal. "Hold it higher! Higher!"

Jerimiah stood on his tiptoes, extending the miniature satellite dish into the vast nothingness. "Do you even have a clue what the fuck you're doin'?"

"Wait!" Steven shouted. "Holy cow. I think I've got 'em." He said softly, as if completely surprised. "Hold it steady now!" He began to speak into the device.

"The CIDE (pronounced City) comes alive at four PM. Over." Steven identified himself as belonging to the 4 PM compartment of Central Intelligence Drug Enforcement (CIDE). Due to the antiquated nature of his radio, Steven was forced to say `over' whenever he completed a sentence. This was necessary because the instrument could only accommodate one way traffic. By saying `over,' the other party knew to speak. If the other party responded to this statement by saying, "Miranda is alive and well," we knew the operation was terminated, and we were on our own.

In this instance, the response was "Make it five, and you've got a date," telling us that all was well. Steven then informed our couriers that we were ready for an immediate evacuation of the drop zone.

When the choppers arrived, we scurried to load the cargo, and then crammed in beside it. The flight to Hondo was quick. We remained silent. We were tired and had no desire to scream over the noise of the rotor blades. Arriving in Hondo, the choppers departed hastily with the cocaine still on board, leaving us to wait patiently in a darkened hangar.

"Well. That went well." I said, while sitting on a cool cement floor and wearing a smirk of relief.

"No thanks to Steven. What the hell went wrong? How can a guy that tracks satellites not know north from south? Would ya please tell me that?" Box complained.

"I have this directional problem. If you asked me to point to a particular satellite, I could tell you where it is, and whether it's in the north, south, or whatever. I just have problems with things that move from one direction to the other. Like when the weatherman says

there's a southwest wind. Does that mean the wind is
blowing into the southwest or from the southwest?
For some reason, north always seems in front of me
and south behind me. I don't know. I have the same
problem with right and left. I don't know. I'm sorry I
let everyone down." Steven apologized.

"It's common sense for cryin'-out-loud. You simply..." Quinn started.

"It didn't seem too common this evening." I disagreed.

"No, it sure didn't!" Debara laughed. "Could you
imagine what it would have been like if Facey (Bill
Casey) had to be told that the operation was scrubbed
because the team was squashed by falling duffel bags."
Debara deepened her voice and said, "I'm sorry Director Casey, but, although the unit was highly trained in
guerilla warfare tactics, we failed to teach them north
from south."

"Quinn, you're a pilot. If anyone should have known
better, it was you." Jerimiah stated.

"If I had a compass. Or if I paid attention to our
flight coordinates. I just assumed Steven knew what
he was doin'. I didn't even pay attention until it was
too late. Shit. It all happened so fast." Quinn took the
defensive.

"Forget it. No one's hurt. We'll learn from this."
Box replied. "From now on, Quinn, you'll situate us on
all interceptions. Bring a compass. If any of you are
debriefed on your way back home—everything went
smoothly. Dig?"

"Yeah, we dig your jive turkey." Lourdes joked, not
fully understanding the slang of the era.

"Shhh. Quiet! Our rides are here. Let's rock- 'n'-
roll." Box ordered.

We ran onto the unkept tarmac, yelling farewells
like relatives departing after the holidays. As we split
up, I turned to watch my friends leave. Debara turned
in her aircraft's entrance and directed a revealing

smile toward me. I smiled back, hoping more than anything that she understood. Box, looking over my shoulder, yanked me into the plane. The door closed and we were on our way.

"You and I need to talk when we get back." Box said in a business like manner.

"Let's talk now."

"It can wait."

"If it's about Debara, don't worry. I've got a girl friend waiting for me in Kentucky."

"Well, it's sort of about Debara. I mean the way you two look at each other. Man! But about that girl friend in Kentucky. Ah—shit, how do I say this?"

"She's cheating?"

"Yeah, I'm afraid so."

"With who?"

"Steve. The guy that sat in front of you in your Italian class."

I laughed in relief. "No way! She's always joking about him. Calling him a geek and shit."

"Well, it looks like she's screwing a geek."

"Jeez, Box, don't mete it out to me slowly, in manageable portions or anything. Is this how you tell a friend his girlfriend is being unfaithful?"

"Hey, I'm sorry. But you need to realize this job takes precedence over relationships. Now that you know about her, you can't trust her with anything. She's a security risk."

"Great. Andy's a national security problem. This sucks, you know."

"I know."

"The agency could have gotten this wrong, you know. I mean, they're fallible too, you know."

"They've got pictures."

"They've got pictures! They've got fuckin' pictures! I don't believe this. Is anything sacred? Have you seen these pictures?"

"Do you really want to know the answer to that?"

I shook my head in disbelief. "This really blows."

"I know."

"Is that all you're gonna say, I know?" Box shrugged, befuddled, so I continued. "I wanta see naked pictures of your wife."

"Excuse me. Is that what this is about? Do you think I took the pictures into the bathroom or somethin'? I glanced at them just long enough to know what it was she was doin,' and with who."

"So what was it she was doin'?"

"I'm not answering that. You're just gonna drive yourself crazy with this. The only thing that's important is that she cheated."

"Wait 'till I see her. And him. He's supposed to be a friend. I'm gonna rip his fuckin' head off."

"Oh, no! You can't tell them you know anything about this. When you see her, just tell her you've found someone else or something."

"I'll do my best."

"No, damn it! You'll do it — period!"

"Is this how you'd handle it if your wife cheated on you!"

"Look, I'm sorry for sounding so cold. I just don't want you getting in trouble. Don't learn the hard way about this. People like you and me have to protect our identities with our lives, because our lives truly depend on it." Box leaned in toward me. "I know you love her. I know this won't be easy. But you have to keep your eye on the ball. She's your past. We're your future. I hate to say your country needs you, but they do. She's small town. She could never deal with what you've become, and I think you know that. Anyhow, she doesn't hold a candle to Debara."

My upper body shook mildly with my giggle. "Great. You sound like my mom. When my dog Gypsy died, she brought a puppy home the next day to replace her."

"Did it work."

"Well, yeah. But..."

But what? Think of Debara as a little puppy."

"I'll expect to see her on my kitchen floor when I wake up tomorrow then."

"Consider it done." Box said, leaning his head back in his seat and closing his eyes.

Morning broke while we were still in the air over Arkansas. Box awakened and began to brief me on the next mission. He told me that we would be flying into Colombia, and that we would be raiding a cocaine laboratory deep within the country. I was concerned with the geographical problems. Especially in light of the comical incident that had just occurred in a state, and a terrain, that we were supposed to be familiar with. Box told me that a CIA friend of his named Bob Terpening presently worked in Langley and was an expert in these matters. Box said that he was so good, in fact, that the CIA waited outside his class room one day, just before he graduated from a college in Oregon, and offered him a job. Terpening was so invaluable to the CIA, that, although he told the recruiters he would be on vacation to Mexico all summer and would be unavailable to take the position, they waited for his return, and called him the day after his arrival.

Box said that Terpening allegedly prevented the United States military from committing a grievous error during the Vietnam conflict. America planned to attack the Vietnamese from a certain island, but Terpening informed the military that, although they had photographs of the island, it simply did not exist. Box said the story was that the Vietnamese had created a fake island to lure the military into an ambush.

His recount of this story eased my mind quite a bit. I repeated this man's name to myself over and over, wanting to remember it in case anything went wrong.

I didn't know exactly what I would, or could do, but it seemed like a name worth remembering.

Back in Murray, Kentucky, I scrambled to get my affairs in order. I was told that immediately following our trip to Colombia, I would be leaving Kentucky permanently. I would need to travel light, so I arranged to have all my furniture picked up by a used-furniture store.

I went out with Andy a few times, taking her to church on Sunday in hopes that her conscience would be aroused. I figured if she confessed her transgressions to me, it would demonstrate that it was only a one time deal. I was feeling scared about my future, and wanted to have someone to turn to that wasn't a part of this operation. I suppose I hung on for all the wrong reasons. I needed her, but no longer wanted her. I didn't tell her what I knew to be true. I was headed into the unknown, and didn't want to hear her say that she no longer loved me.

My fear of the future wasn't too far off. Eleven of us would enter Colombia, but not all would return.

Chapter 10

I was awakened at 3:10 AM by the Motorola STU III secure phone hidden beneath my bed. I plummeted from the mattress, struck my head on an end table and landed on the unforgiving hardwood floor.

"Are you okay?" Dana leaned over the edge of the bed, clutching the sheet to her bare skin."

"Yeah, I'm fine." I picked up the phone and slithered under the bed for privacy. I turned the side key.

"Secure," Boxer said at the other end. The display on the phone verified by showing SECURE.

"Secure."

"The city comes alive at four PM," Box said.

"Who the fuck is calling so late?" Dana asked.

"Shut the hell up," I told her. "It's my mom."

"Good ComSec, Ace," said Boxer. ComSec stood for Communication Security, a word used exclusively by the government.

"Oh, yeah," I replied. "Miranda is alive and well."

"Politico," Boxer responded, using the code word that was to conclude our exchange. "Paducah Airport, five PM tomorrow, Vosotros. Repeat and sever."

"Paducah, five PM, Vosotros, that's it."

"Tomorrow!"

"I thought you said sever!"

I hung up and crawled into the bed.

"Who's Miranda?" Dana asked with a tone of petulance. "The chick who's so alive?"

"You mean my cousin?"

Dana got up and started dressing.

"I'm leaving," she said, skipping on one foot while attempting to lace a shoe.

"What the hell's wrong with you?"

"Do you really expect me to believe your mother called you long distance at three in the morning to talk about your Hispanic cousin? Who do you think you're talking to?"

"Rates go down this time of night."

"Bye, asshole."

"Wait! I'm just kidding!"

But Dana left. In reality, that was exactly what I wanted her to do.

❖   ❖   ❖

Driving my 1982 Corvette to Paducah the following afternoon, I realized clearly, for the first time, the diametrically opposing directions I was attempting to travel. The seemingly harmless balancing act of the night before demonstrated the incompatibility, if not duplicity, of my past and present life.

By late afternoon I was parked in the lot of the remotely located Paducah Airport. As I walked to-

ward the Titan 404 airplane parked on the far side of
the ramp, I saw Box beside it. The sight of him sent my
memory back to the Maryland trip we'd taken together in the black Pantera DeTomaso when all of this
had begun.

I mentioned the trip as I joined him beside the
plane.

"Don't remind me," he responded. "That was the
impetus for my down-slide from a cushy logistical job
to God knows where with the likes of you!" Box spoke
with a seeming nervous energy, although he was
usually more amused than anything else. He looked in
the direction of where I'd parked my car.

"Where the hell is your gear!"

Operation Vosotros was the name given as a counter
to the Colombian drug lords' alliance Nosotros.

As in Operation Lighthouse, the name given to the
interception of Colombian aircraft flying into the
United States, this was a compartment of *Pseudo
Miranda*, and, therefore, operated as a cooperative
and mutually beneficial agreement to the efforts of
both sides. Unlike Lighthouse, however, Vosotros
operations were conducted outside the borders of the
United States, making them far more precarious.

We made our initial stop in Mena, Arkansas, where
we met up with Jeremiah, Lourdes, Rick and Christina.

Mena's airstrip is anchored on all corners by pine-
smothered mountain ranges. Its remote accessibility,
due west of Little Rock near the Oklahoma border,
offered a perfect point of cohabitation for drug traffickers and their predators. Large aircraft hangars
housed anything from drug planes and their cargo to
military weapons destined for Nicaragua. Unrelated
CIA operations were simultaneously performing their
missions out of this obscure locale in utter anonymity.

The 4 PM team utilized this strategic position for nothing more than an abridgement of personnel and cocaine en route to forward bases. While on the ground, personnel was to limit travel and speak with no one. Except for an exceptional few, most adhered to the guidelines religiously. I was, naturally, one of the few.

"Remember, Buch," Lourdes warned me. "Don't speak with anyone."

We all were outside at the airstrip, standing beside the C-130 Hercules military transport that had brought us here. The weather was mild and breezy, with the temperature in the seventies.

"Loosen up, girl," Rick said to Lourdes.

I strolled over to a small green building made of tin. On the roof were numerous antennas. Just behind the cluster of small shed-like structures were satellite dishes of various sizes. I entered the green building abruptly, startling the man working inside. He was so thin you could see the definition of his skeleton. He wore glasses and a button-down white shirt. His pants were oversized, baggy and pleated.

"Close the damn door!" he exploded. "This room has to maintain an optimum temperature of 72 degrees."

But he was reacting only to the threat of his equipment. Apparently my matter-of-fact intrusion had conveyed to him a sense of authority.

"Quite an operation you've got here," I said. You've been handling all our communiques." I read the name of a piece of equipment off its base to buy time and to avoid an ugly reprimand caused by the activation of an intruder alarm.

"So this is the KG-84 Cryptographic machine I've heard so much about."

I continued to talk swiftly as I moved around the room in search of a logical transition out the door. Then I spotted a Safe Driver's Program Award on the wall. I walked over to him and shook his hand.

"Mr. Brown, Equatorial Communications is damned proud to have you represent us in such a distinguished fashion. Mr. Casey himself has made laudable comments about you. I just want you to know that you make us all look good. So...give me some fodder for my next meeting with Claire George."

"Who?"

"Don't kid with me. You know darned well who the Director of Operations is."

He obviously wanted to avoid knowledge of Claire George because he said proudly, "I've kept the C-200s at a 99 percent in-commission rate."

"I'm in Personnel. All of these pieces of numbered equipment get conglomerated in my head. So please refresh me so I can speak well on your behalf. The C-200...why is 99 percent good with that particular piece of equipment?"

"I see what you mean. That is I know that it already has a high reliability..."

"We both know that," I said, inventing my way. "But what would you like me to say in respect to why such a high in-commission rate is invaluable?"

"I suppose," he replied, "it's because so much of the message-traffic originates from, or is destined for, distant places."

"That goes without saying, of course. I thought you might be thinking about something not yet considered by my staff."

With that, I politely left. I looked over at the other team members urgently waving me back toward our aircraft. I meandered back, now thinking more on what I'd just learned than what lay ahead. I hadn't fully recognized the omnipotent scope of what I'd just witnessed: the C-200 Step-up and Step-down equipment was receiving inputs via satellite, decoding them, then transmitting those responses throughout the world.

In the case of *Pseudo Miranda*, aircraft and ground

transponders' Identify Friend or Foe codes matching 4 PM's were changed and transmitted weekly. This enabled 4 PM and the Medellin drug cartel to identify one another in the air and on the ground, avoiding unnecessary confrontations. Although unaware of it at that time, I would eventually learn that most of the communication apparatus supported the Nicaraguan Contras.

"Are you crazy?" Jeremiah questioned. "What kind of rogue behavior was that, going into that green building! It's contrary to team!"

"Rogue behavior is inherently contrary to team. Why don't you take Rick's advice to Lourdes and loosen up."

Box, coming up to us, interrupted the conversation.

"All your equipment is on board, labeled by member numbers. Go check it out. Everyone but you, Anthony. I need to speak to you first."

He then briefed me on the fact that, following his advice, Bill Casey and George Lauder, who was essentially a public-relations man for Casey, had placed me in charge of all field operations except logistical-support decisions. This would not include the pre-planning stage because it was accurately assessed that I performed best when shooting from the hip. Box was to remain my handler, however, and would continue to fulfill his role in the planning division of *Pseudo Miranda*.

Inside the plane, Box informed everyone of what he'd told me. He would repeat the procedure when we met up with the second half of the team at Howard Air Force Base in Panama. For the most part no one seemed surprised. But it was my guess that they might very well be concerned.

The bulky ride of the C-130 Hercules was akin to white-water rafting in a rowboat. By the time we reached Howard everyone was beat.

Debara, Steven, Quinn and Joey were already on

the tarmac. They had arrived from a more direct route originating at Homestead Air Force Base in southern Florida. By now I had concluded that there must have been considerable knowledge about *Pseudo Miranda* by the Air Force Office of Special Investigation, especially when I considered the critical reconnaissance support supplied to this venture by the highest command structures of the Air Force, code-named Olympic Victor for the OV-10 reconnaissance aircraft.

As would be typical of most of our deployments into Panama, the initial journey would prove to be arduous.

Although the agreements formulated in Zurich provided for a round-the-clock availability of Panamanian-based aircraft, outfitted with Identify Friend or Foe transponders and flown by Medellin Cartel drug pilots, apparently none were ready for our use. This was an obvious ploy to provide some of the larger laboratories in the Llanos jungle time to disburse some of their product.

4 PM anticipated this kind of activity. It was in the nature of the endeavor to have to rely heavily on cooperation.

From the onset, it was obvious that Director Casey planned to send a great number of decoy missions to Columbia, making it utterly unfeasible to shut down production every time 4 PM crossed the border. This strike, however, was real, with coordinates already handed down depicting the exact location for what was then considered a large lab—two metric tons of cocaine a month.

The team finally boarded an antiquated C-123 Transport-Vintage Air America and word finally arrived that 4 PM was cleared to Panama City. We prepared for the unknown challenge that lay ahead. The atmosphere was consumed with silence. Introspection was the prevailing mood, with all of us concerned over whether or not we were prepared and whether or not we would react properly to the almost certain pitfalls.

None of us, however, could have anticipated the magnitude of the crisis that lay ahead.

Chapter 11

The trip across the Panama Canal to International Airport seemed too brief. Our American pilot was undoubtedly much more proficient at his job than we were at ours. Plus, we weren't as eager as he was to get where we were going. He placed our craft close to the Cartel's CH-60 Helicopter and our equipment was transferred swiftly. The helicopter, with us in it, began to taxi almost immediately. I was hoping that intelligence estimates on all *Pseudo Miranda* labs were accurate; I didn't hold our Washington back-up personnel in high regard.

The helicopter was owned by Pablo Escobar and flown by a Spanish-speaking pilot. Identity could be signalled to others involved in the *Pseudo Miranda* operation only by Escobar's specific tail-flashing, which is to say the color-sequence on the rudder. The flashings for each family, including Escobar, Ochoa and Ocampo, were changed periodically for immediate and exclusive identification. The changes were updated through Mena, Arkansas. Right now, the flashing on our helicopter was green and white with the number 777 overlaid.

At about 11:30 a.m., our craft landed for servicing in the mountainous region of Northern Colombia due east of Baranquilla. Members of our team, armed to the teeth and ready to defend against ambush, began disembarking as the propellers wound down.

Then, from the surrounding jungle, came countless numbers of gun-carrying individuals riding American-made, pickup trucks and Japanese, motorized, dirt bikes. They looked like bandits.

Although it appeared to be an attack, my gut instinct told me that it wasn't. But I immediately ordered 4PM members back into the helicopter.

They hesitated, as though waiting for Box's approval.

Box, sensing the potential for a breakdown in the command structure, immediately supported my order, even though doing so went against all of his previous training. Everyone returned.

Everything had happened within a few seconds. We were all now lying on the floor of the helicopter, carefully looking out windows.

Box spoke, panic in his voice, "I hope you know what the hell you're doing."

"Look over there," I said, pointing at a truck. An ambush would imply that these people surrounding us could be representatives of the Revolutionary Armed Forces of Colombia, an organization that had been carrying out uprisings against rich Columbian land owners. If that were the case, they could have carried out such an uprising right here and, I guessed, be in an emotional state.

"What about it?" Christina asked nervously.

"Yeah," said Boxer, "what about it?"

"I wasn't sure at first," I said. "But that's a fuel-servicing truck. They don't seem to be in a panic. I'm thinking now they belong to Escobar."

Jeremiah responded in anger, "How do you know the FARC hasn't killed the driver and stolen the vehicle?"

"Our pilot was cleared to land here with the pre-set IFF code. Unless the fucking FARC knows about PM and knows exactly where we were going to put down, we should be okay. Anyhow, I see something else now. Look over there in the trees. Anyone attacking this airstrip, including the FARC, would have first knocked out those sniper pods. But the trees don't look as though they've taken any serious gunfire lately."

"All right, then," Joey added with sarcastic relief, "Maybe the fact that the pilot is talking and laughing with that gray-haired guy in the Jeep might also be a good sign."

"Oh, yeah," I agreed quickly, leaning my head back and blowing a large sigh of relief. "That, too."

"So you weren't absolutely sure of anything, were you?" Box said.

"The only thing I've been absolutely sure of is our inability to play Audie Murphy in the middle of the Colombian jungle."

"Good call, Ace."

❖ ❖ ❖

The airstrip was owned and operated by Don Fabio Ochoa. The people who'd appeared to be bandits were, in fact, exactly that—the notorious Cocaine Cowboys. These bold enforcers of Medellin drug-cartel law acquired their name from a purported ability to shoot enemies with exacting precision while perched on their vehicles and traveling at speeds in excess of 70 miles an hour. My decision not to confront them had obviously been a wise one.

The Colombian pilot, reentering his cockpit, seemed oblivious to everything that had happened. A veteran of the drug trade, he'd probably grown numb to the sensation of surprise.

I certainly hadn't. And I sincerely believed that the team could find safer ways to get their adrenal rushes.

I snapped myself up from the floor and headed out of the helicopter, calling for Lourdes to follow me.

Outside, I headed toward the front of the aircraft where I was met by the older bandit who'd been talking with the pilot. He was a stout, pudgy man in his middle forties with a gray-and-black beard grown over several previous days. He took my arm firmly and attempted to guide me back aboard. I resisted, saying, "Lourdes, get your ass up here."

"Tell this guy I need someone in authority! Translate."

She did and the bearded man responded in Spanish, telling her that he was indeed the commander of this group. He identified himself as Colonel Borda. In Third World Nations, men who could choose their own title inevitably choose colonel; in our country they would have been emperors. His uniform wore him, crumpled with some of its pockets turned indecisively outward. I decided that he was a decidedly uncivilized man who was content to be the leader of a band of dangerous nobodies.

"Colonel Borda, my name is Anthony VesBucchi. I'm the United States Government's appointed leader of this group. I need to make a request that one of my translators ride up front in the cockpit of this helicopter in order to render continual communication with the rest of us in the back. My reasoning is simple..."

Colonel Borda was perfectly capable of understanding English. He began to bellow, inaccurately pronouncing my code name and flailing his arms.

"You're VesPucci, of the CIA. Your group is Miranda Team!"

"Sir, I need this request granted or..."

"You get in plane. Everything go smooth."

I could smell an aggravating combination of raw beef and licorice-flavored aguardiente on his breath. And I was definitely not appreciating the fact that respect for my leadership position was not being reciprocated by him. But, on the other hand, I was not forgetting that Colonel Borda and company were toting automatic weapons, namely MAC-10s.

"Interrupt me one more time, Colonel, and this group you call the Miranda Team is going to turn the area into a thousand-hole golf course. I don't particularly give a shit what your rationale is for not wanting my translator in the cockpit. But that's

precisely where she's going. Whether you realize it
or not, we came within milliseconds of cutting your
men in half. Capiche?" I added, somehow believing
that the Italian word might assist his understanding.

There came a formidable pause. Then, with a face-
saving grin, he pulled a bottle from a pocket of his
rumpled jacket.

"Have some Scotch! Then we go wherever you
like."

"Do you mean you're coming with us?" I asked
with surprise.

"I'm your guide," he said matter-of-factly.

Chapter 12.

The trip to the Llanos region was magnificent. Colombia, from above, appears as richly flowing in all hues
of green as any country in the hemisphere. In order to
avoid Colombian radar, the helicopter skimmed the
terrain, giving us a close-up view of the aesthetic
qualities of the landscape.

Then, the chopper altered its course slightly and
followed the Magdalena River on a south-easterly
track toward Puerto Triunfo, approximately one-hundred miles east of Medellin. The scene below changed.
Jungles patched with pastures began to crop up. Small
bodies of water mirrored the belly of the helicopter as
it swooped down from the hillsides. We all rested, but
no one got enough sleep.

Finally the CH-60 nosed forward as we approached
an unlikely airfield in the midst of the jungle. As the
craft touched down, we could see another entourage
of welcoming bandits. But this time Lourdes, relaying
information to us from the pilot, convinced our team
that all was well. We had reached the optimum staging point established at the onset of *Pseudo Miranda*.

Quinn, our navigation expert, assured us that our location was correct.

The group of bandits swarming around the aircraft this time was known as the Muerte a Secuestradors or Murder to Childnappers. The organization had been formulated as a result of the kidnapping of Don Fabio Ochoa's youngest daughter by M-19, the April 19th Movement, a revolutionary group of the socialist variety.

Almost as fast as we could depart the helicopter, tents and gas generators were positioned to form a well-crafted camp site. Four tents were pitched. Three were for a fatigued PM team. The fourth was to shelter Colonel Borda.

But the colonel had been drinking steadily and he was preoccupied with diverting my attention in order to cut our cocaine yield. I wanted the others to get their rest, but I gave up on mine and followed the pudgy, scraggly-bearded man to his tent where he raised his bottle in invitation.

"No, thank you," I said.

Borda exited the tent and began to rant and rave, demonstrating his resolve to prevent other team members from sleeping if I continued to refuse his invitation. I demonstrated the universal gesture of defeat by letting my shoulders droop and followed him.

"Okay, okay," I said wearily.

"You drink now?" he asked with a touch of surprise, slapping an arm around my shoulders. He held the bottle to my mouth and said, "Bazookas!" It was the name given to the coca paste that was notorious for blowing your mind when smoked.

I took a gulp.

He did the same and handed the bottle to me, shouting, "Bazooka brains!"

I was momentarily taken in by his sloppy charm. I proved it by taking another drink and then shouting back to him, "Cannonball!"

But I was beginning to realize that there was no way I was going to distract this intoxicated leader of bandits away from his objective.

Box, who'd obviously trailed us, suddenly stepped into the tent.

"Buenos noches, Colonel."

Box then proceeded to chop a downward-thrusting overhand right to Borda's jaw, sending him into sudden unconsciousness.

He turned to me, grinning.

"Let's get some shuteye."

❖ ❖ ❖

At dawn, most of the team slept, still exhausted, but I'd gotten up at daylight and walked to the top of a small hill where I sat down on the ground to view the valley below. Moments later I was surprised when Debara joined me.

"Am I bothering you?"

"Not at all." My guard was often up with Debara, but not at this moment. She sensed it.

"Take a look," I gestured in the direction of the valley below, at the rolling fields, the streams, the camels, giraffes, kangaroos, buffalos, llamas, elephants, hippos and ostriches.

Debara sat down at my side, breathing, "Wow!"

"Those animals are found only in places like Africa and India...at least that's what I thought. God, they're beautiful, aren't they?"

"From here they seem so majestic. Down there it's nothing more than survival of the fittest."

"Like up here."

"It's still nice to fantasize that we could be a part of a simple world again...at least in a vicarious sort of way."

I nodded. But I was again aware of the very real nature of this higher space we occupied. At the base of the hill on which we were perched, surrounding the perimeter, was a moat. On the near side stood an enormous metal fence laced with electrical current. Access to the concave surface of the hill was limited to crossing over a bridge with a gate or coming in by air. Three sides of the strip were bordered by immensely thick jungle, which made defense of the area relatively simple. Aircraft had to come in and leave in the same direction. Occasionally, when the bridge gate was opened for personnel and vehicles, some of the more domesticated animals would meander through. Because of that, the top of the hill was speckled with docile farm beasts.

"I hope I'm ready for all of this," I said to Debara, finding a need to confide my feelings to her. "When this whole thing began back in Maryland, and even during that sadistic training in Nevada, I somehow never recognized the absolute reality of what we're going to do. If I fail, you could all be Dixie Cups." I paused. "I just don't want people thinking we died in the pursuit of peddling drugs. I want my life to mean something. I want all of our lives to mean something. I probably sound like the millions of dreamers that came before me."

"You sound human. Finally." She paused, then added, "I didn't intend that to be mean."

"I know." I felt a hand tightening into a fist. "It's just that I'm more successful when I'm showing people another exterior—when I'm extroverted, spontaneous…"

"Hey. When we're working, you need to be that way. But you've got to have some avenue of release from that, somewhere, sometime. I bet you can be real personable when it's necessary. And selfless. Well, I'll take that last back. I mean maybe much of what we're doing is selfless."

"I'm not convinced of that, not at all. But…what is it I'm worried about? Being labeled a drug-pusher? I've been wondering about something. Do you think

Jesus feared being called a nut or a blasphemer?"

"I'm sure he did fear it. But, listen, if your goal is to be like him, you're in for a world of hurt. All of us are worried."

"I know what you're saying. But that doesn't make it any easier. And…I appreciate our discussion, believe me. But it only distracts me. And I have to maintain a certain mind-set, a certain energy level, to be effective."

"Okay!" she said, laughing, emerald-green eyes sparkling, showing her perfect white teeth beneath the thick, darkly brown hair. "We'll go another direction. How's this? I think, Mr. VesBucchi, that the federal government should fund abortions!"

"Now you're talking," I replied, finding myself returning to character.

We stood up and started back in the direction of our encampment.

From somewhere ahead of us there came the ominous staccato sound of machine-gun fire.

I dove for the ground, pulling Debara with me.

❖ ❖ ❖

I reached for my weapon, an automatic Colt 45, telling Debara to stay as she was. No Colt 45. "Damn!"

I bounded to my feet and ran toward my tent. There was no one else in sight. Inside, I grabbed my handgun as well as its holster and belt which also carried additional clips and the bonus of grenades. As I came out of the tent, both Box and Borda appeared from their shelters. Several voices screamed loudly from beyond.

We scrambled in that direction. As we came around the front of the forward-positioned tent, I saw Joey sitting dejectedly at the tent's opening with his M-60 in his lap.

Strewn in front of him was what was left of a now-indistinguishable creature — meat and hide and bones and blood-soaked fur.

"I killed a horse!" Joey wailed. "A hoooorse!"

"Shit," said Quinn, her short blond hair appearing dirty even in the clean morning light, "You murdered a llama, you idiot!"

We gathered around the carnage. Box, interlacing his fingers behind his head, said to me, "Your problem, Ace."

I turned to Colonel Borda. "Is llama edible?"

Borda responded with a jolly, "Absolutely!"

I turned back to Box. "Not a problem."

But as we were to learn, the exotic animals populating the area, including llamas, had been imported by Pablo Escobar to create his own personal zoo. Eating the assassinated llama was definitely out of the question.

Chapter 13

Operation Vosotros rules dictated that the team be given a limit of three days to complete the intervention of the southern cocaine laboratory, the location of which was known only to team members. Colonel Borda continued his attempts to distract and deter us from accomplishing that mission. We were authorized to confiscate fifty percent of any cocaine production for a given period. But we were not guaranteed it. And there was no doubt that Borda would be properly rewarded by the Cartel if our mission would run out of time.

I quickly grew tired of his game and instructed my people that we were proceeding. But I decided to orchestrate the operation differently than planned — with an extra twist.

Instead of following the original plan to fly directly to the lab, I instructed Quinn to change coordinates so that they reflected a decoy mission to Letica, a small, dilapidated shanty town sitting on the bank of the Amazon River. From there, our team could theoretically launch a strike on any one of several locations.

The helicopter flew south by southeast, crossing dense jungles. The llama incident seemed to have relieved everyone. The ridiculous mistake that invariably accompanies any first-time mission was now behind us.

As the chopper began its descent, the powerful Amazon came into view. The mighty river was churning up mud and turning once-mystic water milky gray as it carved its way across the continent.

Box shouted over the noise of the rotor blades.

"The Sicilian Mafia often looked for refuge on that river."

"It's like traveling with the fucking National Geographic!" Quinn exclaimed.

Then, as though realizing her impulsive remark threatened our Command Structure atmosphere, she added, "I mean this is very educational. Really!"

Box only smiled, signalling the fact that her natural enthusiasm was okay. Quinn smiled back. The rough edges were softening.

I made sure that Colonel Borda and the pilot, sitting in front with Lourdes, could not hear me.

"We'll stay in a group of at least three, when we land. Exactly an hour from touchdown we'll return to this helicopter and head to the target zone." Team members understood that they would use that hour simply as part of the twist in this new decoy mission.

I looked forward at Borda.

"It'll be my job to shed the colonel. We're close to striking the primary target. Let's be careful!"

When we disembarked the CH-60 on the outskirts of Leticia, we were surrounded once again, this time by children who had learned that it was customary for the Colombian elite, including drug barons, to offer gifts and food to the poor when visiting among them. Our large helicopter was signal enough to them that its occupants must be among that elite.

Colonel Borda had reached under his seat, where normally the windscreen protective covering was stored, and pulled out a large canvas bag. Now, outside the aircraft, he opened it to reveal that it was filled with coins. He began giving them to the surrounding children by the handful.

Jeremiah, his dark face with its strong jaw usually reflecting grimness, suddenly got caught up in the excitement created by this show of generosity. He ripped the bag from Borda's grip and began showering the kids with cash. His face relaxed so that he appeared years younger. He continually looked at the rest of the team, grinning at our laughter, unable to control his childlike jubilation. The colonel, however, was not amused. He had intended to reserve a portion of the money for sexual activity which could be purchased in this community.

But Jeremiah emptied the bag, then, his eyes full of tears, stepped back beside Borda. It had not been just the excitement.

"My father would have loved to have done that if he could have afforded it. Do you have more money for these children, Colonel?"

Borda smacked a palm against his forehead and muttered several expletives. I decided that he would still be intent upon finding his sexual interlude — even if it meant using his own money.

Debara bent down to hug one of the cutest of the dirty little boys.

"You've got yourself some new friends," she said to Jeremiah.

"Now that I'm out of money?"

"It's your personality they love, Jeremiah," I said, "not your checkbook."

"Thanks, KaBuch."

Then, to dupe Colonel Borda into thinking he had plenty of time for his assignation, I said to the others, "Remember—everyone be back here at noon tomorrow."

Borda took off quickly. Several of the team did the same, but leisurely. Box, Rick and myself closed in on the pilot to engage him with useless but diverting conversation.

Exactly an hour later, everyone who'd gotten off the helicopter — except Colonel Borda — had reassembled beside the aircraft. I asked the pilot to get inside. He refused. I put the muzzle of my handgun to his skull and walked him in.

The chopper took off with Colonel Borda's seat empty. Our destination was the jungle region south of Tranquilandia.

❖   ❖   ❖

The CH-60 landed about 2,500 feet from the location of the cocaine laboratory, at the mid-section of a small hill that jutted out considerably, its surface covered with fern-like bushes. The aircraft's IFF Transponder had already identified itself as a *PM* insurgent. We got off and proceeded on foot from the north in the direction of the lab. Three hundred feet from the target, I signalled everyone down.

Crouching, surrounded by team members, I gave instructions.

I wanted a frontal assault in the shape of a half-moon. On either end would be the best of our personnel, which meant Jeremiah and Rick. In the center would be Joey, armed with his M-60 tree killer. Behind Joey, wearing his ever-present fishing hat, would be the quiet-spoken Steven. He needed to trail because he was the SATCOM, responsible for satellite communications. If a serious problem were to occur, he would radio the States for help. Or, if the problem appeared to be potentially fatal, he would deliver the news of our impending demise. Box and I took second point, just inside Rick and Jeremiah, with Debara, Lourdes, Quinn and Christina paired on either side of Joey.

I signalled the go-ahead with a wrist-flick of the hand holding my Colt 45. We started forward again.

I felt tension igniting inside me now. And I was remembering the conversation with Debara as we'd sat on the crest of that hill earlier in the day.

I glanced back at Debara. She was watching me as we moved forward. The expression in her lovely green eyes told me that she knew what was in my mind.

For the moment, I concentrated only on traveling through the jungle. As Viet Nam infantrymen before me had learned, it was not an exact science. Maintaining proper spreading was nearly impossible.

But we finally reached the edge of the lab clearing. I knew that Jeremiah was about to break through. Before he did, I waved everybody down again.

I repositioned Joey, Rick and Box so that the three of them formed a straight line.

The laboratory was positioned in a corner of the clearing. It was constructed primarily of wood. Long horizontal timbers covered with thin metal and some sort of grassy vegetation ran across the roof, which was long and narrow with a very shallow angle. The sides were open and revealed the poles that supported the building. The entire structure was approximately 70 feet long and 20 feet wide.

I had one concern: where were the Campesinos?

The Campesinos ran the labs and farmed the crops. They weren't paramilitary. They weren't capable of slipping away undetected as the Viet Cong had done in another era and in another part of the world.

I whispered the order for everyone to move ahead slowly.

We could now see why this lab was capable of producing up to four tons of pure cocaine a month. The assembly line consisted of cocaine paste acquired from Peru and Bolivia as part of the *Pseudo Miranda* setup. The resultant crystal was then dissolved in sulfuric acid. Filters were used to remove many of the impurities. Ammonium hydroxide was then added, followed by another filtering process. The base that had been created was made into a powder by combining hydrochloric acid with ether, the most important ingredient of all.

We reached the lab and determined that it had indeed been abandoned. A feeling of relief settled over all of us, along with a sense of security. Weapons were lowered to our sides as I delivered instructions to gather up the purified cocaine, approximately 500 kilos of it, and place it in the center of the clearing for destruction.

"According to Miranda guidelines, we're not supposed to harm any of the facilities in any way," Box reminded me.

"Too bad," I told him. "As a matter of fact, I'm thinking maybe we should demo this whole piece of shit."

Almost immediately, all hell broke loose.

A flash, an intense, penetrating heat and a roaring high pressure were its calling card. The loud noise was heard only by those far enough away not to feel the initial cruel heat.

The six-inch mortar round landed and exploded at Jeremiah's feet.

I was close enough to be knocked unconscious by the concussion. The next thing I knew Christina was shaking me violently. I started pushing myself up groggily, looking for the enemy and not seeing him.

"Don't get up!" pleaded Christina, still flat on the ground.

But I was on my feet now, running toward the dismembered remains of Jeremiah. Looking at what was left of him was like looking at the llama back at the camp.

I twisted around, shouting, "Joey, over here! I want some plastique!" There wouldn't be time, I knew, to give Jeremiah a traditional burial.

"The rest of you, back to the chopper!"

Box came running with Joey, who handed me enough C-4 explosive to blow up half the hillside and then hurried to the southern boarder of the clearing and began thrashing the area with his machine gun. Rick assumed command position of the rest of the team and led them back in the direction of the helicopter as Joey followed.

Box and I gathered up Jeremiah. We placed the torn-up body in a vat of acid as another mortar round sailed into the clearing. When it exploded, no one was near enough to be hit.

I took a grenade from my belt and methodically wrapped it with the plastique.

"We've got to get out of here!" Box shouted. "Come on!"

I yanked the pin from the grenade and dropped it into the acid.

"Run! Now!"

We sprinted back into the jungle, firing blindly behind us. A barrage of gunfire sounded from the clearing.

Then there was silence as we hurried over the grassy ground glistening with dew beneath a thick canopy created by tree limbs and leaves.

We paused, listening, making certain now that no one was pursuing us.

"What happened?" Box asked with total disbelief.

I shook my head.

"Who are these bastards?"

"All I know is that we're picking up the proverbial prison soap," Box responded, using his euphemism for getting fucked.

We had no answers, at that moment, as to whom our attackers might be. We could only surmise that the Medellin Cartel had double-crossed us.

It was very quiet now. But I knew that sulfuric acid was eating away the plastique which held the handle of the grenade. When the handle sprang outward, the timing mechanism would be activated.

I heard the grenade explode. I'd forgotten the enormous volume of ether stored at the facility we'd just escaped. A huge chain reaction began as the lab became Mount St. Helens erupting. A huge fireball engulfed the area as the lab was blown away. Debris was strewn for at least a mile. The thick jungle canopy was all that protected Box and me from serious injury.

Suddenly bullets began to fly at us again, as our attackers circled to cut us off.

Moving almost blindly now, skin lacerated by the unforgiving brush, we finally traversed our way back to that small hill where the helicopter had landed.

It was gone.

Chapter 14

A desperate numbness enveloped us, paralyzing us to indecision. We paced back and forth, unable to settle in any one direction.

We could soon hear the choppers distinct pulsating signature. It appeared in a precise intermittent pattern. The effect of the helicopter, as seen through the canopy, was similar to freezing the blades of a fan by slowly blinking your eyes in a repetitive fashion. We charged toward it as it hovered at a 60 degree angle to us. It moved away abruptly.

We watched helplessly as the other team members, leaning outside the craft, motioned us to follow. We darted after them. Finally, exhausted and with no breath left, we staggered to a halt. Just as we were about to throw our hands up in frustration, Box noticed the helicopter descending. With a grin and a deep gasp, he bolted for the rendezvous. We followed with the final ounces of our energy, expecting to fall face first into the mechanized angle, but the aircraft still lacked clearance to completely descend through the trees.

There's always the winch system, I thought. They could simply drop a cable and hoist us up.

Fifty feet from the aircraft, we slid to a halt. Turning sideways, we faced one another. We could see both the aircraft and our inevitable pursuers. In dismay, we stared at a cable dangling from the cargo door. It was eight feet short of reaching the ground. The aircraft was not equipped with a functional winch system. We would have to jump and climb our way to safety.

"Go ahead, Box! You first! I'll cover!"

"Bullshit! You get your ass up there. You won't need to wait for me!"

"Listen, just get your ass..."

"I can't climb! Never could! My daddy said it would come back to haunt me. And here it is just as big as shit."

"Good luck Box," I said, clutching his arm.

"You, too." Box said solemnly. "Now get you butt outa here."

I attacked the cable, leaping as high as I could. I'd hoped to leave enough room for Box to follow immediately. I barely made the end of the cable and had to climb, using only my arms, as I swung back and forth.

Intermittent gunfire filled the air. I removed my Colt 45 Automatic with my right hand while holding on to the cable with my left, and attempted to cover Box. It was an exercise in futility. The 45 caliber handgun was useless in the vast jungle. The pendulum effect of the rope only added to the futility. It was Joey who provided our assailants with a lesson in deforestation as he shredded the jungle with his 50 caliber tree killer.

Box hurled his body at the cable three or four times, leaping more forward than upward. The cable continued to sway out of his reach. I feverishly attempted to coax him onto the cable.

"Don't run at it! Stand below me! Jump straight up!" I screamed.

"What!"

"Straight up!" I signaled, pointing my thumb upwards. "Straight up!"

"No shit asshole! What the hell do ya think I'm doin'! Help me, damn it!"

"Stand below me!" I pointed downward. "Below me! Below me!"

"Okay. I think I got it," Box calmed down and gestured with his finger to the bottom of the cable. Standing directly below me, he exploded, concentrating every fiber of his body into a twelve inch vertical leap. He finally made firm contact with the cable. Box clenched my calf, digging his nails into my skin as he climbed. My grip slipped momentarily, as Box blindly felt for the cable. Just in time. The pilot began his ascent.

The helicopter's angle was insufficient to allow unobstructed clearance through the jungle. Our bodies battered into the jagged tree tops.

With no feasible location to set the aircraft down, we remained dangling precariously until the pilot finally reached a clearing some 15 miles from where he first lowered the cable. By this time, we were physically exhausted and on the brink of losing our grip. With no gentle way of lowering us in advance of the landing vehicle, we were bounced on to the rain soaked ground. I crawled toward Box, who was lying face first in the mud. Placing my hand to his back, I was able to feel the rhythm of his heart. I was too tired to speak. Rick and Steven carried us into the helicopter for the return trip.

Chapter 15

No one spoke as Box and I, saturated in blood and earth, stared blankly upward, our heads resting in the laps of Quinn and Debara respectively.

As the helicopter pilot executed another unexpected nose-in approach, Lourdes radioed back to Rick that the Colombian Special Operations Group (GOES) had transmitted the detection of an unauthorized aircraft — our plane — in the area. The GOES unit was traveling in a De Havilland DCH-6 Twin Otter, capable of speed that would make it futile for us to try to outrun. The CH-60 by this time was traveling over Tranquilandia. The aircraft slowed to a crawl, as if searching for something. There weren't any airstrips, nor any buildings or inhabitants, visible in the area. The pilot's actions were a mystery. In the middle of wide open emptiness, he had initiated an approach.

"Lourdes, what the hell is going on up there!" radioed Rick.

"What's going on?" I inquired, fearful that the worst may not yet be over.

"I'm not sure? The Colombian Government is on our tail. But for some ungodly reason we're setting down in the middle of nowhere?" Rick explained.

I grabbed the intercom from Rick's hand, and was about to demand answers when the aircraft touched down. The pilot rushed to the rear of the aircraft, leaving the helicopter running, and adamantly demanded we leave the plane. We remained still, astonished that he would even suggest we deplane in the middle of nowhere. Then, an armed Colombian appeared, seemingly from nowhere, but actually from a tunnel in the ground hidden by a fake tree. He hastened us off the aircraft by snapping the gun barrel against some of our shins. Box and I needed assistance to gain our balance. As this tall, awkward man herded us beneath the surface of the earth, we stood anxiously at the head of a long and narrow staircase. The closing of the lid of the tunnel brought absolute darkness. Finally, a dim light filtered in, illuminating the barren cubical we occupied. The stair case was cast in iron and dropped straight down through the middle of the floor. Three sides were made of eight inch thick reinforced concrete, typically associated with bomb shelters. One wall, however, was more reminiscent of military SCUPS (Self Contained Universal Personnel System), an underground military facility used to protect the United States military from chemical attack.

In the center of the wall was a six foot wide impenetrable window that protected the facility's guard. To his right and left, and at his rear, were three separate compartments that could be accessed only by an electromagnetic locking mechanism possessed by the guard. With a window view of all compartments, he could monitor anyone that he admitted, and control their progression through the staging areas.

The first room required that the occupants disrobe and shower. There was little time for embarrassment, so we simply gendered off, standing back to back, and did what was necessary.

The next stage involved the donning of an anti-static wardrobe, essentially a white cotton-like jumpsuit and black rubber boots that tied around the leg.

The final compartment removed any latent static with what might be described as a gigantic cassette eraser. We were instructed by the guard to remain perfectly still when the walls began to converge from two opposing sides. The walls came within a foot of us before stopping. Air blew across our bodies before a monotone buzz was emitted, providing for the completion of the process. The experience numbed us all.

We finally reached the door that had necessitated

the complicated process. None of us had uttered a word. We had not yet realized that our protection was so important that the cartel had risked giving us access to their previously unknown underground laboratory.

The door finally opened, revealing a pristine cocaine manufacturing plant. Huge rooms with rubberized floors and counter-balanced explosion doors were filled with sterilized Campesinos. Each of the large rooms was designed to self seal in the event of an explosion. The counter balanced doors, with rubber coated cylindrical weights plainly in view, would slam closed in a millisecond if an explosion were to occur. The occupants would be instantaneously sealed in with the violent explosion, preventing the spread of fire to the rest of the facility. Each phase of the cocaine production process occupied a separate room, diminishing the possibility of error.

As we went from room to room, careful not to trip over the twelve inch high threshold at each door, we came upon a stockpile of cocaine that, heretofore, per intelligence estimates, was not considered achievable for a single lab. My conservative calculations placed the stockpile in the 20 ton class.

The cartel's operational plan for protecting these subterranean laboratories was to self destruct the primary access cavity. Based on the likelihood that the GOES unit had detected the camouflaged entrance, it had become necessary to permit us into the covert operation. We were left to wait in the cocaine storage room, the least likely room to incur an explosion.

The storage room was unlike the remainder of the building in that it doubled as a bunker. It was designed to accommodate up to 20 people for durations in excess of six months. Cocaine wrapped in thick green polyethylene covered an entire hundred foot wall, obscuring several abundantly stocked shelves from plain view. Bedding was visible only by the

rectangular seams contouring one wall at two levels.
These beds tilted out, one over the other, suspended
like the shelves of a refrigerator. Fully functional
bathrooms were located at opposite ends of this spa-
cious bunker. Recreation came in the form of table
tennis and pocket billiards, both of which were dis-
sembled and stacked in the corners of the room.

Our internment gave everyone ample opportunity
to discuss the day's events and render opinions. That
this incident would likely have occurred irrespective
of command structure, pointed to a deep seated problem. Box and I were the only members of the team not
prepared to defray direct responsibility. Verbal assaults flared and might have been easily defeated,
however, if it were only a question of responsibility.

"Why the hell didn't we stick to the original plan?"
questioned Quinn.

"If Jeremiah were here he could answer that question," Rick paused momentarily. "Loud and clear!"

"Why did we change our plan?" asked Lourdes.

I sat up for a moment and then returned to my seat
without saying a word. With my left hand to my
forehead, elbow supported by the armrest, and eyes
fully closed, I sat expressionless as the attack persisted.

"A loose cannon, isn't that what he called you? That
shit may work with your college frat buddies, but it
doesn't fly with us. Look at you. If you had anything
to say you'd of said it. There must be nothing to say.
Otherwise you'd say it, wouldn't ya!?" Rick asserted
as he hung over me.

I turned my eyes up at Chavez wondering why he
was doing this to me, and then returned my attention
to the armrest.

"Why was the lab empty? Where were the
Campesinos? I don't get it. I don't get any of it?"
Christina said in frustration.

"They know the answers! You can just bet that. I'm

sure there were plenty of explanations in those intelligence briefings Box has been attending. I can only assume that information was disseminated to VesBucchi."

Box glanced over at me, not knowing how, or even if, he should react. I stared emptily at Box, gradually lowering my eyes once again to the floor. Box had never seen me act this way. He folded his arms and glared at Rick. Box was calculating his response carefully, not yet fully satisfied that I wasn't manipulating the mood for ulterior reasons, such as rebuilding morale.

"I can't believe it? There were intelligence reports on all this and we weren't told? You let us just walk in there without warning us or coming up with a plan or something? I don't believe this?" Lourdes rambled.

"It sure sounds like you do." Debara offered sarcastically.

"Sounds like I do what!" Lourdes replied.

"Sounds like you've already made up your mind. Rick goes off on a tangent about some presumed intelligence reports and you've got them withholding critical information against self interest. My God, girl, but you're gullible!"

"Who's side are you on?" Rick inquired.

"Four PM's side, you asshole!"

"It's time you face reality, girl. These two bozos almost got us all killed!"

"They did? Who the hell came within a cunt hair of starting a war with the cocaine cowboys!?" Debara retaliated. "So, enlighten me. What exactly would you have done?"

"Certainly not what Bucchi did! That's for damn sure." Rick responded.

"Could you be a bit more specific?" Debara pressed.

"I'd need to see the intelligence reports first, then…"

Box cut him off at the knees. "There weren't any such reports, you idiot! You hold the intelligence community in much too high regard. Stop reading that

damn Tom Clancy shit. In the real world we rely on
quick thinking. That's why Bucchi's in charge. If he
hadn't reacted the way he did, you'd be strung up by
the balls with piano wire. And less I forget" Box
walked over to Rick, standing toe to toe, with his bent
index finger shaking tensely in Rick's face. "If you
ever talk to me that way again I'll, I'll... You don't
want to know."

Lourdes looked erratically about the room, realizing she'd chosen the wrong side. "Look, I'm sorry, I
guess I'm a little worn from this whole affair."

"Can I say something?" Steven motioned with his
hand waving in the air. "First of all, the finger pointing
thing is just stupid. Nothing's gained from it. None of
us would have wanted to, or for that matter been able
to, do a better job. So let's drop it. Unless we've
forgotten', we just lost a very good agent. And for
some of us, a very good friend." Steven's mouth began
to quiver with emotion. He bent his head and folded
his arms, as he rocked back and forth. Whenever
Steven had anything to offer, he received every body's
undivided attention.

Word was passed in by a Colombian courier informing us that we would have to remain there for the
evening. The down time was dedicated to saying what
could be said, based on a limited shared history, about
Jeremiah and what he meant to us. I didn't share any
thoughts, even when probed. My mind was preoccupied with remorse, and consumed with second guessing. I reconstructed the day's events endlessly, hoping
not to find an alternative to what I did. Box crawled
over to the side of my bed when all were asleep to tell
me that I did it right. When he knelt at the head of my
bed, he noticed tears rolling gently off the side of my
cheek, falling to the thin mattress.

"Tomorrow's a new day," he said, and slipped back
to his own bed. I never moved, nor acknowledged his
presence, but it did matter. I seldom let my guard

down because it made me most vulnerable. But I knew, as did Debara, that it was a necessary part of being strong—admitting to yourself that you're not. I also knew that tomorrow I would be able to put back on the facade that made me so successful.

The following morning we awoke to a damp, clinical odor. A guard entered the room at around eight to instruct us to bathe. He was too late; we had already showered and were waiting to depart. The guard left and returned promptly with the fatigues we'd removed upon entering the facility. They were washed and had had the static removed. We re-entered the first chamber at the front of the structure and changed back into our fatigues. The guard had already placed our weapons below the original staircase and simply pointed up, signifying his desire for us to depart. The hatch was already open. The difficult transition from florescent lighting to the bright sun was made easier by the fresh air that poured into our lungs. The land was as we'd left it. The reality that the world had continued on despite our own tribulations, was a harsh reality check.

Chapter 16

Colonel Borda wasted little time with his "I told you so" speech. Rick grabbed him by the shirt collar and threatened to throw him into the rotor blade of the awaiting CH-60 Helicopter if he persisted. Rick's action offered him a chance to forget yesterday's dispute. We boarded the chopper bound for Puerto Triunfo, specifically a ranch called Hacienda Napoles.

Although we had no knowledge that we were about to be delivered to Pablo Escobar's doorstep, Debara and I remarked on the commonalty of the region. The numerous small lakes and non domestic animals scattered about seemed familiar.

I expressed my concern:

"Flying in Escobar's plane. With Escobar's pilot. Over Escobar's notorious stomping ground, can only mean one thing. Trouble."

"Why trouble?" Box said hesitantly, leaning in toward me.

"We blew up his lab. Remember?"

"What's this *we* shit? You got a frog in your pocket?" Box chuckled. Suddenly everyone began to laugh uncontrollably, giving their own renditions of the lab going boom.

"What's going on back there?" Lourdes radioed back.

"Nothing..." Rick began to say when Quinn relieved him of the intercom.

"Nothing, you gullible geek!" Quinn said in a continuous laugh.

I snatched the mike from Quinn's grasp and gave her a smirk. "Everything is just fine. In fact. It's just perfect. Quinn was just having fun with you. Quinn, Lourdes says she's gonna kick your dike ass when we land." I joked, hoping to get a response from Lourdes.

"Don't tell her that. Does she think I really said that. Holy cow. She's gonna kill me!" Lourdes replied in a panic stricken voice.

Knowing full well that I was playing, Quinn picked up the mike, "You best run when we get off this chopper."

The helicopter began its descent before I could tell Lourdes that we were just kidding with her.

The aircraft landed in a field bordered by tiny lakes and the Magdalena River. Anticipating an ugly scene with Quinn, Lourdes began to run away from the aircraft, heading in the direction of one of the small lakes. Colonel Borda, attempting to stop her, raced behind her. The sight of the pathetic man trying to keep up with the gazelle-like Lourdes had us all laughing.

Short of breath, the Colonel turned back toward the team and wailed.

"Caribe! Caribe!"

No one reacted.

"Fish!" the colonel screamed.

Rick was the first to react.

"I believe Caribe means Cannibal?"

"Oh, my God. Piranha!" Box, Debara and I yelled simultaneously.

Quinn, feeling she was to blame, ran frantically at Lourdes hollering "Piranha! Piranha!"

Since Quinn was the reason for Lourdes running in the first place, Lourdes dove into one of the small lakes and began to swim, M-16 and all. I placed my finger on the trigger of Joey Bali's gun which was still slung over his shoulder and fired off several rounds. The sound of hooves trampling throughout the countryside further impeded our communication. Lourdes began to tread water, realizing that she wasn't going to make it across. I said:

"Me alone!"

I ran past Quinn to the shore of the lake. I didn't want to panic Lourdes, fearing that she would generate too much turbulence hurrying back to the shoreline.

"Hey. Don't tell me that getting shot at doesn't frighten you, but the thought of fighting Quinn does? Come on in now." I didn't want to tell her that we were kidding either, fearing she would choose to enter into a long dialogue with me before coming ashore.

"I just wanted to show her that I could wear her out. Then I'd pounce on her." She said in feisty, childish tone.

"Well, you won. Quinn realized she couldn't catch up and quit a ways back. Now, come on in."

Lourdes swam to the shore without making much ripple. As she crawled on to the rocky bank, everyone sighed in relief.

"What's wrong?" inquired Lourdes.

I just gave her a big hug. Lourdes pushed back
gently.

"What is it? What's wrong?"

Many of the lakes and streams throughout Cartel
property were swarming with piranha. They were
placed there for the expressed purpose of deterring
and hampering infiltrators. The local Campesino
would send a farm animal into a body of water before
crossing himself. The lakes were erratically strewn
about the rolling hill sides. The entire area covered no
more than a few miles. This was the staging area for
clearance to the home of Pablo Escobar.

Although the lake Lourdes was swimming in was
not laden with piranha, it did domicile, to a small
degree, the veracious eater by way of the many connecting streams, which abounded in piranha. Lourdes
and I returned to the group, pausing on the way to
speak with Quinn. Quinn, sweating profusely, placed
her hand at the back of Lourdes' head and pulled her
inward, apologizing all the while.

"God, I'm so sorry Lourdes. That was so stupid of
me."

"Will someone please tell me what's going on!?"
Lourdes demanded.

"Can't we just show how much we care without
you being so suspicious about our motivation?" I
persuaded.

"Now, I'm really worried."

"It's really nothing. There may have been some
piranha in there. Really very slight chance. Hardly
worth mentioning." Quinn stuttered.

"Ooow." Lourdes paused as she twisted her pelvis,
exposing her shredded fatigue trousers.

"I thought I felt something nip at me when I climbed
out of there."

Her pants and flesh dangled like strips of bacon. It spoke well of her threshold for pain. Before the team moved on, Steve treated and bandaged her wounds.

We switched aircraft once again. We were to enter Escobar's estate aboard two smaller Bell Helicopters.

The flight into Los Napoles was a short jaunt. Flying north along the Magdalena, we passed over numerous cars and busses crossing into the unrestricted portion of Escobar's property. The camels, giraffes, kangaroos, buffalo, llamas, elephants, hippos, and ostriches of our earlier camp site were plentiful, offering an exotic experience for visitors. Indeed, this was Escobar's treat to the average folk of Colombia. The only creatures not offered here, that were visible at the camp, were the carnivores: jaguars, lynx, cougars, and leopards.

The choppers landed a short distance from Escobar's palatial estate. As we exited the craft, we were escorted by armed guards to the rear of the ranch, past a large pool with jacuzzis at either end. Gazebos sheltered several vintage 1930's/1940's automobiles of the gangster movie genre. Thomas sub-machine guns served as taps for beer barrels and Colt 45's replaced the handles on the sliding glass doors. The most conspicuous amenity of all was the marble Aphrodite (Greek goddess of love) that buttressed the side of the pool.

The house was capable of accommodating 120 people comfortably and showed that the acquisition of wealth for wealth's sake was one of the primary motivations for drug lords. Incongruent furniture and artifacts were piled on to the walls like a big game hunter mounts his kill. If a common theme existed, it was probably Victorian, only because it conveyed a sign of wealth to the Colombians. Down two flights of stairs, in a vast game room, we were told to relax and be comfortable. A guard was posted outside the door to assure our "comfort."

"Steven. Will that thing transmit a signal from here?" I inquired, pointing at the miniature satellite dish attached to Steven Hall's bulky radio.

"No way. Why?" Steven replied.

"I just wanted to send back a message that we wouldn't meet our rendezvous. It's no big deal. Don't worry about it."

I was considerably worried though. I didn't want anyone in Langley to overreact and exacerbate the problem.

"Anyone for a game of pool?" I asked nonchalantly.

"Sure." Joey said enthusiastically. The fact that I wanted to shoot a little stick sent a non verbal message that we weren't in any danger. The enthusiasm caught on and everyone began to have fun. Rick found a juke box and played the only artist on it, a Spanish singer named Roberto Carlos. Quinn raided the bar, one of four, and began to serve Black Label scotch to everyone. Debara and Steven slid the slot machines close to where the tables were, and, with a little "Jerry Rigging," we were pulling one-armed-bandits for free.

After drinking only one shot, I pulled Box aside very subtly and told him that I'd had enough of waiting. Unbeknownst to Box, I'd removed a vintage, nonfunctional German Luger from above the bar. I told Box to follow my lead as I pushed him toward the door to where the guard was standing.

"I'm not taking this crap any more. These idiots are gonna learn that we're in control here and we won't take being imprisoned or prevented from doing our job. Not to mention being killed. Now open the damn door." I stated harshly in a lowered voice.

"I notice you doing all the talking, but it's my ass up front."

"Next time you come up with a plan, you get to live."

"What!"

"I'm just kidding. Now keep your voice down and get going."

I told Box to pretend to be drunk, but not to be too belligerent. Assuming that the guard would try to stop the first person by placing the gun to his belly, I would counter by placing my gun to the guard's head. It went like clockwork. Then the guard unexpectedly spun Box around and placed him in a headlock, pointing his MAC-10 machine gun to Boxer's temple.

"For God's sake, Box! You're not supposed to let him spin you around like that." I disappointedly criticized in an almost playful manner. "Damn! I wish I knew some Spanish."

"That's it? That's your plan! You have to know Spanish to make this plan work!" Box rambled in a raspy voice brought on from choking. "Rick's right! You are an idiot!"

Placing my gun firmly to the guards head, with my eyes affixed on his, I began to count.

"Uno-Dues-Tres-Quatros."

The guard immediately relinquished his weapon. Obviously, he was not authorized to kill any of our team. Consequently, he was not prepared to risk his life on a shallow bluff. The counting in Spanish probably made him quite nervous because he was unaware of all the other things that were being said.

"I thought you said you didn't know any Spanish?"

"I don't. But I know a little Italian. And it's basically the same thing."

I led Boxer up to the main level where a meeting was transpiring. We entered an enormous study decorated in a much more traditional fashion. We moved about in virtual obscurity, not following the path we were led in on. I did not have a specific intent in mind, except to send a message to the highest level that *Pseudo Miranda* would fold if this type of treatment continued. Box was toting the MAC-10, and I carried the useless Luger. Although a maze of escape tunnels existed beneath the ranch, countless surveillance cameras overlapped the perimeter of the immediate property and the dwelling itself was equipped with motion detectors and monitors at the window and door entrances only. Once inside, you could move about freely without fear of detection. At least, that's what we thought.

Sliding down the hall past an Italian marble fountain built flush with the wall, I busted into a meeting with the Luger in outstretched arm, snapping firmly in all directions. Box trailed after immediately, covering the entire room.

"Now, what do we do?" Box looked over his shoulder at me. "It's that Spanish problem again, isn't it? Why the hell didn't you just bring Chavez?"

"By the time I came up with this idea, he was already drunk!" I argued.

"What plan, with the possible exception of shooting everybody, would not require a translator!?"

"This one." I replied sarcastically. "Who in this room doesn't seem to fit the drug trafficker image?" My focus fell upon the only white man in the room. I grabbed him by the back of the collar and demanded he tell me what was going on. The gentleman whimpering at the end of my grip was a "Business Man" pure and simple. His narrow framed physique and Coca Cola glasses epitomized the true villains of America's drug infested streets. His disassociation with the actual product that provided him the standard of living he'd become so accustomed to, was born out in his soft, pale skin, manicured nails, and Mariani of Beverly Hills suit. Before I could ascertain what was going on, numerous armed soldiers of the M-19 flooded in. They were alerted to the meeting by none other than Pablo Escobar Gaviria, who had his own viewing screen of the main meeting room in his bedroom suite. Many gatherings involving the discussion of money laundering took place in the absence of the three family patriarchs. The hashing out of minute details was typically left to representatives who would zealously carry out the will of the family.

Pablo Escobar was receiving his own brand of intelligence reports on what had happened to our team a day earlier. He was about to summon Box and I when we came to him instead. Soon after the M-19 disarmed us, Pablo Escobar came down the curving staircase into the cathedral ceiling meeting area, stopping first to ensure that all had been defused. Escobar was a sophisticated looking man of unusual stature for a Colombian. His wavy black hair, parted on the side, coupled with the well-groomed mustache painted evenly along his lip, said a lot about the way he saw himself, and the way he wanted others to see him. His attire was casual, likewise his posture, as if he wanted others to think of him as unpretentious. Speaking in shortened sentences with breaks for translation, Escobar asked politely for Box and I, whom he referred to as friends from the American government, to join him at the pool for drinks.

By this time, the M-19 had re-secured the other team players who had made it as far as the staircase after they discovered we were missing. With permission from Escobar, I returned briefly to the lower level to let everyone know that we were fine. Upon returning poolside, I discover Box laughing with Escobar. I wasted little time in destroying the mood.

"Who the hell do you think you are attacking us like that! The rules were established in Zurich and you agreed to those rules! If you want things to return to the way they were only a few months ago, I can make that happen!" I pounded my open hand on an antique automobile while being simultaneously translated.

"We were not the ones who ambushed you." Escobar asserted in an aristocratic manner. "The Cali Group is retaliating for our assault against them. The same

assault that your government funded to produce the
Pseudo Miranda Program. I am terribly sympathetic to
your loss. Believe me when I tell you that. *Pseudo
Miranda* serves our vested interests as much as it does
yours. We will strive to preserve it as much as you."

"Where were your Campesinos when we entered
the lab?"

"I think he just answered that?" Box reminded me
in hopes that I would not agitate.

"No! He answered the "who" part of my question.
But he has yet to tell me how his people were able to
slip away before the onslaught."

"Yes. We have a network of former Cocaleros (Coca
farmers) spread throughout the jungle, who's sole job
is to report unusual activity to our laboratories."
Escobar explained, sensing my path to the next question.

"Aren't your labs equipped with IFF? Don't bother
to answer. Just tell me why the hell they didn't re-code
to warn us!?"

"Would you trust us if we did that? No, you
wouldn't! You would assume that we were chasing
you away from a large seizure!"

Escobar was absolutely correct in his assessment.
His forthcoming opened up a needed dialogue and led
to agreements that would preclude a repeat of the
events that took place in the Llanos jungles. Neverthe-
less, one problem was yet to be resolved — at least in
my mind. I had no intention of departing without
reciprocity, fully cognizant that we could never be
fully compensated for our loss. I politely asked Escobar
to follow me back into the house. Walking directly into
the meeting room, I pointed to the American:

"I want him to accompany us right now on our next
intervention."

"What are you nuts." Box whispered to me. "Let's
not push our luck with this guy." Box smiled and
looked over at Escobar.

I ignored Boxer's plead and pushed Escobar for an answer.

"So when do we depart?"

Without so much as an objection, Escobar acknowledged the need for reciprocation.

"Do what you need to do." Pablo motioned to Colonel Borda. "Give him what he needs." He then approached me, offering his handshake. "I'm glad we had an opportunity to meet one another. Don't take this too far."

An ambiguous warning at best, I thought.

"Okay, Colonel. Get my team. We're back in business!" I enthusiastically proclaimed. "Let's go, you geeky mother fucker!" I laughed, hauling the American in a headlock. "How many people did you kill today asshole?"

"I don't know what you're talking about! I haven't killed anyone. You've got the wrong guy. I swear!"

"Wrong-oh buck-oh. I've just the right guy."

Box had never seen me take advantage of a defenseless individual. Usually my adversaries were more capable than I. As Box continued to analyze, he concluded that this person represented all that was dirty about the drug trade. Most of those that benefited from the drug trade were wealthy; most of the users were middle class or below. All of them, in Boxer's estimation, had 'blood in their mouths' from the innocent people who died in an effort to prevent coke from getting to their table. Box's thought was how ironic the struggle was when good men and women are slain in an attempt to prevent ignorant people from hurting themselves.

The team formed up minutes later at the helicopter pads. Accompanied by Colonel Borda and "The Accountant," I instructed Quinn to take the lead pilot and direct him toward the coordinates of the mission's secondary target. Lourdes and Chavez separated in order to have a translator aboard each Bell helicopter.

The new target was in the Northern Andes, due east of
Baranquilla, not far from one of the homes of Don
Fabio Ochoa.

The trip required refueling of the aircraft along the
way, making for a long flight. Much of this time I
dedicated to the psychological torture of the accountant. At one point tying a string around the testis of the
frightened man and asking him if he'd ever seen the
movie *Scar Face*. The thought of being pushed out of
the aircraft with his testicles tied to the door put him
into an hysterical cry. I tried to remain cold even
though it made me feel lower than the man I was
attempting to frighten from the business. I withdrew
from the punishment and began to ask some rather
innocuous questions.

"So, where the hell do you work?"

"What's the difference. You're gonna kill me anyway!" He continued to sob.

"Why don't we just shoot 'em and get it over with."
reacted Joey, placing his gun barrel in the accountant's
face.

"Great. Now you've got him balling again!" I said
in frustration. "Hey! I'm sorry! Look at me! I'm sorry.
Really. Take some deep breaths. That's it. In and out.
In and out. Feeling better?"

"Yeah. I'm Okay."

"So. Who are you laundering money for?"

"Bank of Boston in Miami."

"That's my bank! Kill this sonuvabitch! I'm just
kidding. Put the gun down, Joey!"

As we approached the sight, I radioed ahead to the
lead chopper and told Quinn to pull up 300 feet from
the lab in plain view. Once cleared in 'Green' on the
IFF, she did as I instructed.

"Follow our lead," I advised.

Pivoting the helicopter to the side, my group fired
over the heads of the Campesinos, scattering them. I
then had Joey fire upon the lab. Without hesitation,

Joey riddled the area with bullets. Boxer's group followed suit, demolishing the lab in several ensuing explosions. When the firing stopped, my chopper whizzed over the top of the burning lab, dropping grenades. Box trailed in behind us doing much the same. Everyone was cheering.

"That's for you Jeremiah!"

I radioed once again to Quinn, this time to have her direct us home. By the time the helicopters touched down in Panama City, over five days had passed. The feelings were as mixed as they could be. Exuberance over destroying the two largest labs identified by the Air Force's Strategic Air Command (SAC) under Operation Olympic Victor, named for the OV-10 Aircraft, recognition that an underground network of labs could exist that far surpass conventional lab production, and, of course, remorse for our fallen comrade.

Once at Howard Air Force Base, it was time to say good-bye, if only for a short while. The realization that our very existence was so fragile in the midst of this ominous task, created a solid bond that would have otherwise taken years to develop. Good-byes really could mean forever.

Everyone departed on the same course as their arrival. Except of course for the accountant, who stayed aboard the Colombian aircraft in Panama City.

The last leg of the trip from Mena, Arkansas offered time for Box and I to prepare for our debrief in Paducah, Kentucky. Careful evaluation led to one unavoidable conclusion. We had to show force and resolution when south of the border, and we had to limit our visits to only "Big Game." When I arrived back in Murray, Kentucky, I immediately became Ken Bucchi once again, except for a part of me.

A part that had changed forever.

Chapter 17

Immediately upon my return to Murray, Kentucky, I attached a U-Haul to the rear of my Corvette and prepared to move. Andy had been with me all day, helping me pack my memories. Knowing what I did of her infidelity, I deliberately hid my feelings, deciding it was a good test of my ability to maintain my secret life. At the last moments, I began to cry in her arms, as much for the loss of innocence and security that college represented as for the loss of a woman that I would never hold again.

As I drove across country to Bellingham, Massachusetts, I thought that the promise of a wife and kids was gone forever. I believed that I was ready to sacrifice much of myself for this operation. What I didn't realize is that I could never be entirely that altruistic.

Over the next few months, I traveled from Arizona to Mississippi, intercepting tons of cocaine in the middle of the night. These excursions typically lasted no more than 48 hours. With few exceptions, Box drove me to Andrews Air Force Base (AFB), Washington, DC, bound for any number of bases throughout the south. These bases included, but were not limited to; Davis-Monthan AFB, Arizona; Holloman AFB, New Mexico; Kelley AFB, Texas, and Columbus AFB, Mississippi. Mena Air Field was used whenever travel in and around Arkansas was necessary.

For at least an hour each day, I would make myself available for approach, which meant going somewhere that provided anonymity for myself and any courier that wished to deliver the latest instructions. Rarely was Box that courier, so the need to exchange encrypted messages was commonplace. Box had given me a key to a briefcase and a schematic featuring random holes on a plastic covered piece of paper. Whenever a courier would exchange coded messages with me, I would follow him or her, inconspicuously, to where the briefcase was kept. If I was unable to accompany the courier at a given time, I would respond to the coded message inappropriately. When I did follow, the courier would hand me a briefcase that mated to my key. After opening it, I would immediately remove the new key and replace it with my own. I would then overlay my schematic at a predesignated position on the coded sheet. The sheet would include the latest instruction, and the overlay position of the next message. After memorizing the message, I would switch my schematic with the new one enclosed in the briefcase, and take the old message, burning it in a small metal box that was provided in the briefcase, placing the box of ashes back into the case. When this was not practical, I would tear the message up and take it with me. Throughout this period, the courier would stand watch, and advise on any dangers.

Initially, this cloak and dagger activity was exciting, and made me feel that I was a part of something very important. After a while though, it became encumbering. I found myself having to lie to friends and family about my whereabouts and my unusual behavior. The more often it would happen, the more incredulous the lies became. I felt dirty and pathetic lying to the people about whom I most cared.

I soon decided that it would be easier to have one lie that I could use to explain short absences. I created a fictitious woman in Holliston, Massachusetts, that I would visit and sometimes stay with for a day or so. If the excursion were anticipated to be longer, I would claim that I was traveling to Kentucky to visit friends and look for a job.

On one of these occasions, I received a message to take a written entrance examination for the CIA. The message gave no explanation, and I was unable to contact anyone concerning the purpose of my taking such a test at this juncture, so I did as I was instructed.

Mark Rizzo, still unaware of my second life, took me into Boston and showed me where the government building was located. As we ate at the Quincy Market, I told him that I always wanted to work for the CIA, but that my chances were probably remote.

"Why would you think that anyone working for the CIA had any more ability than you?" Mark asked.

Mark Rizzo has always been quietly confident in his own abilities as they compared to others, and assumed that I was likewise confident in my own. In reality, I sometimes wondered what I was capable of, doubting my talent, often surprised that I was worthy. I disguised my wavering confidence by endeavoring to do more than even others thought I could. Mark never had anything to prove, which explains why his life has always been more settled than my own. Although we probably both lived vicariously through each other's lives, neither of us ever wanted to, nor could have lived the other's life. Our lives followed completely different tracks, but were always on the same course. We remained the closest of friends for decades, crossing tracks numerous times on route to our own destinies.

"If it were a test of skill—dealing with people and such—I think I'd fare pretty well. But this written examination crap? I don't know," I replied.

"What do you have to lose? You shouldn't worry about the geek portions of the test anyway. I don't think you want a desk job with them, do you?"

"No. But I'll bet that's all they're testing for."

Mark seemed to sense that I knew more than I was saying, but didn't probe.

"Why do you say that? Did I miss something?"

"You never miss a thing. Just remember I took this test, okay."

"Mind like a steel trap." He said. I wished that this secrecy could end between myself and those for whom I cared most. I always felt like a looking-glass, with all my deceptions glaring and transparent. I felt especially so with Mark and my parents.

I enjoyed the day with him, as I always have. He is arguably the funniest person I've ever known, and the easiest to speak to outside of my mother. His humor runs the spectrum, excepting possibly the blatantly sexual. He has never judged what I've done, even though much of what I've done is alien to his very nature. He's an anomaly of sorts, Christian in belief and practice, yet fully understanding and accepting of my life, which has been, for the most part, un-Christian-like for years. But, then again, maybe that's not such an anomaly after all. He was always exceptionally bright, but naive when it came to the world of crime. I could actually meet with agents while I was with him, and not fear detection. Many times I wondered if he was indeed cognizant and simply allowing me the opportunity to do what I had to do. I once recounted an event I'd witnessed in a mall that involved the subtle passing of a package. The transfer, made in a newspaper, had actually happened to myself in his presence, and I wondered if it would trigger a memory. If it had, I would have come up with a logical explanation, but it didn't.

"Ever since I can remember, I've always wanted a job that required the wearing of a suit," Mark said.

"Really? Why would you want to do that?"

"I guess I noticed that the people wearing the suits seemed to make the most money."

"With the possible exception of porno stars," I clarified.

"And sumo wrestlers," he added.

The following day, I took the examination which lasted several hours. The room was filled with Coke bottle eye ware, and pocket protectors. I paid no attention to the instruction given, and placed little effort in my work. The only thing I remember about the test is a section that required the examinee to create sentences from a fictitious language. I recall making a sincere effort in this area as I was intrigued with its uniqueness. Intrigue didn't provide me with enough intelligence to figure it out, however. I was already working for the Company, so how important could this test be?

I would later discover the intent of the test. If any of the team members later claimed an affiliation with the CIA, the Company would deny employment by pointing to the test taken, which had been failed by the alleged employee.

It was early in February of 1984 when Box caught up with me in Framingham, Massachusetts, at a huge night-club called *The Other Side*. I was out with a friend named Chris, whom I told that I'd met a girl, and that I was going home with her. He was accustomed to me departing abruptly, leaving him stranded, but he never became comfortable with it. This was the last time he went out with me when I drove.

I found myself at Andrews AFB shortly after dawn. Box didn't seem to have any idea where it was we were heading or why.

"Don't you find this a bit strange?" I asked.

"More than a bit, I'll tell ya, I don't like this at all."

We flew to Wright-Patterson AFB, Ohio, located near Dayton, refueled, and headed south. We made stops in Paducah and Mena to top off tanks and transfer passengers, then continued southward on a journey to the unknown. After Mena, we traveled alone. When our path took us more southerly than easterly, Box became concerned.

"This has never happened before. I always know what we're doin' and where we're going. Always."

"I'm sure everything's fine."

In truth, I wasn't at all sure, but I figured I'd better get used to this scenario. After all, it wasn't as if I could do anything about it. Looking out over the puffy clouds, I realized my life was no longer my own. I'd surrendered it back in Chicago. In the CIA, they call this being habeas corpus.

We touched down once again, this time in southern Texas. When the T-39 came to rest on the Chase Naval Air Station runway, we were leisurely transferred to a small Huey Helicopter. We later discovered that we were waiting for clearance onto a large ranch in Beeville, Texas.

"So what do you think this is all about?" I inquired of Box.

"Beats the shit outa me."

I yawned deeply, even though I'd slept along the way.

"This job's gonna give me an ulcer."

"I wouldn't worry about that. Ulcers take time to develop."

"That's real comforting. Thanks a lot."

"I'm just kidding."

"Why is it your sense of humor only flares when we're in deep do-do?"

"Who needs humor when everything's fine."

We landed in a large field with trees scattered throughout. As we exited the chopper, a short, grey haired man, wearing a hunting hat approached. He aggressively interrogated us on the operation.

"I want answers, gentlemen, and I want 'em now. Are you, or are you not, assisting cocaine and heroine into our country? Has this country been supplying weapons to the Colombian drug barons? How involved are we in the illicit drug trade? Gentlemen! He only authorized not making arrests. That's it! If we have to violate their constitutional guarantees, then so

be it. Then we won't make arrests. But we don't help
them, for God's sake!"

As he spoke, Box tapped my leg lightly and glanced
off to my left. My head turned slowly, stopping, as my
eyes fell upon a group of hunters. My focus rested on
the tall gentleman in the middle. I couldn't believe
what I was seeing. The man, dressed in hunting fatigues and toting a shotgun, stared patiently back at
me. I blocked out all that was being said to me. I began
to gain insight as to why we were brought here.

"I'm talking to you!" The gentleman in front of me
exclaimed.

"Yeah, I can hear you. Hey, look buddy. I don't
have the foggiest idea what you're talking about.
We're not helping anyone traffick drugs. We're just
putting them outa business by taking away their protection against illegal searches and seizures. All right?
Now, I don't know who the fuck you are, and I don't
wanta know. So, if you don't mind, I'd like to get home
because you're giving me a splittin' headache."

"You get this administration in trouble, you're
gonna have more than a splittin' headache."

"Well, they better send someone more intimidating
than yourself."

"Oh, shit." Box interrupted. "He's just tired, Mr.
George. I'm sure he doesn't even know who he's
talking to. Do ya, Anthony?"

"Why? Who is this?" I asked, feeling a bit ignorant.

"Never mind who I am," the man retorted. "You
remind me of myself when I was your age. You like
automobiles, don't you?"

"Not all of them."

"Fast ones. I know. I know." He said smiling. Then,
he became more serious.

"Learn when it's appropriate to shift down. I'm a
tough corner at a hundred and twenty. You can't run
it flat out for very long doing what we do for a living.
Believe me. Learn that before it's too late."

I didn't respond. For once, common sense seemed the best policy.

On the return trip to Washington, Box refused to discuss the meeting. He finally loosened up as we drove back to Massachusetts.

"Who did that look like to you?"

"I have no idea. You're the one that called him Mr. George. For all I know, he's Mr. Ed's talking mule cousin."

"No, not him, you idiot. That was Claire George. I'm talking about the guy standing about thirty feet from us."

"Claire George?"

"Please tell me you've at least heard of him?"

"Could we skip the ritual name calling and just tell me who the hell he is."

"Your boss? Director of Operations? Stop me if any of this sounds familiar. You're serious? How the hell did you ever get this job?"

"He's not my boss. My boss would know what the hell was goin' on. In fact, my boss is obviously above him. This operation, and everything we're doing in it, came right from Casey's mouth, and I was there to hear it! So don't give me that crap about him being my boss! If he's such a big fuck, why doesn't he ask Casey himself? Better yet! Why doesn't Bush ask him. He works for him, for cryin' out loud!"

"So, it was George Bush." Box said somberly.

"Yeah. Who the hell did you think it was?"

Box let out a large breath.

"I think we just witnessed the escalation of *Pseudo Miranda*. Level two: establish deniability."

"I don't get it. Why not have this conversation with Casey and let him deceive them?"

"Because that would put it too close to the presidency."

"That doesn't make sense, Box. That doesn't make any sense at all."

"I know it doesn't! All I know is that things just got more convoluted and probably more dangerous. We have to tread a lot more cautiously from now on."

"Whenever you do that you get hurt. Box, I'm telling ya. Keep it together or get the hell out. You're gonna become a liability if you don't remain aggressive. Nothing's changed. Everyone's just getting their ducks in line. It's probably a good sign. It probably indicates that they've decided they're in it for the long haul." I paused to pat Box on the back as he drove. "I know what you need."

"I do too. And I'm goin' home to get some."

"No, not that."

"What?"

"Cow tipping."

"Oh, no! I'd rather take my chances with the Colombians than tip another side of beef with you. It's too cold anyhow. There aren't any cows around this time of the year. Are there?"

"No. But I'll keep your interest in mind the next time we're in Texas."

"You do that, Bucci."

Back in Bellingham, I began to place a more conscious effort in building my cover. The meeting hadn't frightened me, but it seemed prudent to push my identity deeper than it already was. I put together a resume and began to peddle it around, doing what was necessary not to get hired.

One of my courier messages informed me that I was to initiate the process of applying for a slot in the Air Force's Officer Training program. The message didn't express why this was necessary, but I assumed it had something to do with deepening my cover by making it appear as though I was an airman, especially while abroad. Not knowing the exact reasoning behind it, I took it upon myself to apply for the Army's Officer Candidate School as well.

After completing the initial application process, I was given instruction to ready myself for another *Vosotros* operation. I felt more prepared to cross the border this time. This deployment would teach me, however, that there is no such thing as enough preparation in an intervention mission.

I headed to Kentucky.

Chapter 18.

Wickliffe is a rustic town on the Kentucky-Tennessee border. The Westvaco Paper Mill provides the town with both its main source of employment and its pungent aroma. My late uncle, George F. Buckley, was the company's CPA, and a bit of a celebrity around town. George had treated me like a son, and I shall never forget it.

He also introduced me to the Gevedens. The patriarch of the family, Charles, was at one time the county attorney, Ballard County's version of a district attorney. The motivating force behind Charles is undoubtedly his wife, Pat, who paved the way to his seat in the state senate. I know them affectionately as Mr. and Mrs. G.

Chuck, the youngest of the Geveden siblings, was the first to greet me on my unannounced visit.

"Mom! Dad! KaBuch is here!" Chuck called out as I rolled up in my Corvette.

"Hey Chuck! How's the glandular problem?" I said facetiously.

"Six foot-three. Want to play a little one on one?" He challenged me to a game at which I used to thrash him. Now, with his imposing stature, he apparently felt he had the advantage.

"What's the matter? Chicken?"

He was seven years my junior. There was no way he could beat me.

"Let me change into my shorts. Grab my suitcase, Chuckles."

"Kabuch! How are you? We didn't know you were coming." Mrs. G. welcomed me at the door.

"Kabuch." Mr. G. said with an extended hand. "What brings you this way?"

"I'm gonna look for a job in Murray, and see my girl at the same time. But first, I'm gonna whip your son in a little game of round ball."

"Don't be too sure about that. He's grown a lot since you last saw him."

"I know. I hope you saved that piano case, 'cause you're gonna need to bury him in it after this game."

"Oh, I think he's already out grown that." Mr. G. replied.

"You two are terrible." Mrs. G. said, laughing.

I stayed with the Gevedens for a day and a night. Mrs. G. cooked a country ham for dinner, and biscuits and gravy for breakfast. I never ate so well. We sat around in the evening and reminisced about the five years I'd spent in Kentucky, and the great times we shared with my Uncle George.

I narrowly won the basketball game, but for the last time. My body would degenerate over the passing of time, not from natural causes, but rather from *Pseudo Miranda* experience, and Chuck would continue to grow.

I drove to Paducah shortly after breakfast, telling the Geveden's that I'd see them in a few days. Box was to meet me when my plane touched down at Kelley Air Force Base, Texas.

I walked tentatively toward the T-39, which sat on the ramp with its engines running. I poked my head in the aircraft, not positive that this was my ride.

"Hi. I'm Anthony. Who is it I'm supposed to speak with."

I didn't realize until later that I would never have gained access to the ramp if I hadn't been cleared in advance by the crew.

"Get in." The pilot said coldly.

I was alone in the cabin as we took off. It was strange not having Box along. I felt more at liberty when he was around, his constant reminding of my zealot behavior provided me with an imaginary line that served to guide me.

We began our approach into what was supposed to be Kelley Air Force Base, but instead turned out to be Randolph, located some thirty miles away on the opposite end of San Antonio. As we touched down, I looked out on fifty-some-odd, guppy looking, trainer aircraft, called T-37's. Years later I would command this fleet of aircraft and the people that maintained them. We taxied to the end of the runway, and waited, engines running, for clearance into Kelly.

We eventually received clearance and reached Kelly, taxiing to a hangar that displayed the numbers 977 preceding four other digits, referred to as Hangar 17. Box met me with the most incredible audacity.

"Where the hell have you been! What the hell kept you?"

"I had a compressor stall on the number two (engine), which slowed me down a bit." I answered sarcastically. "What do you mean, what took me so long? What the hell do I have to do with the timing of anything? I did my part. I was at the airport on time."

"Just get in the plane, please."

"You know, it really pisses me off when you don't apologize for criticizing me by mistake. Which one is ours?"

"That one." Box said, pointing limply to a pint-sized, vintage transport.

"We're goin' in that? You're kidding me? There's

no way we're gonna make it in that. What the hell is that anyway?"

"It's a C-47."

"Don't the names of these aircraft follow sequentially?"

"Whata' ya mean?"

"You know. C-123, C-130,135, 141, etc., etc.."

"Yeah. I guess that would make this pretty old, huh?" Box said, nerves creeping into his voice.

We entered the aircraft somewhat distressed over out impending journey in this obsolete relic of World War II. With its narrowing tail slanting downwards toward an insignificant wheel, the plane was outfitted with one row of seats on one side, and two rows on the other. The seats were modified with race car harnesses, supporting both shoulders with wide nylon straps. It didn't reassure me to know that the technicians found it necessary to add such a safety feature. It was probably easier to add harnesses than to fix some major flight control problem.

As I boarded the plane, I thought of how I would one day cherish the memory of Boxer's petty disagreements with me. His persistent bickering was a security blanket, a constant reminder that all was fairly normal.

We flew for hours due south, stopping intermittently for servicing at small airfields along the way. One pit stop occurred at an airfield in southern Honduras at an American air base situated near Toncontin in the midst of what appeared to be a jungle. I had noticed a trend: wherever there were encircling mountain ranges covered in trees, there was likely a CIA staging area. Regular army personnel had massed here to train transplanted Nicaraguan Contras, only to send them back across the border to die. I wanted no part of anything I saw there. It turned my stomach to watch para-military training on shows like "60 Minutes." I hated, this type of mentality. Killing,

under the most profound of circumstances, can become a necessity, but should never, under any circumstances, become enjoyable. Those that train
people to kill, excluding a recognized government's
sanctified forces, have lost their sense of humanity. I
realized that much of what I was doing might seem
hypocritical in light of this philosophy, but killing, in
my case, was a manifestation of the war on drugs,
and not the thrust.

Day had given way to night by the time we finally
approached Howard Air Force Base in Panama. The
runway lights were the first thing I'd seen all day that
told me I hadn't left the twentieth century entirely.
With each landing, I prayed silently to God. I didn't
frighten easily, but it paralyzed me to know that I was
not in a position to defend myself against a foe. This
antiquated hulk of scrap metal was most certainly
such a foe. I poked my head into the cockpit periodically during the trip, only to catch the pilot thumping
a gauge or leaning out over the windscreen, apparently in search of a landmark.

Our aircraft followed a pick-up truck with *FOL-
LOW ME* written in yellow lights hung over the
vehicle's rear window. We parked on the Hot Pad,
where aircraft carrying dangerous materials or explosives are normally placed. Our pilot informed us that
he was instructed to have us remain while the rest of
our people were being shuttled over to us.

I looked out the window while we waited patiently
for our team's arrival. Parked adjacent to us were a
couple of C-130 transports.

"Damn. I never thought I'd be happy to see one of
those pigs again." I said relieved.

"I don't know what the hell you're so happy about!
I'm piloting you all the way into Colombia!"

The pilot was a chubby man with pulled back hair
that concealed a balding crown. His clothes were
loose, with an Hispanic flavor to them. He chose not to

give his name, but certainly had no misgivings about telling us how great a pilot he was.

"Shit! Don't worry about this bucket of bolts! I've flown bigger pieces of shit into tighter spots than this."

"Look, buddy, we're not looking to have you fly us into anywhere tight. If we have to fly with you to Colombia in this death trap, it's only to a nice runway owned by one of the *PM* players." I said rationally.

"The PM players? Did someone let the cat outa the bag?" He taunted. I hadn't considered the fact that he was just a pilot, oblivious to the purpose of our cross into Colombia.

"Look. You do what you do best and fly the plane. Ask any more questions, and I'll do what I do best." I responded in frustration. I was more upset at myself than him.

"Don't go getting your ovaries in an uproar. I just like to know as much as possible about a mission, that's all. You may not believe this now, but I'm a good person to have on your side. I've pulled a lot of asses outa the fire in my time."

"Yeah. Of course what you're not telling us is that you probably put their asses in the fire in the first place." Box amended.

I said softly to Box, "Let's be careful. Don't forget, there's a lot of fires in Colombia he could put our butts into."

"You carry on for ten minutes, and I say one thing — and you're blaming me?"

"Remember Zurich. We can't take the chance that this guy hates black people."

"Funny. Very funny."

A van arrived carrying our comrades. Debara, Christina, Lourdes, Joey, Rick, Quinn, and Steven had been assigned to the mission. Jesus was recovering from an allergic reaction to a large scale fire ant attack, which he suffered during an interception that I was not a part of. He was put out of commission for weeks as a result.

"Hey, good looking," Debara said cheerfully.

"Hi!" Box and I responded — along with the pilot, who had a cockiness that far surpassed any realistic expectations.

"Three good looking men. What's a girl to do?" Debara said flirtatiously.

"Puke?" Quinn answered Debara's rhetorical question.

"You know, my mom says that the most sincere compliments given to women, come from women. Joey, who's the best looking man here?" I said in jest.

"Quinn." Joey replied.

"Boy, you're pushing it with me." Quinn reacted, only slightly serious.

"I can see this is gonna be a fun trip," the pilot stated.

Actually, we were again becoming comfortable with one another. We were able to speak our minds without worrying about adverse retribution.

I had been traveling for ten hours when we finally entered Panama City, Panama. We landed at the international airport in Tocumen and awaited word to cross into Colombia. Specifically, we needed to fly into Colombia, shadowed by a Noriegan aircraft with a scheduled flight plan. The wait was short, and we lifted off, bound for a small air field in Aracuara, Colombia, some 900 miles away. The C-47 had an expanded flight envelope due to wing bladder and fuselage tank modifications.

The basic plan of the operation was to fly toward Aracuara, diverting along the way to a small air strip located near the Magdalena, south of Medellin, in the Andes Mountains.

We flew between, not over, the Andes Mountain range. Again, the aircraft's limited flight envelope restricted the altitude we could achieve. At certain points, our wing tips flirted with disaster, coming within meters of the mountain's walls. My confidence in our pilot's competence grew with each near miss. This "seat of your pants" flying made it infinitely more difficult to detect our radar signature, explaining why it was not necessary to provide us with an aircraft capable of greater altitudes.

Time passed quickly in the air, as conversations hit new levels of absurdity. We laughed and argued at high pitch, often ignoring the white-knuckle piloting of our transport. When our altitude dropped suddenly to tree top level (we had flown most of this leg of the trip at reasonably low altitude to avoid detection and because of the limitations of the aircraft), we became keenly aware of our rather precarious position.

"What the hell's goin' on up there?" Box worried aloud.

"Nothing! Just looking for a sign." The pilot shouted nonchalantly.

"A sign?" I questioned. "Like from God?"

"Like from the road, I think." Quinn submitted.

"What! This crazy mother's gonna get us killed!" Box shouted.

"Someone with good vision and good Spanish get your ass up here pronto!" The pilot demanded.

"Is this guy serious?" I asked, still in disbelief. "Quinn. Get up there and help him."

"I don't speak very good Spanish."

"You're a pilot. If he really needs to read street signs, speaking the language is the least of our problems."

Quinn rushed to the cockpit, expecting the worst. When she saw that most of the gauges were inoperative, and that the jerry-rigged fuel system indicated, with warning light, that we were dangerously low on fuel, she called out in horror.

"What!" The pilot reacted.

"Look at this mess! We're gonna ditch! We're gonna ditch!" Quinn responded hysterically.

"We've got plenty of fuel. That gauge only measures the pre-configured tanks. Of course, if we don't get our bearings soon, we will run outa fuel."

"Does this thing have a fuel transfer set-up?" Quinn asked rationally.

"A what?"

"Fuel transfer? You know, from the wings to the fuselage, and then to the engines. You know it's quite possible that your wings have already drained. The wing tanks are normally set up to pump first, then the fuselage. If that's what happened, we're low on fuel." Quinn explained.

It was all technical mumbo-jumbo to me, but I did understand the part about still being low on fuel.

"Is she right?" I asked, my head and shoulders leaning into the cockpit.

"There's one way to find out. I could turn off the fuel pump, bank the aircraft and gravity feed for a bit. See if one of the engines fails."

"Oh, that's a great plan." I said satirically. "Where are we? Oh wait, you don't know that, do you?"

"You catch on quick." The pilot smirked. "All I know is that I flew the course I was supposed to, passing over the Corridera Central, and I never saw the strip."

"The Corri-what? What the hell is he talking about?" I asked Quinn. "Give it to me in English."

"The Andes. We flew over them. No fuckin' runway where they said there would be one."

"You know the Andes are a pretty big mountain range! Maybe you missed it! Did you ever think of that! That you mighta' missed it!"

"Yeah, dipshit, I thought of it. You wanta' fly around at nine thousand feet looking for a runway in the sky! We run outa' fuel up there, you can put your head between your legs and kiss your ass good-by!"

"All right, I get your point. But now whata' we do?"

"Pray." He said, twisting back around to face forward, and sliding back into his seat.

"Okay. Quinn, get in back with everyone else."

"I thought I was needed up here?"

"Just go back and tell everyone to prepare for a rough landing."

"What are you going to do?"

"I don't know. Pray, I guess."

The pilot had flown a course more southerly than he had intended. The topography soon became much greener, and the mountains shallower. We were moving into a rain forest, which was not on anyone's agenda. Suddenly, a squawk on the radio asked us to identify ourselves.

"So, where's it coming from?" I asked.

"Don't know. But at least it's a safe landing."

"No, it's not. We can't be discovered." My speech quickened. "Drop down even further."

"What, are you fuckin crazy. Look how low we are!" he shouted. I ignored his concerns.

"First find out where they're calling from, so we can get our bearings."

The pilot radioed back, and was told that the signal came from Puerto Leguizamo on the Putamayo River. Moments later, we lost contact.

"Great! That's just fuckin great! Now what the hell do we do?"

"You're the bad ass. Put us down somewhere safe, and my SATCOM man will call for help."

"That *was* help!"

"No! That was the end of the whole operation! As long as I have a breath in me, that ain't gonna happen! Now put the fuckin plane on the ground and shut up!"

"You got it, boss."

We flew along, praying that our IFF transponder would locate a PM installation, whether it be an airstrip or a lab, just somewhere safe. It was a pipe dream, but neither of us wanted to consider the alternative. The chances of landing in a remote field and being extracted safely were slim at best. We altered courses several times, continually rethinking our present location. Then, a loud bang rocked the aircraft.

"What the hell was that?" I asked gingerly.

"That, my friend, was the number one engine." Then another loud bang. "And that was the number two." He kept his cool, as we miraculously flew over a ravine with some semi-landable terrain. The plane breached a small mountain peak.

"You can start kissing that ass right about now. One of our mains is stuck." The pilot was referring to the main landing gear. If one hangs up, you have to pull up the other to prevent a cartwheel landing.

"Here we go!" the pilot screeched as we dropped into a ravine, bouncing and sliding our way through the field. Bushes and debris blasted the front of the aircraft like artillery shells. I tossed and jerked for what seemed a life time, waiting for an explosion, or worse, to flip. We plowed over vegetation. The projectile began banking off obstructions like a pin-ball, as we began to decelerate. We came to an anticlimactic rest when our craft's right wing engaged a small, brush covered hill.

I drooped forward, exhausted and relieved. The first thing I noticed were my hands quivering uncontrollably. I tried to unfasten my seat belt, but I couldn't get my hands to cooperate. I looked to my left, and stared at the blood trickling from the pilot's head. He was unconscious and in need of help, but I couldn't gain enough strength to assist him. I closed my eyes, thinking, in my irrational mind, that I'd regain my energy if I rested for a minute or two. I didn't know

that I had a concussion, and that the grogginess would
not immediately dissipate. I also didn't know that
sleep was counterproductive, if not deadly. The hot,
humid air rolled in over the shattered windscreen,
encouraging my sleep. I started to fade. I felt no pain,
but suddenly I imagined I saw a Black Panther perched
on the nose of the aircraft. I gaped at this mystical
sight, drifting in and out of consciousness, before
slipping away completely.

The next thing I remember, were my heals dragging
over the metal floor of the aircraft. My back of my
head was cradled against Rick's chest as he pulled me
from the mangled wreckage of the C-47.

"The pilot," I said with a tired voice.

"He's fine. Just relax," Rick comforted.

"How's he doin'?" Box asked.

"Seems okay. Let's get them some water," Rick
advised.

I attempted to gather my wits and stand erect. I
stumbled, then reached for the ground with bending
knees and extending arms. Now on all fours, I asked,
"Is everyone all right?"

"We're fine. You two are the only ones that got
hurt." Debara eased my mind. She rubbed the back of
my head with her hand as she knelt along my side.
Ducking her head under mine, she looked up at me
and continued: "You had us all scared."

"I saw a Black Panther."

"What?"

"A Black Panther. He watched over me." I'm not
sure why I worded it this way, but I did.

"He saw a Black Panther." Debara announced to
everyone.

"Where?" Box inquired, doubtful.

"On the nose of the plane." I said to Debara.

"He says he saw it on the aircraft."

"He's delirious. Panther!" Box said, leaning down
to feel the knot on my forehead. "Wooo! You got some

schnozzle there!" He turned away and walked toward the aircraft. It looked as though it had been there for years, enveloped by plant growth, its tail severed. It began to rain, steady but light.

"I suggest we take cover in the hull and crash for the evening. Well, maybe crash is not the best word. Ahh. Let's sleep in the plane."

Debara assisted me to my feet, and walked me to the plane. "I did see a Panther." I said.

"I believe you. I do." Debara responded.

"It could have been a guardian of sorts, you know." Christina suggested.

"You mean like an angel. Right?" said Lourdes.

"Yeah. I mean God controls what he wants to control. Why not tame the wild beast to demonstrate his presence. An angel doesn't have to do any more than carry a message." Christina asserted. "Of course, you could just be hallucinating from that bump on your head."

"How to stick to your guns Christina." Joey teased.

Everyone carried their bumps and bruises into the aircraft and slept for the evening. We came equipped with a few days worth of C-rations and some essential camping equipment, making our night's stay hardship free.

Shortly before sunrise, I awakened with an uneasy feeling. While everyone slept, I walked out into the alien environment, not knowing what drew me there. With a grey haze cascading off the mountain top, I slipped into the virgin hillside. I walked some hundred feet to the perimeter of the jungle, and looked back at the wreckage. It had already begun to meld into its new surroundings. The jungle would someday claim it for its own, swallowing it up like so much earth. The tail section stood on its end, like an idle to be worshipped, about a hundred yards aft of the fuselage.

Turning toward the jungle, I felt drawn into it. At first, it seemed nothing more than a curiosity. I had never experienced a forest so thick. The sunlight, as it rose on the rest of the region, barely reached the ground here. The surface plants were comparatively thin, making a hasty traverse somewhat manageable. The deeper I penetrated, the more I wondered how far I would go before turning back. I could no longer see the clearing where we'd crashed our plane. I paused, debating my return, when I heard a faint moan. The forest was alive with the sounds of birds and monkeys, but this sound was distinctive. It called to me. Chills ran up my spine as I turned back into the forest. I searched tentatively for the Panther. The jungle floor was moist, dew dripped from big leafed plants onto my unprotected head. I drew my gun and pushed back some shielding plants. I became fraught with an untenable fear, causing me to hastily retreat. I stopped and crouched, spinning evenly with my Colt 45 leveled at an invisible enemy. I paused, directing my weapon toward the elephant leafed plants that obscured my vision. I knew that whatever my mind's eyes had picked up was behind that wall of leaves. I had seen something, that's for sure, but what? What had I seen? Whatever it was, I had instantaneously thrown into my unconscious. Was this cat so mysterious to me that I feared confronting it. I was confident in my ability to shoot it before it ever laid a paw on me, so it couldn't be that. But what if it were more than just an ordinary cat. What if it were symbolic of a fear, or worse, sent by God. I didn't feel I was ready to meet God on this morning.

I moved with caution, placing my weapon in the hair-trigger mode. I breathed deeply twice, calming my heart as much as possible, as I pushed passed the big, bright green leaves.

A woman, stripped naked, was tied to a tree with safety wire, her throat slit from ear to ear, and her eyes plucked out and placed in her mouth. A man, also tied to the base of a tree, was skinned from his nipples to the top of his forehead. His skin was tacked to the tree behind him. In his lap was a baby, dead, having been stabbed through the chest. The man's eyes seemed to stare at me.

"Hmmm." I heard the sound that had drawn me here. It was that man calling to me. My eyes filled with tears, as I told him how sorry I was. "Oh God, what do I do?" I asked aloud. He moaned one more time. "I know." I told him. "Your family — they're at peace." I attempted to ease his mind. Tears, now draining from my eyes, blurred my vision. I reluctantly wiped them away, as they screened some of the horror from my eyes. I moved close to him, easing my gun to the back of his head. "Our Father, who art in heaven..." I sighted the Lord's Prayer, slowly and succinctly, contemplating what I was about to do, hoping that he would die naturally. He didn't.

"Hmmmmm!" He moaned one last time.

"God, please forgive me." I shot him through the temple. I sat on the ground, blood dripping from my face, numb, but somehow knowing that I would get through it. I reasoned that the Panther and the feeling of being drawn into the forest, were somehow connected, and that I was supposed to be in this place at this time. My coping mechanisms were running at full throttle. I wiped my forehead, streaking the blood across my face like Indian war paint. Calls began to ring out in the forest apart from those animals and birds frightened by the gun fire.

"Ves! Anthony!" They called out in desperation. Although I heard their cries clearly, I was unable to respond. I searched for the energy, breathing deep as a preamble to a scream, but not finding the will nor the inclination to do so.

I remained quiet, listening as the voices closed in on me.

Chapter 19.

I could discern Joey's voice as he searched the veiling leaves.

"Tony!" He called out. Then in a more fragile voice, "Come on Buch, where are you, man?"

"Here. Over here." I answered.

Joey plowed through the rubbery leaves, stopping when he saw the bodies. He stood only a few feet from me.

"We gotta get outa here, Tony. Whoever did this may have heard the gun shot. Come on. Let's get away from this insanity."

"We've gotta bury 'em. My God, Joey, look at 'em. For God's sakes, who would do this? Who could? We gotta bury 'em." I demanded in a mournful tone.

Joey, considering the dangers of calling out in the furtive, skulking jungle, canvassed the immediate area for possible culprits, then concealed himself between two larger trees.

"Over here!" he yelled.

"This way! It came from over here!" Lourdes responded. She came through the leaves and called out again.

"Here! He's here!" Her smile immediately changed to terror within twenty feet of the dismembered corpses.

"What happened?" She asked. "Joey? What happened?"

"What the hell's it look like happened! Some people were fucked up by some sick mothers, and Tony put one of 'em out of his misery."

"Is that what happened, Ves?"

"Would you shut the hell up!" Joey stopped her from interrogating me. "Do you think he did it!"

"Of course not!" She shouted, now bawling.

"Then shut the fuck up! Nothing else matters!"

"We gotta bury 'em." I said.

Joey leaned toward Lourdes. "He wants to bury them."

"With what?" Lourdes asked.

"Good question. Look at 'em. He ain't leaven' until we plant them."

One by one, everyone came on the scene, including the pilot. Joey gathered everyone together and attempted an explanation. I glanced up periodically to find each of them intermittently looking over their shoulders at me. I felt like a freak show in a circus.

"All right." Box began, speaking rapidly. "Rick, Steven, Quinn, you (the pilot) and myself will grab some dirt. Use your knives or anything sharp to help you dig quickly. Lourdes, Debara, muster up some rocks if you can—as many as you can. We'll have to make the graves shallow. Bury the child with its mother. Joey and Christina, move around, look for anything that doesn't fit."

Joey cleared his throat and signaled Box in my direction. Box nodded, and then came to my side.

"We're gonna give them a proper burial. You just relax and let us take care of this, okay."

"No. I wanta help." I said firmly.

"If you think you're up to it. You can help find some rocks."

"I'll help dig the father's grave."

"Okay. I'll help you."

We worked slowly, ripping and gnawing at the earth. The more I dwelled on the cruelty of this event, the more violently I thrust my knife into the dirt. I scooped the soil like an armadillo, venting my anger in my labor. Box exerted a similar energy, his way of reassuring me that I wasn't going mad. I couldn't bare to watch as Joey cut the man's skin from the tree and laid it back in its somewhat natural position. I continued to look away as Box and Rick laid the bodies in their inconsequential holes. The

dirt began to cover their faces before I turned around
to assist in the burial. Several rocks were placed over
the graves and Christina marked them with crossed
branches. As Christina said a mindful prayer, I asked
the Lord if I'd made the right decision. I then asked
him to allow this family to look down on the earth
one last time to see that someone cared. We huddled
tightly, holding on to one another. We were becoming polarized from the rest of the world by reason of
circumstances, and I liked it. The tougher things got,
the closer we were drawn together. Even the pilot,
who now seemed like one of us, threw his arms over
those that stood beside him. We waited for a moment,
staring down at the piled dirt, when I heard it. "Huh."
I smiled.

"What?" Box asked.

"The music." I said, assuming he must have heard
it.

"What music?" He continued.

"That beautiful music. The trumpets—the brass.
Oh, how soothing." I closed my eyes, and swayed back
and forth, not considering the absurdity of music in
the thick of the jungle.

"I hear it." Lourdes said convincingly, as she began
to mimic my motion. Box followed suit, probably
deciding that I had gone crazy. His clumsy dancing
started me laughing, though I continued to move. We
were all dancing now, and laughing. We were released from this place, lifted up to a level not achieved
through drugs or self-determination. Something di-
vine had happened, and no one was questioning it. We
departed as if something good had happened here,
not considering our next move until we later reentered
the camp site.

We gathered up all the food and water that we could
carry, and headed north. At the edge of the forest, I

looked back to the wreck, wondering if we had actually died there, but didn't yet know it.

The pilot led us due north, telling us that we would soon come upon the Macaya River, where we would find help in the form of the drug smugglers we originally searched for. Quinn confirmed the connection between this river and a secondary target she was given back at Howard Air Base. She could not, however, assure us that we were where he said we were.

"What makes you think we're near this river?" Debara asked. "We could just as easily have passed into Peru last night, you know."

"The radio transmission." Quinn responded. "If we were in Peru, they would have asked us more than just to identify ourselves."

"I hope you're right," added Box.

"But…?" The pilot started.

"But? But what?" I asked.

"The eyes."

"What eyes?" Box pressed.

"The ones in—you know…her mouth." He said with caution.

"That meant somethin', didn't it?" Joey said anxiously.

"Yeah." He gasped. "It means you talked about something you saw. Something you weren't supposed to talk about. It means betrayal."

"So how does that mean we're in Peru?" Box asked.

"Its symbolism is used by the Shining Path." I answered.

"And they're in Peru I bet." Joey injected.

"Now the question is how far into Peru." Said Debara.

"Well, let's not give up hope that this torture is common to the Colombians, too." Lourdes attempted to build our confidence.

❖   ❖   ❖

We walked for about five hours. Reaching the bank of
a river, we hunkered down and considered our options. The worst scenario was that this was the
Putamayo River, the best scenario was that it was the
Macaya. In either case, we would have to cross it. We
feared using the radio. If we were in Peru, it would
take too much time to remove us from the area.

The section of the river was much too rapid to cross
safely, so we decided to travel the bank in search of a
safe crossing. We had tracked about a mile eastward
when we discovered a portion of the river that flowed
with far less current. It was still much too deep to wade
across. A decision had to be made as to whether or not
we should leave behind all that we carried, excepting
the weapons. "We shouldn't have any need for water,
what with all this rain." I said. "And food seems quite
plentiful around here. Joey could shoot a monkey or
something, if we get desperate. So that's not a problem.
I for one, will feel a lot better over there."

"We're gonna cross? Is that what you've decided?"
Christina asked.

"Let's go," Debara cut to the chase.

The pilot waddled in front of us, still wheezing
from the journey. "If we're gonna do this, there's a
couple things you need to know. First, swim with the
current, on an angle to the opposite shore."

Quinn interrupted him. "Great. Mark Spitz with
glands."

He shook his head and continued. "And the other
thing to remember, is not to thrash the water. You
never know when you'll run into a school of piranha."

"No problem. We'll send you first, and they'll be
too stuffed to bother with the rest of us." Quinn said
harshly.

"What's your problem, bitch? I don't need this
attitude of yours."

I separated the two, throwing my arm around the pilot and walking him to the edge of the water. "I wouldn't press my luck with her. She can do more damage than some flesh eaten' fish, believe me."

I entered the murky water directly behind the pilot. I was never much of a swimmer, and was astonished at the grace of the pilot, as he side stroked his way across, never rippling the water with his feet. He had a rhythm, short kicks that did not rupture the river's surface, and extending arm pulls that moved voluminous amounts of water. No matter how I attempted to emulate his stroke, I couldn't maintain my calm, kicking and pawing at the water in spurts of panic, whenever I lost buoyancy.

As I approached the opposite shore, I developed an anxiety attack. I kicked and tore at the water with short choppy strokes, before swallowing a mouth full and sinking below the surface. I was only twenty feet from the shore. I emerged, coughing. I could almost touch land, but it seemed unattainable. The pilot offered help.

"Stand up," he said, sincerely confused with my struggle.

I reached for the river bottom with my toes, and was relieved to find I could protrude my nose above the water. I had time to grasp a couple of refreshing breaths of air before Steven flopped on top of me, pushing me below the water again. Soon, there were nine of us churning in six feet of water, pulling for the shore.

Except for Lourdes and the pilot, everyone was completely exhausted. We laid sprawled out on the bank, convulsing as we struggled to stabilize our breathing. We regained our energy, and drove further north, traversing the mountainous region was grueling, and we soon were once again consumed with fatigue.

"Does anyone have a clue where the hell we are?" I asked, sapped of all my strength.

"If that was the border back there, then we're somewhere in the Amazons region." Quinn started. "It's a big area, with few breaks in the jungle. The chances of us going on unnoticed aren't very good, though. We need to do something, and soon. I'm not sure what, but we can't stay out here indefinitely. There are poisonous snakes, carnivorous animals, and, let's not forget, the Campasinos. They don't carry IFF. They're not going to know who we are."

"Well, we're not goin' to be extracted from here. The forest is just too thick." I replied. "Let's sleep here tonight and attempt to find a clearing tomorrow."

We were without blankets, so we nestled under the thickest canopy we could find and readied ourselves for slumber.

"You know. This reminds me of when I was a little kid and my dad would take me, my brothers, and a bunch of the neighborhood kids camping in the woods near Beaver Pond. Of course there, you could see the stars and light a fire without fear of being killed. How circumstances change."

While the others slept, Debara and I talked for a couple of hours. We never once considered tomorrow. Speech turned to intimacy in the tropical night air. I knew immediately that this was not something I would regret come daybreak. Unlike so many females I knew in college, Debara was a woman, emotionally and mentally. She understood herself, and held no unrealistic expectations of me. We came to each other honestly, without masks. I held her close to me for the longest time, clinging to a moment that I wished would last forever.

My internal alarm clock awakened me before the others. I started to slip away from Debara when she likewise woke.

"Where you going?" she whispered.

"It wouldn't be good if the others saw us like this."

"I'm sure they heard us kissing and panting last night."

"Probably, but..."

"I know. Come here and give me a kiss good morning," she offered sweetly.

I did, and it felt right. I had fallen in love over the past few months, and didn't even suspect it was happening.

"I'll see you in the morning."

"Not as well as you saw me last night," she played.

"Sshhh! You kook."

The following day it rained. A steady flow of water could be heard pelting the thick jungle canopy. Water dripped and splattered on our heads, but we were sheltered by the natural umbrella of the forest. Ironically, in this drenching weather, we desperately sought an open field. For Steven's equipment to have the slimmest chance of effectively contacting the CIA in Mena, Arkansas, we would first need to find our way out of this jungle and into a sizable clearing. To compound our plight, the clearing had to be virtually obstruction free, meaning no more ravines.

After a few hours of drudging our way over the hilly terrain, I expressed my malcontent.

"This isn't working. Steven! Is there any other way of getting this shit to work?"

"I've gotta bounce the signal off a satellite. That just isn't possible from in here," Steven replied reasonably.

"What if we held that dish up above the trees?" I questioned.

"If the tree was on a peak, sure. But how the hell are we gonna do that? Even if one of you could climb one of these trees, the cord won't reach the top," Steven reasoned.

"It would if you climbed up yourself," I said, realizing that this was our only hope.

"There's no way I can climb..."

"Okay! Let's find a tree on a peak. The next hill looks promising. When we get there, I'll climb to the top. It'll be up to the rest of you to persuade Steven up the tree behind me."

"The radio isn't that hard to figure out. Maybe someone else can do it," Steven suggested.

"Good try, but we need this to work the first time. I don't want someone half-way up a tree trying to figure this thing out. No, you've gotta go."

"Okay. I'll do my best."

"No. We don't want your best." Box insisted. "We want your ass up that tree."

"You can do it, Steven. You swam that river, didn't ya?" Lourdes supported him.

"I wasn't terrified of swimming."

"Good lord! I want a show of hands of anyone else who's afraid of heights." I said in an increased tone. No hands were raised.

"That figures. The only two that have needed to climb something in a crisis have had phobias."

❖ ❖ ❖

As we climbed the hill, I was proud of our team's determination, yet uneasy with our obvious, and collective, lack of experience. Box, who was pulling up the rear, glanced up at me, grinning tensely as sweat poured off his brow. He dropped his head back down, and continued his struggle up the hill.

"We're almost there! Just a few more yards!" I yelled encouragingly.

Turning, I was startled to see a boy, maybe nine years old, standing directly in front of me. Fear canvassed his face, as his eyes swept back and forth across our group. I sensed that he wanted to run, but feared exposing his back to us. He carried a small handgun. It was raised, but hung flaccid. I could have killed him with little effort. I called to the others, who were unaware of our visitor.

"Halt," I said in a soothing voice. "Everybody halt. No talking, no talking. We've got a small friend right in front of us. Mind you, an armed small friend. Just relax. I'm going to attempt to disarm him."

Box's voice had an edge of disbelief in it.

"Are you outa your fuckin' mind! Look where we are at, for God's sake. This is not your average little boy."

I spoke softly to the boy, "It's okay." I lowered my weapon to the ground. He's Spanish, I thought.

"Whoever's nearest me with good Spanish, please tell this kid I'm unarmed and don't wish to cause him any harm," I said softly. I was now in a crouched position, having just placed my weapon on the damp ground. Lourdes began to speak, distracting him a bit, as I stood up.

I heard nothing initially, as my arm was smashed backwards. It was like being hit with a baseball bat. Pressure filled my arm, no real pain. I wasn't even sure if it was my arm that had been shot. Before I could consider the extent of my injury, I heard a barrage of gun fire.

"No! No! No! I'm fine! Stop shooting! Stop shooting!" I screamed, hugging the ground as the bullets wailed over my head.

The shooting stopped. Box leaned over and grabbed me by my injured arm.

"Do you think you used enough fire power!" I shouted. "Would you like my gun? Maybe there's an ounce of flesh left we can still shoot!"

"We shot over his head," Box said solemnly. "We just chased him away." He turned my wrist, exposing my forearm. "I thought you were dead. I really thought..."

As I sat up, I saw Debara crying in the arms of Christina. So many things raced through my mind. I knew that she loved me, and that she must have thought, as everyone probably thought, that the little

boy had killed me. I also knew that I could never bear
to watch her get hurt, and, as a consequence, our
work together would soon have to end. Looking at
Box, I could see that he was thinking the same thing.
As the field leader, I could never send her into harms
way.

"We've got to stop the bleeding." Rick said.

"Yeah. Get me a tourniquet." I said.

"Hold your arm out." Rick gently demanded. I did,
expecting to feel a soft cloth being wrapped around
my arm. Box held my biceps, blocking Rick from my
view. Then I heard the distinct sound of something hot
contacting something that was not.

"Hhhmmmmmm!" I cringed and grunted. I could
smell my flesh melting, but never pulled away, figuring that an Indian would know more about these
things than I. The bullet, a 7 mm shell according to
Joey, deflected off a bone, and exited at an angle. The
damage to my arm was negligible, but the bruise, or
fracture, to my bone, prohibited my making the climb.

"We better step it up a bit," Debara advised. "That
boy couldn't be too far from an adult."

"Let's just pray he's a part of the look-out patrol
that Escobar told us about." Box replied.

"We're almost to the top of the hill." I said. "We'll
call from there."

My legs and back were in spasm by the time we
crested the hill. I asked for volunteers to make the
climb to the top of a very tall tree. There were no
shortages of volunteers.

"No, Rick. We're gonna need you down here to
boost lard ass up the tree."

"You've got Box." Rick said, suggesting that Box
could lift Steven into the tree.

"It'll take more than Box to get him up to that first
branch." I insisted.

"How 'bout me?" Quinn asked.

"You're too short. Look at the spread on those

limbs." I answered. Joey began to ask about himself, when I replied: "The same reason."

"I can do it." Lourdes demanded enthusiastically.

"Then do it." I answered sharply. "Steven, wrap some cord around her waist—not too much, and face the dish (mini-satellite dish) to her back. When the cord becomes nearly extended, we'll yell for you to stop climbing. Then we'll send Steven up. He'll match you step for step until you reach the top. That way, Steven climbs only as much as he has to." I explained very pragmatically.

"Okay. Let's go."

Lourdes climbed at a very brisk pace, pulling and hoisting herself ever higher with marsupial grace. Within minutes, she had made her way into the sky, and it was time to push Steven into the tree. I was unable to assist, so I watched as Box and Rick strained to boost him to the first limb. Steven grappled, with legs dangling, to pull himself beyond the branch, but could not do so. As Box carried Rick atop his shoulders, Rick attempted to push Steven over the limb.

Eventually, Steven, in a very undignified manner, conquered the limb.

"Take your time. You can do it." Lourdes encouraged from the tress. "Don't look down. Just keep climbing."

"Move, you fat ass!" Box yelled.

"This proves we didn't evolve!" hollered Christina. "It would have taken more than a few billion years to forget this much about climbing!" She shouted before busting out laughing.

"Don't worry! Just take your sweet-ass time!" Joey shouted.

"Why don't you get your ass up here!"

"That's it. I'm shooting his ass down." Joey said,

loud enough to be heard. He then fired a round a few feet from where Steven stood in the tree.

"What are you, fuckin crazy?" I reacted in amazement. "You could have killed him?"

"Yeah! Well, look at 'em climb now." Joey pointed to the tree, where Steven was halfway up.

"That was real bright, Joey," Lourdes yelled. "He's doin' his best, you know."

"Well, now he's doin' better!" Joey claimed.

"The time we may have saved in his climbing may be lost in the time it takes the Campasinos to find us." Debara said.

"Well. I'm not sure that that's such a threat. And that little fucker has probably already told them every thing they need to know about us. Half of Colombia knows where we are by now," I answered.

"So you're saying I did a good thing?" Joey asked.

"No! You stupid shit. Don't ever do that again! Or it'll be you that gets his ass shot!" Box threatened.

Steven had made his way high enough into the tree to allow Lourdes enough free cable to scale to the top.

"Are you there!" called Steven. Lourdes replied in the affirmative. "Now hold it up as high as you can above the tree!"

Lourdes did as she was instructed, reaching fervently into the vast nothingness.

"Oh, my God!"

"What's wrong?" Steven asked.

"Nothing's wrong! It's beautiful!" she exclaimed. "It's absolutely beautiful."

"Really?" Steven, forgetting why it was I'd sent him up there in the first place, said in the voice of romance.

"Really what? What are you two talking about!" I asked.

"She says it's beautiful! The landscape!"

"Shoot that mother fucker down!" I said sarcastically to Joey, loud enough for Steven to hear.

"I'm doin' it!" Steven shouted back. "I'm trying to get a signal. This equipment isn't designed for this. There's no way this is going to work."

"Stop your whinin' and do your job!" Box ridiculed.

Steven continued to mumble. "I don't see your ass up here. That's 'cause you can't climb. You can't swim either. You just scream a lot. Wait! I got something. Hello? Hello?"

"Aren't you supposed to use a code!" I reminded him.

"Damn it! Yes. That's right. `The City Comes Alive At Four PM.' Over!" Steven had made a satellite connection with Mena, Arkansas. He now attempted, in as few words possible, to work out a plan to get us out. The biggest problem of course, was where we were. Steven broke away from his conversation for a split second to ask the pilot if he had removed the emergency transmitter device from the aircraft. The pilot said that he had, and that it was fully charged and ready to go.

"Great!" Steven responded. Now the awkward part. How to send an American military aircraft into the area, undetected, and extract us from the jungle. A helicopter would move much too slowly and carry too large a signature on radar to successfully cross the border unnoticed. A fast, sleek aircraft would be unable to maneuver in these tight quarters, and would not have sufficient cargo space to transport us. Steven was in the middle of discussing these extremely important details when he fell out of the tree. "Wooo! Ah Shiiiiit!" he crashed through the limbs, twenty feet to the ground.

"Are you okay?" I asked, as he lay twisted, the cord wrapped around his body.

"Oh God, I think I broke something."

"What? What did you break?" I probed.

"I don't know. But I know I broke something."

"Let's straighten him out a bit, and check for damage." Box directed. We gently laid him flat and searched for severe lacerations or broken bones, but found none.

"Get your ass back in the tree!" Box insisted.

"I can't. It's broken."

"You're fine, now get up there."

"No. The SATCOM system. It'll take me a while to fix it."

"We don't have a while," I said gravely.

"The last thing he told me was to set that emergency transmitter ten minutes after he gave me the signal. Of course, I won't be able to get the signal now."

"Great. If we set the signal too early, we could be detected by the Colombian Special Operations bozos. Set it too late and shwush, there goes our ride! And if he doesn't receive your reply, he may not send an aircraft at all!" I looked up the tree and told Lourdes to come down. I continued to stare at the perch that Steven once sat upon.

"How in God's name did you fall out of the tree? Would you please tell me that? In all my childhood I never once fell out of a tree. Not once!"

"What do you want me to do with this." The pilot asked, holding a little black box out in front of him.

"He said ten minutes. Let me think." I sat on a log, unable to come up with a logical answer. Instead, I waited for it to feel right. I pictured Arkansas trying to contact Steven. I added time for him to contact Langley, which would in turn have to make a secure call to an Air Force commander. Time would then be needed to detour an Air Force aircraft with a scheduled sortie, and fly it to our general vicinity. I allotted twenty minutes for this to transpire.

"Okay. Turn it on." He did, and we waited with eyes and heads drawn skyward. Approximately fifty yards away was a tiny clearing, not large enough for the landing of a fixed wing aircraft, but large enough for a visual sighting of our team. We made our way toward it.

We stood poised on the edge of the clearing, hesitant to cross the threshold. We squatted below the brush line, distressed over our incapacity to deal directly with the situation. We were at the mercy of happenstance, unable to decide our own fate.

"Hey!" Box whispered. "Fat boy." He directed at the pilot. "What should I call 'em?" Box asked Christina who wore an angry look. Box turned his attention back to the pilot who was protruding into the clearing. "Move your fat ass back."

"Call me Mack from now on." He seemed a bit hurt. "Yeah, I'm fat. But you didn't see me wheezing after our little swim, now did ya."

"Wish we could say the same for our little hike in the woods. You sounded like a damned wildebeast." Quinn said.

"Hey, you mentioned glands before," Lourdes began, "maybe he's got glands?"

"Glands. That always kills me." I joined in. "You'd think that at least one Jewish prisoner of war had a glandular problem."

Taking offense, Rick said: "They were starved."

"Oh. So there *is* a connection between eating and gaining weight."

"I don't have glands, Mack said. "I just love to stuff my face." We began to chuckle mildly.

With his stilled hands raised at a ninety degree angle to his body, the pilot suddenly looked alive.

"Wait!" With his head tilted to the clearing and arms still stiffened outward, he paused. "What the hell!"

"What is it? A plane?" I searched.

"Not quite."

"What then? Talk to us, damn it!" I said aloud.

"Hear that crackling sound?" he asked, as we listened to what sounded like a Harley Davidson motorcycle. "Those are jet engines."

"I thought jet engines roared?" I said.

"They're near stall speed, aren't they?" Quinn stated.

"Bingo!" the pilot rasped. "This crazy pilot is flying by his ass to save our butts." He then rose to his feet, throwing his finger into the air. "There!" he shouted, running into the clearing with waving arms. Everyone followed except for Box and I. I couldn't believe it. I had never seen anything like it. It was crawling, dark and foreboding, across the tree line. In my mind, the operation had just expanded incalculably. The SR-71 program was one of the most compartmentalized programs in the Air Force. Yet, here it was in support of *Pseudo Miranda*. The Air Force now had a gigantic butt to cover if anything were to go wrong.

Watching as the SR-71 pilot risked his life for people he would never meet, I was never so proud of my country and the people who served it.

Moments after the pilot gained a visual, he slapped his engines into after-burner and launched into the cosmos. Several seconds later, the aircraft was gone from sight. We were obviously very important to someone very powerful, if we commanded such resources. This passing thought comforted me just long enough for the rescue craft to arrive.

We were soon on board an Ochoan helicopter, bound for Guaviare, and eventually home.

Chapter 20.

In Bellingham, I applied to a number of different management positions with my friend and neighbor, Kevin Racine. Kevin and I had been close friends since childhood. He was tough, and had fought through the pain twisted feet had caused him as a kid. His feet had been medically corrected, but he was still a resilient fellow determined to succeed in life. The thing I most admired about Kevin was he never apologized for his childhood disability, nor complain of the pain when participating in one of our games of mangle football. It was a tough neighborhood.

The neighborhood that my father, Bennedict, had helped build had changed depressingly. When I was a kid, my father had taught all the children of the neighborhood how to play a variety of games. Many of the kids, I felt, had adopted him as their own. Especially the Ferrelli's, Kenny and Joey, who lived across the street. It was a neighborhood of ethnicity, with Italian the strong suit. The Tagliaferri's, notably Kevin and Paul, formed part of the clan. Even the Racine's were mostly Italian.

I can still recall my father compressing and leveling the snow in the back yard immediately after a storm. I'd look out the second story window late at night with my older brothers, Benny and Danny, as my dad, with his hand powered roller, would labor for hours building the best hockey rink ever. After rolling the snow, he would build a circumference wall, flooding the inner sanctum to form an outdoor hockey rink, complete with nets and boards made of snow. It also carried with it the luxury of direct access to food, beverage, and, of course, first aid.

My father was also the point man for developing and building the Little/Senior League baseball and Pop Warner football programs. The political climate which downgraded the importance of winning and learning, and rewarded under achievement and non-success, eventually drove my father out of organized sports, but, fifteen years later, I still bump into people who are compelled to tell me what my father meant to them.

He had been the glue that held the neighborhood together. Ironically, it was the introduction of drugs that had torn it apart.

My mother, Dorothy, has always been the emotional foundation of the family. I credit her with my having gone to college. My mother was, and is, always there for me. She is the most dependable woman I have ever known.

My first memory of my mother is during the Kennedy assassination. I didn't understand what had saddened her, but I sensed it was important. She would often call me Kennedy instead of Kenny thereafter. He was likely the last Democrat to receive favorable press in the Bucchi household.

I acquired my sense of humor and extroverted personality from my mother, and my determination, resilience and pigheadedness from my father. The combination was useful to the wheelings and dealings of the CIA, but less becoming to the opposite sex. When times got tough, as they did, I could always rely on my parents. I credit my life to them.

❖   ❖   ❖

I completed the application processes for the Air Force and Army Officer programs. I knew the fix was in for the Air Force and the Army would certainly never want the likes of me. I was becoming concerned that Pseudo Miranda was floudering; more drugs were getting through than were being inercepted. I had only two recent interceptions and no interventions during this period.

On April 15, 1985, I was diverted while enroute to Texas for another interception. Box met me in Paducah and informed me that George Lauder of the CIA wanted to see me in Boston in two days. Box didn't reveal the exact nature of the meeting, but he hinted it involved he and I traveling to Panama in May.

After driving twenty straight hours, I finally arrived at the Quincy Market, located near the Boston Common. I was exhausted and expected to me met promptly. I wasn't. I ordered some fried clams and devoured them as I waited anxiously for Mr. Lauder's arrival.

The profession had made me very sensitive to people who seemed interested in me beyond a normal glance. A man soon approached from the double doors at the end of the room. He was very Ivy League with his draped, crumpled brown suit and preppy tie. Lanky, he had a face that had as many folds as his suit. Although attempting an indirect focus, he made directly for my table. No hand shakes were extended.

He promptly entered into a lecture on the proper conduct for meeting with Director Casey. Not again, I thought! He continued with his advice, speaking aristocratically, making sure to cram as many polysyllabic words into each run-on sentence as possible. In the middle of this excruciating lecture, I arched my back over the chair and bellowed a contemptuous yawn.

"Did you hear what it is I just said?"

"You mean the Casey thing?" I said mechanically.

"It's that type of perfunctory response to a portentous matter such as this, that will cause you great tribulation."

"And me without my thesaurus." I replied, eyelids drooping. "Look, I'm tired. I've driven twenty-six hundred miles in three days. I haven't slept, bathed or brushed my teeth in over twenty-four hours. I've been living on Diet Coke's and Oreo Cookies since Kentucky. And, except for James Cagney, I've never been too awe struck by mere mortals. So, if you would just wake me when he arrives, I would be most appreciative."

I laid my head on the table, between my folded arms, and closed my eyes completely.

I was awakened with a smack to the head. I was to

see Frank Dupero infrequently during my CIA tenure, but it was always a displeasure. I responded to his rude welcome with a curt reception of my own. Snapping my hand from the table, I clenched his esophagus with the tips of my fingers, pulling his head hastily to meet mine. My finger nails drew trickles of blood as I reeled him inward.

With his desperate face next to mine, I said, "Anthony? What's yours?"

I then released my grip and laid my head back down between my arms.

He clutched his throat, and gasped for air.

"You're damn lucky we're in a public place," he rasped with an injured vocal chord.

"I feel lucky," I said.

Mr. Lauder re-entered the picture, and informed me to look sharp. Bill Casey was about to arrive.

"What the hell happened to you?" he said to Frank, slipping from his deliberate speech. "Here he comes. Try not to draw attention to him."

Bill Casey was entering and Lauder was worried that I would draw too much attention. Even though I had become very astute at picking out people in a crowd, I could not readily detect Casey's security men in this crowd.

As he sat down, I smirked, knowing as I did how politically aware these Bostonians considered themselves to be. Yet, here was the world's biggest spy walking among them, and they weren't discerning his presence. Of course, with the luxury of hindsight, I wonder now if they simply weren't impressed.

Mr. Casey never so much as removed his hat as he delivered a succinct briefing on the momentous changes in the operation.

"I don't have much time, so listen carefully." He muttered. And I did listen carefully, attempting to glean what he said through his inarticulate mumbling.

"Mr. Ochoa (mispronounced: Aw-choh-wa) has specifically requested you to meet with him at his ranch in Northern Colombia before he meets with Antonio Noriega in Panama City next month. Mr. Escobar (mispronounced: Es-choh-bar) was very impressed with you. That chance meeting you had with him has opened up new territory for us. That's good. But remember. This is the Supreme Don of the hemisphere. Escobar is a schmuck compared to this guy. Whatever Don Fabio says, goes. Get in good with him, and the sky's the limit for us. He requested you by name!" He then whispered loudly. "Do you know what that means?"

"That he knows my name."

"What?"

"Nothing. Go on, sir."

"We've been trying to get close to this guy forever. We've determined that he's the only one we can trust working with. But he's Colombian through and through. No American has ever gotten into his inner circle. Except..." He caught himself before revealing something he shouldn't have. "He doesn't speak any English whatsoever, so pick who you want to accompany you."

"Lourdes."

"What? Oh, not now. Talk to George."

"What's this meeting about?" I asked

"As you probably know, we're not doin' so well with our intercepts. Too many places of origin, satellite problems, fuckin' Air Force, you name it. I want you to persuade the Don to fly all *Pseudo Miranda* flights through Panama." He removed a piece of paper from the inside pocket of his overcoat and showed it to me. The paper read *Bottle Neck*. He then placed it back into his pocket and continued, first muttering something incomprehensible. "He's gonna know this doesn't make much good business sense, so you'll have to convince him that *Pseudo Miranda* dissolves if we continue to lose. I wish I had more time with you. I don't. Do you understand what it is…? Good. You're doin' very fine work for us, Mr. Bucchi. Keep it up."

"Yeah. Sounds do-able. When do I go?"

"George will handle that. Don't let the brevity of this meeting mislead you, this is very important to our country's security. "

"No, sir."

"George will fill you in on the Air Force stuff and the money issue too. I gotta run." He stood up to a crouch and shuffled out the door.

"The Air Force stuff?" I asked Lauder.

"You'll be attending the Air Force Officer Training School on the Medina Annex of Lackland Air Force Base in San Antonio, Texas. We will then send you for further training in Illinois."

"You're kidding me, right?"

"No, we're not. We need to provide you and the others with airtight alibis now that this operation has achieved a new level."

"So I train and that's it, right?"

"No, that's not right. As long as this operation is in affect, you'll remain an active duty member of the armed forces. In name only, of course. Everything will be taken care of once you've completed your training. While in training, you're on your own. This means that you could readily flunk out if you don't apply yourself."

"Why not just put the fix in there, too?"

"We need to first know that we can pass you off as a military officer. If you fail, we'll place you else-where, and continue to do so until you fit in perfectly."

"So, what's in mind for Box?"

"He's Langley. If anything were to go wrong we'd fire him and accuse them of running the show with some other government employees in positions of opportunity."

"Like myself."

"Like yourself. From now on, Frank will relieve you of any money you acquire when you first touch down in Homestead, Mena, or wherever."

"How does that differ from what we've been doin'? I mean it's not as if we're becoming inundated with currency."

We had only received money on one occasion. Why this sudden change in logistics? In the past, one of us, usually Christina, would accompany the drugs to Tonopah, Nevada, where they — and on this particular occasion, the money — were then stowed underground. The drugs would still make their way to Nevada, but now any money that we acquired would go to parts unknown. The fact that the CIA might want some untraceable money to help fund other operations in no manner surprised me, nor did it bother me. The acquisition of money becoming the focal point of *Pseudo Miranda* did concern me, however. Warning sirens were wailing in my head, but I ignored them, hoping that the operation would continue to diminish the flow of drugs into the country.

"There is no difference, so don't worry about it. Just do your job, and let us concern ourselves with the technical matters." Lauder assured me.

"Is that all?" I asked bluntly.

"No. Just keep up the good work."

After lounging around Bellingham for the rest of the month, I soon grew restless. I wanted to be thrown back into the fire and fly to Colombia. For all the horror and sadness I had experienced there, I still craved the pressure and excitement. Regardless of all the ethical dilemmas, I felt what we were doing what needed to be done, and it was important to my country's security. I knew that *Pseudo Miranda* was not the final program in the war on drugs, but it was a crucial step, and I was honored to be an integral part of it.

I was about to fly back to Colombia, to the home of the true Supreme Don of cocaine, Fabio Ochoa.

Chapter 21

It was early May and my patience was wearing thin. I had made myself available for message traffic for hours on end, hanging out in the malls or taking lonesome walks through the wilderness around Beaver Pond in hopes of being contacted. I was playing a *Star Wars* video game at a local arcade when a courier finally caught up with me.

The date was set and I was off to Colombia.

When I met up with Box and Lourdes in Arkansas, they had plenty of questions about my meeting in Boston and what it meant to the operation. Box seemed as puzzled as I was about the changing events.

"You got me," he said. "I completely understand the need to involve the General (Noriega), but all this stuff about money. I don't know."

"Why would they think there'd be more money in this, anyhow? It's not as if it'll continue to drop out of the sky. Don't they have numbered accounts in the Caymans for all that?" I asked.

"Off course. That guy must have had a need for cash. Maybe he didn't trust the numbered system. I don't know, but I guaran-damn-tee it, the rest of the pilots have it wired to an island," Box insisted.

"Then why Frank Dupero?"

"Who?"

"Oh, I don't know. But you can bet your noodles something's cookin'."

"Yeah. And I bet it has something to do with Noreiga," I said.

"What are you two talking about?" Lourdes asked impatiently.

"If we knew, we'd be glad to tell you," I responded.

Box gave me a briefing on exactly what we were supposed to accomplish over the next couple of days. With the assistance of a LORAN system in Acandi, Columbia, set up by the CIA, the drug planes could safely fly out of Colombia and into Panama's Darien Valley, the location of Noriega's cocaine laboratories. This would provide a continuous safety beam to vector low altitude flights into America.

My job was to convince Ochoa that security necessitated this action, and, off the record, let him know the underlying motivation on the part of the CIA. Simply, this would enable us to capture the prescribed portion of the market that Pseudo Miranda established back in Zurich. Without said seizures, Pseudo Miranda would become defunct, and we would be forced to revert to our antagonistic relationship.

This information would need to remain with Ochoa, while he convinced Noriega and the other traffickers that this was simply good business. Noriega was not to know that the CIA suspected that he would capitalize on this opportunity to strike separate deals of his own, like piggybacking drugs onto large shipments, and accepting bribe money from the Cartel in exchange for safe passage. Therefore, Noriega would be paid large amounts of United States currency by the CIA for his assistance. This would convince him that our government knew nothing of his usurious compensation from the Cartel. In this way, the CIA would avoid the potential for blackmail if Noriega were ever placed in a position of compromise. Noriega would simply believe that the CIA was attempting to facilitate a better means of tracking drug shipments into America.

We flew in a Lear jet through Panama directly onto Ochoa's sprawling ranch on Colombia's Caribbean coast. Mack was once again our pilot.

"You're sure you know where you're going this time?" Box asked Mack.

"Nicaragua, right?"

"Yeah," Box replied. "Head for Nicaragua and we're sure to end up in Colombia."

The runway stretched for at least a mile, leaving the Lear plenty of room to negotiate a landing. Two pick-up trucks converged on us as we taxied to a halt. Several men casually exited the vehicles, toting chalks for the airplane's wheels. They secured the craft in place and opened the doors.

I paused for a moment to view the ranch. The rolling hills reminded me of Maryland, speckled with cattle and spotted with trees and shrubbery. It seemed normal, even though I detected buffalo among the scattered herds.

"Are those buffalo?"

"Oh my God!" Lourdes yelped, staring at an elephant only a hundred yards away down the runway.

"What's wrong with you people? It's an elephant. Haven't you ever been to the zoo before? Don Fabio's got lions, tigers, elk, deer, zebras, giraffes, chimps, monkeys, you name it." Mack said.

"How do they keep them off the runway?" I inquired.

"Sometimes they can't. But they've got electric shock and barbed wire." Mack informed us.

Mack was restricted to the airplane, but the rest of us were led casually to the vehicles. As we drove up a staircased hill toward the low house of Don Fabio, we passed a lake where carnivorous animals were imprisoned on a man made island by way of the water that surrounded them.

The Ochoa home was like the mansions of Beverly Hills, tradionally Spanish, with many ninety degree angles that created pockets of natural atriums as the structure crossed itself. Inside, the art and furnishings were traditionally Spanish.

We were greeted by a young man with long, dirty blond hair parted through the middle. As he spoke very little English, we relied heavily on Lourdes' translations. Except for Fabito (meaning young Fabio), we were unescorted. From the moment we met, he was articulate and polite, with a stately grace about him, even though he was barely five years older than myself. He acquainted us with the many unique features of the landscape, always more offering than demanding. I felt I was being coddled, as if some ulterior motive lie in wait.

We appeared to have free rein of the ranch. Occasionally, I saw people attending to the property and livestock, and a helicopter flying overhead, but I never saw an armed guard. I suppose the remote location allowed sentinels to be posted on the perimeter where they couldn't be seen. Oddly, this lack of security made me feel safer.

Fabito took us to a garage where a brand new Porsche 911 Cabriolet sat nestled between several vintage Harley Davidson Motorcycles, he mentioned his brother Jorge, who was, at that time, imprisoned in Spain. He asked what the CIA might be able to do to help him. We gave no answer, except to say that we would mention his concerns to our superiors. He seemed satisfied, but guarded, as he casually led us to a fenced-in area, where his father was watching a horse being trained.

We came to a stop at the wooden gate of the corral. Young Fabio stood silent, respectful of his father's position. I was reserved and patient, utilizing the dead time to admire my new surroundings. I saw no bulls, but the bleacher seats and pen gave evidence of the Spanish people's zest for bull fighting.

My eyes were curiously drawn to the pristine looking horse as *Don* Fabio, with his two keg girth hung extensively south of the belt line, grabbed hold of its rein, and, with the trainer steadying the disinclined animal, rolled himself aboard. It took every scrap of discipline I could muster to withhold the laughter within me. I knew that I needed only to look in Boxer's direction and I would immediately erupt into a tearful cackle. I pinched my leg and imagined I was mowing my lawn when a burst of pressurized air discharged from Boxer's nose. A torrent of air blasts stuttered out of our noses and mouths. Lourdes promptly tried to cover for us.

"You mean to tell me you two finally got that joke? Unbelievable!" She then said something to Fabio, obviously convincing enough to leave him unfazed at our behavior.

Still laughing, I said, "A pig that good, you can't eat all at once! That's a good one, Lourdes."

We ceased our laughter as Don Fabio pulled his horse beside the fence. A hat cast a shadow across his face as I strained to see him clearly through the nagging sun's rays. Still perched in the saddle, he began to speak softly to me. It became apparent that this would be as personal as it would get on our first encounter. I squinted with my head cocked, unable to erase the awed look from my face. His chubby facial features and short, somewhat hooked nose, were eerily reminiscent of Marlon Brando. I respectfully recited the CIA's interests, worrying that I had omitted something vitally important, yet not wanting to delay him too long. In remaining on the horse, Don Fabio had ingeniously communicated the non-verbal meddage that I needed to be brief.

He understood all of our demands, yet did not convey his position on any of them.

"Are we forgetting something?" I asked Boxer.

"No. Wait!" Box leaned toward me, whispering.

"You know this isn't any way to conduct a meeting. What have we accomplished? Is he gonna do it? How much, and when? We need something more than a few stares and a nod or two."

Boxer's whispers became more intense.

"I can't go back to Langley with some stares and a nod."

At this point, Don Fabio high stepped his mount away from us, with Fabito in close pursuit.

"Now we'll have to wait for him to return."

"I don't think so." I said.

"What the hell do you mean, you don't think so? We can't go without..."

"Sure we can. And we will." I turned and began to walk away. "We've got our answer. He'll do it."

"How do you know that? And how are we gonna know when we travel to Panama if he does?" Box challenged.

"Don't be ignorant. We found out about this meeting didn't we? Anyhow, if he immediately objected, he would have said so. Let's not force his hand before he's thought it out. If I'd pressed him for absolutes, he may have been forced to reject our offer. In this way, he can make any decision appear to be totally in his best interest. He knows he has to do this. But he doesn't want some young snot-nosed American telling him that he has to. I want him to feel comfortable dealing with me. Right now, he's gotta know that I completely understand what the appearance of our relationship must be."

"That's not how you dealt with Escobar," Box pointed out.

"Different people. You gotta make the call early. First impressions. Quick judgments will keep us alive in this business. Provided their insightful, of course." I answered. "Oh Lourdes. Good job back there. You saved our butts." I turned around to look at her. "How did you keep from laughing?"

"Did you see that poor horse?" She said sympathetically.

Box and I began laughing once again. "I should have guessed." I responded.

As we walked in the direction of the estate, a pickup truck pulled up. Fabito shouted from the bed of the truck:

"Come! Come!"

Box and Lourdes rode shotgun as I climbed in the back with young Fabio. He was all smiles, as he extended a hand for what appeared to be a congratulatory shake. He nodded repeatedly, making me feel somewhat uncomfortable. I felt like the unwitting entrée at a pigmy tribal dinner. I didn't want to return a smile, concerned that I would add embarrassment to my list of problems.

As we drove past the lake I noticed some large, circular Quonset huts. I asked what prevented the carnivores from crossing to the mainland. No matter how Fabito attempted to explain, I demonstrated my lack of discernment by shaking my head and shrugging my shoulders. I knew what it was he was attempting to explain, but I wanted a close up and personal look. What I got was a window into Fabito's ruthlessness.

Fabito tapped on the truck's rear window and signaled the driver in another direction. We soon came to a stop at the bank of the lake and he leaped from the vehicle and waved to a man on the hill. The man was prompt in his obedience, as he ran down the slope with his loosely fitted clothing sailing in the wind. He conferred with Fabito and then left, returning with a tiny lamb. Fabito carefully took hold of the lamb, cradling it in his arms. He caressed its head gently, demonstrating an authentic compassion for the cuddly creature. He then lobbed it into the water.

I gasped and watched as the baby lamb struggled to keep its head above water. Lourdes kicked off her shoes and headed for the water, hoping to deliver the helpless lamb from the scurvy of the vicious piranha. I lunged for her clothing, catching two fingers in one

of her fatigue pant belt loops. It was enough of a grip
to slow her progression. I soon had a firm, two-handed
grip on her. She lashed her arms violently as the water
began to churn and boil around the pitiful lamb.
Lourdes screamed and then cried, her body collapsing
limply at my feet.

I grabbed her firmly by the shoulders, digging my
thumbs into her blades.

"Stand up and pull yourself together, right now. Do
it damn-it."

She threw her arms to one side of me, attempting to
brush me aside. I quickly locked my arms around her
waist, pulling her backwards, as she flailed her arms
and screamed defamatory remarks at Fabito. He never
broke eye contact with us, nor did he demonstrate
emotion. I felt he was studying us, learning.

I walked Lourdes to the truck and turned to witness
Box staring puzzled at Fabito, who stared benignly
back. Placing Lourdes in the front seat, I walked to
Boxer's side.

"Let's go," I said.

"You gotta ask why, don't you? Why are all these
things necessary. He was happily grazing — you know,
content. And then he throws him into the…" Box
paused, and turned his arms outward at Fabito.

"Why?"

"It's just an animal for God's sakes. What's with
you two?" I insisted.

"It's not about that! He could have simply told us!
Don't you see? It's not just the lamb. None of it means
anything to these people. You and me, we're just
sheep."

"So for the price of a lamb, we found out something
very important about this guy. A small price to pay if
you asked me."

"Unless you're the lamb."

"Well I'm not. Come on Box. Do you think they
surgically remove the lamb's leg for leg-of-lamb? Huh?

Anyhow, who ever said the lamb was a more important species than the piranha?"

"A lamb that good, you can't eat all at once." Box said with a short, snide smile. We ignored Fabito as we trotted back to the truck.

Fabito escorted us to the Lear, where we found Mack sprawled out on the wing.

"You're gonna crack the wing spar, you fat ass!" I howled.

"Just gettin' an even tan." Mack said. "You meet the man?"

"Yeah. We sure did." Box answered.

Young Fabio bid us goodbye pleasantly. He assured me that his father would support the CIA's needs, and apologized for the lamb incident. I knew the latter was void of any sincerity, so I likewise doubted the veracity of the former. Nonetheless, I shook his hand and thanked him for his most gracious hospitality.

Aboard the jet, Lourdes repeated her anger at Fabito for torturing the lamb, and me for instagating the incident in the first place.

"That was horrible. I can't believe you two."

"Shut up, you piece of shit!" I cursed her. "You hardly shed a tear for Jerimiah, and you have the nerve to cry over this! It's a sheep! I've seen you seat cheeseburgers, buffalo wings and Mcfish sandwiches. So this lamb's somehow different? It's not as if it's on the verge of extinction! It's a sheep, for God's sake! You know, Bhaaaaa. Lamb chops!"

I calmed momentarily.

"You better damn well grow up, 'cause this won't happen again. Man is the only creature never to be killed. Period."

"How 'bout the condor and the Bengal tiger, or any other endangered species. I suppose if he'd tossed one of them into the water, you'd be defending him," Lourdes screamed.

"First of all, I'm not defending him. He's a sick bastard. But showing weakness in his presence doesn't accomplish anything. And, second of all, if you want to save the condor, make him part of the American diet. You don't see cows and chickens on the endangered speciers list, do you? When's the last time you personally saw any of those animals, anyway?"

"I haven't. And it's probably because they're so scarce."

"Then you wouldn't miss them, would you?" I explained.

"You're right," Box said solemnly. "We should have ignored it. We should have walked away without any emotional outpouring. He won that round. It's gonna be hard to call his bluff in the future."

"That's why we have to reverse the tables on him some day," I said inanely, not knowing that such a day might come.

I returned home, but it wasn't long before I was enroute to Panama City, Panama.

Chapter 22

I slept in the T-39 on the tarmac at Mena Airport while the pilot awaited clearance for takeoff. Spanish pilots were practicing touch-and-goes with their American trainers for hours on end. I finally stepped out onto the tarmac for a moment to stretch my cramped limbs. During an elongated yawn, I detected a large prop aircraft at the end of the taxi way, directly in front of a large hanger, unloading its cargo of several large brown duffel bags. Upon completion, numerous large crates were loaded onto the aircraft. Engines were cranked and the plane was soon taxing. This all took place in the span of minutes.

"What the hell was that all about?" I asked Mack, as he came out to join me.

"Don't you know?" He said inferringly.

"Drugs?"

"Yeah. And weapons out."

"To where? The weapons, I mean."

"That, I don't know — and don't want to." He lit a match for a cigarette, and shuffled away from the aircraft. "Lots of drug money in this state," he said, still moving away from the T-39.

I walked away, not criticizing him for lighting a match near the aircraft.

"Why here? Wouldn't it make more sense to hide it in a place like New York or Miami?"

"Where do you think the biggest bond market in the country is? Here! Right here! Low interest rates and no questions asked. The state gets a lot of capital that would otherwise go to the Caribbean, and the traffickers have a safe way to launder millions of dollars. Everyone's happy. Except for us, of course. We sit on the ground for four fuckin' hours with our heads up our ass."

"That's a pretty amazing revelation coming from a guy who doesn't have two nickels to rub togther."

"What do you mean? I have plenty of dough. You ought to take some notes. I'd peg you for a drug dealer in a New York minute."

❖   ❖   ❖

We were finally given runway time and were on our way to Panama, where I picked up Box at Howard Air Force Base. We were alone on this excursion; apparently Don Fabio and Noriega insisted on their own translators.

"Is Don Fabio already in Panama City?" Box asked.

"This is all too Helter Skelter for my liking," I replied. "If he is already there, who knows what they've already discussed."

"What does it matter?" Mack called back. "They can talk to one another anytime! As long as you get what you want, be happy! We're beginning our descent into Panama City. Fasten your seat belts."

We dove like a kingfisher, perpendicular and precise. My organs fell slower than the rest of me, tossing my stomach into my rib cage. The bottom of the aircraft seemed to evaporate. My feet felt for the floor, looking for something firm.

"What the hell are you doing?" Box screamed. "Hey! You're killing us back here!"

"He passed out," I yelled.

I stood up to a crouch and launched forward. My arms instinctively flew outwards, smashing against the metal divider that separated the passenger section from the cockpit. My pectorals stretched as I tightened them to resist falling. The aircraft suddenly leveled without warning, throwing me on my back. My body whirled sideways, my face smashing into a metal seat support. A sudden lurch of the plane sent me rolling into the aisle, then headlong into a seat back. I turned about, my personal odyssey at an end, only to hear Box laughing hysterically. I imagined how I must have looked, and began to laugh uncontrollably as the aircraft touched down.

"What the hell was that all about?" I wondered aloud, still giggling.

"Who knows. But I'd pay to see it again." Box laughed.

After taxing to a halt, Mack came to the rear of the aircraft.

"What the hell happened to you?"

"What do you mean?" I asked, vainly patting my face in search of obvious marks. As I felt about my nose, I sensed pain at the bridge. Glancing at my hand, I said loudly: "I'm cut! Shit! Box! Does it look bad? Did I break it?"

"With a beak like that, who can tell." ·

"You went from Italian to Jewish on a single trip." Mack joked.

I reamed him out.

"Do you have your pilot's license? What the hell was going on up there? Come clean! You were a crop duster before you became a company man, weren't you? Up there, demonstrating all the moves that made you famous. You're so fat, the plane probably noses over whenever you let go the stick! You fat piece of..."

"I was told to conduct an emergency landing." He said dumbfounded.

"Oh— —Sorry." I said, feeling stupid.

"Fatness runs in my family, you know." He explained, his pride slightly bruised.

"The problem is no one runs in your family." Box teased unsympathetically.

Three jeeps, traveling in a "V" shape configuration with emergency lights flashing, greeted us. They had military personnel aboard. There was no need for subtlety; we were meeting with the head of state. Relying on hand-signals to direct our progression out the door and into one of the jeeps, we drove in the open sultry air directly to the Caesar Park Marriott Hotel, located on the banks of the Gulf of Panama. The walkway into the hotel had water on either side running flush to the building's foundation and flowing around the sides. The lobby was a tropical atrium, open and elegant. A railed balcony ran along three corridors, offering visitors a romantic view of the palms below.

We were introduced to a gentleman we would know only as X-7. Later, I would be told that his name was Mark, or possibly John, Butler. When we first met, he was mustached and blue-eyed. Later, he would become brown-eyed and clean shaven. His height and weight would also change during the evening, making identification difficult. He was to function as a liaison, or buffer, between Ochoa and ourselves. This was one of Noriega's requisites, agreed upon by Director Casey. The only requirement was that Box and I were to have a visual of Ochoa and Noriega before the meeting took place.

We had a military escort on the elevator to the top floor and along the hallway. X-7, now bearded and with hair to his mid back, met us and instructed us to fold our arms in front of our chests and nod when we were satisfied that we had a positive ID on the two gentlemen. I had only seen the General in several photographs and was concerned that I would not be able to readily recognize him, but my worries were soon placated when I immediately recognized the man affectionately known as "Pineapple Face." We both nodded at once and were escorted back to the lobby.

Over the next two hours, X-7 would return to the lobby only twice. First, to ask Box a logistical question of little significance and, second, to tell us that everything had been agreed upon. He gave no specifics and slipped away into the black of the still balmy night.

Having envisioned intense negotiations of which I was an instrumental part, I departed with feelings of uneasiness and disappointment. Yet, there was a certain comfort in knowing that there was at least one critical element of *Pseudo Miranda* for which I was not ultimately responsible. Nonetheless, things were steadily becoming more convoluted. This decision would ensure a bigger take than we had been getting heretofore. How would the traffickers react at the distribution level?

I had a bad feeling.

Chapter 23

Box and I connected with Debara, Joey, Rick, Steven, Lourdes amd Quinn at Howard Air Force Base. Debara informed us that we were to strike a Colombian lab near the Meta River, due east of Bogota in the plains region of Llanos. Stretching into Venezuela, Llanos is filled with faded green meadows, caterpillaring hills and sparse shrubbery, with an occasional plot of trees.

I made a decision that Mack would fly the mission in place of the pilot who had flown the others into Panama. Mack didn't hesitate to jump into the cockpit of the C-123 and begin his function checks and pre-flight, while Box and I quickly changed out of our "civvies" into military fatigues. Debara briefed us on the specifics of the mission, which included the need to dispose of all the ether found at the lab. This particular lab was the ether storage site for several larger producing laboratories in the area. Under the guide-lines of *Pseudo Miranda*, precursors of the cocaine product were treated as the product itself, giving us an opportunity to effect several labs with a single raid. After being briefed, I expected the worst.

An encrypted message soon arrived from SATCOM telling us we would launch at 0530. We made use of some Aerospace Ground Equipment (AGE) to keep us comfortable and slept for the few hours before take-off.

❖ ❖ ❖

We flew east across the Gulf of Panama, turning slightly south as we vectored off the Acandi LORAN system. Turning due east once again, we crossed the Gulf of Urabe, maintaining an easterly track across northern Columbia. The aircraft shook and flexed, sometimes appearing to buckle, as we narrowly tipped the moun-tain tops. Tiny clumps of green sponges advanced on us, swelling to towering trees as we neared each peak. Two enormous lakes of listless blue loomed in the distance, splitting into five as we drew closer. Soon, the Magdelena poured into view, slicing through the Andes. Our course was now due south, toward Bogota.

The Magdelena appeared to split and we flew the general course of the vein, passing directly over a large mirrored body of water. The flying became more unprotected in the wide open geography of the Llanos.

"I sure hope you know what you're doing, Quinn." Mack called out.

"Why? What's wrong?" She answered.

"This." Mack pointed through the windscreen. "No way of evading radar out here."

"I don't know what to tell you." Quinn explained. "These are the coordinates I was given. Can't you drop down lower?"

"We're already a thousand feet off the deck. I don't go any lower unless I know the area better."

"No. Don't go any lower." I interceded. "Box says Escobar has a lot of the air traffic controllers out here on his payroll. They contact his people before notifying the authorities as a standard operating procedure." I walked to the rear of the plane.

"Just fly to where you're supposed to, and call out if there's any trouble."

"Roger that, captain." Mack said.

We were soon over a large grass runway beside the Guaviare River. Although Mack expressed concern that there would be no service facilities for the weary C-123, with my knowledge of Escobar's extensive resources I was not in the least concerned about our being stranded in Llanos. The airstrip had no tower and, according to Mack, no one had made any attempts to contact us by radio. We taxied blindly to an arbitrary spot and, as the engines wound down, waited tensely for some sign of life.

An hour passed and there were no attempts to greet us. Then, from the cockpit window, we observed the rapid approach of two military jeeps, stacked with armed troops. They crossed their vehicles at the nose of the plane, obstructing any attempts at flight. I ran to the back of the aircraft, calling for Mack to lower the cargo door.

As the door became parallel to the earth, I could clearly see three rifles pointed upward toward me. I changed my mind about leaping off the aircraft.

"What the hell is going on?" I screamed frantically. "Do you know who we are? Lourdes! Lourdes!"

"Here! I'm right here." She answered from behind my shoulder. "You want me to interpret?"

"No, I want you to strip naked and do the cha cha."

I turned to the sloping doorway and the waiting authorities.

"Tell these gentlemen who the hell we are."

"Who are we?" Lourdes whispered, almost apologetically.

Still facing the police, I said calmly, "We are close, personal friends of Pablo Escobar. He's expecting . . ."

Their audible chatter drowned me out.

"El Padrino? El Padrino?"

"What are they saying?" I asked Lourdes softly.

"The Godfather."

"Really! The Godfather!" I climbed down the sloped door and yelled for Steven to bring his radio. Their weapons were still aimed at us as Steven tentatively shuffled down sideways to where I was standing.

"Call him." I said sharply.

"Call who?" He asked.

"You know. Escobar. Get him on the phone. And ask him if this is the way he treats his loyal friends. Go ahead. Call him."

Steven handed the satellite dish to me and I in-turn

dished it off to Rick. Standing in the open space, Rick twirled it about until Steven acknowledged that he had a clear signal to the predesignated channel. Finally, from an unsecured telephone line at Langley, Steven was told something rather amazing.

Looking into his bleached face, I asked what was the matter. "Strange. I don't see how it's going to help. I really don't." Steven muttered.

"What did they say?"

"He said to have them look at the pilot."

"Oh God. Please don't tell me the pilot I got rid of?"

"Shit. I didn't think to ask."

"It wouldn't matter anyhow. Where is Mack anyway?"

Mack was conspicuous by his absence. Everyone else was on the field but him.

"Do you know our pilot?" I asked the apparent leader of the armed group.

"Which one is he?" Lourdes translated his response.

"Mack! Somebody get Mack, ASAP."

Quinn soon returned with Mack, persuading him with a hand twist and finger bend. When the head of the authorities did not recognize him, Mack seemed relieved. The officers then gathered us all together and began to search the plane. Meanwhile, I asked Mack why the Colombian authorities would know who he was.

"You probably left the person they'd recognize in Panama. Are you sure Langley understood you were being held up by the police?"

"I'm not sure of anything. And what do you mean by `held up'?"

"These guys will loot us, torture us for information and kill us," Mack informed me. "We better do something, quick!"

"Shit!" I replied, placing my hand into my left pant pocket and lifting my untucked shirt, exposing two grenades. "I could blow them into the next century with these. Grab one, but be casual. When I say `now,' you toss yours into the plane and I'll throw mine at the bozos in front of us. Okay?"

"Okay." he answered.

"Wait! These are supposed to be the good guys. I can't do this. Are you sure they'll rob us?"

"What do you think they're doing out here in the middle of nowhere?"

"Catching drug dealers?" I suggested weakly.

"You do what you want with your ball. Mine is going in the hull."

I needed time to think, time to gather my wits about me. I needed a delay tactic, something simple to buy time. "They want drugs, I'll give 'em drugs."

My mind was racing.

"Lourdes! Translate." I approached the military group.

"You're looking for the cocaine?" I said openly. "I can give you tons! My offer is ten percent, and a guarantee that I won't have you killed."

"Have *us* killed, gringo?" The short, dark skinned man said in Spanish. "We want it all, and *maybe* we don't have *you* killed."

"Told you." Mack said from behind me.

"Wait. Just wait." I cautioned. I walked up to the man who had addressed me.

"Would you like me to show you how we hide it?"

"Yes." He answered.

I led the five men to the front of the plane, while I furtively removed the grenade pin.

"Here." I pointed to a small opening in the floor where load masters secure their cargo. As the man in charge knelt forward over my right shoulder, I planted the grenade into his chest.

"You lose."

The man could readily see the live grenade, and rose slowly to his feet with my hand still against his chest. I turned him so that the others could see his dilemma. They raised their guns crisply to my head.

"I let it go, we all go! Boom! Boom!" I used sound affects for understanding. "Drop them! Drop them! I'll kill him! I'll kill us all!" They argued among themselves, unable to agree upon their next course of action.

"Lourdes!" I wailed.

"Yes! I'm here!"

"Tell them I'll let them all go unharmed!"

She yelled it out three or four times as they made their way out the rear of the aircraft. The man in my grip said nothing, even as his men drove off in the vehicles.

"Let's get the hell outa here!"

I threw the man out the rear of the aircraft, having already removed his MAC-10. He flapped his arms attempting to stabilize himself. Spiraling to a stop, he sloshed face down into a small pool of water, where he lay in humiliation.

"Bap! Bap! Bap! Bap! Bap! Bap! Bap! Came sounds in the distance. Then a large explosion. The man in the puddle lifted his head, water dancing off his face. He clenched his eye lids, trying to determine his present state of health.

In the cargo bay, we were unable to see what was going on directly in front of the plane. All of us except Mack, who had a bird's eye view.

"Holy Cow!" Mack said. "Come look at this!"

I didn't need to. The man in front of me told the whole story, as he scurried desperately away from us, futilely attempting to escape the wrath that had already killed his cohorts. As he fled, I couldn't help but feel pity toward him. His life was over. There was only the question of how much torment remained for him. Three pick-up trucks soon curtailed his progress, corralling him like Indians circling the wagontrain.

Colonel Borda and his army of killers had finally found us.

"Joey." I said normally. "Can you hit him from here?"

Joey cracked his neck to the right.

"Pick a part of his anatomy."

Colonel Borda now stood beside me, assuming that I was enjoying the entertainment as much as he.

"It's good?" He asked in English.

I continued to ignore him, feeling comfortable and safe in his presence. By now, separate ropes had been tied to each of the man's feet.

"Make a wish," Borda joked.

"Now." I said to Joey.

Joey fired two consecutive shots. The man fell backwards. At the same time, the trucks churned mud high into the air as molten lava from a volcano, pulling away in opposite directions, shredding the body irregularly. Even from our distant vantage point, I could see the showering of blood. The vehicles spun toward us, dragging the torn carcass, blood smearing across the thick bladed grass.

"Did you hit him?" I asked Joey.

"Twice between the shoulder blades. He didn't feel a thing." A pause. "God, I hope not."

"You no fun!" Borda exclaimed with his ongoing assault on the English language.

"Service our aircraft and get a helicopter to us now!" I asserted.

"I come with you, you know?" he said.

"I know. Believe me, I know."

Box was noticably upset.

"Why were we abandoned again by you idiots? I thought we worked all this out. Remember? No surprises! This is bullshit! What if they'd killed us! Huh! What then!"

Lourdes gave him Borda's translated response.

"We didn't know that you were landing at this particular runway today. When they came, we hid out in the woods like we always do. They were on you before we knew that you were even here. We couldn't attack without killing you also. This was good the way we handled it, don't you think?"

"No, I don't think! And someone's gonna damn well hear about it!" Box insisted, referring to someone in Langley, not Colombia.

"You won't tell Mr. Escobar?" Borda asked.

I saw a weakness, and moved in.

"You delay us or cause us any more harm, I'll have Escobar make a wish with you. Understand? Now, let's go."

As we gathered our gear, I asked Mack why the Colombians were at work on the tail section of the aircraft.

"Haven't you seen them do that before?" He said. "They're changing the registration number to match one of their own. They do it any time we bring one of our own in. In case it's discovered."

"You mean they have a C-123 in their arsenal?" I was flabbergasted.

"Of course. It's one of the more common CIA planes."

"I don't follow you?" I said, now even more puzzled.

"Arr! You crack me up!"

We flew the helicopter west by southwest, up the Guaviare River, to the base of a low mountain range. We touched down in an open field surrounded by hills. I wondered if there was indeed a lab out here.

"Why here?" I asked. "There's nowhere to hide one."

"Quinn!" Box said stoically.

"We're in the right place, I promise you," said Quinn. "Keep in mind, these coordinates don't land you on top of the snow. We should be due north about five hundred meters or so. That means it's just over that crest right there." She pointed to a pith of trees on the hill facing us.

We scaled the mound on foot, reverting to our bellies as we neared the top. Crawling through the tall airy grass was almost relaxing. As we transitioned into a thinly wooded area at the crest of the hill, we advanced in crouched positions. When the lab came into view, we were spread seventy-five feet across. There was tropical growth, and an oasis, probably man-made, circumferencing a long, wood-framed structure. Between the forest and the lab, there was a short open field consisting of nothing more than grass.

Through the dense growth, I could barely make out what appeared to be people, hastily rolling barrels into the center of the clearing for disposal. We had already made positive identification with IFF, so there was no doubt that they had chosen to fly the ether out instead of destroying it. If they had wanted to destroy it, there would have been no need to move it. And, with IFF confirmation, they knew that they were in no danger of arrest, making destruction of the vital fluid nonsensical. They were instead trying to salvage as much as they could before we took half. The clock was ticking, making safety a secondary issue.

There was no time to re-situate anyone. Giving hand signals, I began.

"Joey! Debara! Secure the rear of the building!" I looked right. "Rick! Steven! You two make a long swing to the right." Finally, I spoke to Lourdes and Quinn. "Cover all of us on our approach! Lourdes, you and Quinn remain about fifty yards back and support any retreat we may have to make. Okay?"

"Roger. We got your cover." Quinn said boldly.

I signaled with a swirl of an arm for Rick and Steven to go. I would have preferred a sharpshooter in support of both flanks, but at least Joey was protecting the right. When Steven and Rick made it safely to the trees, I sent Debara and Joey after them. Debara smiled at me, as if to say all was well. I gravely demanded that the others shoot anything that appeared threatening.

Soon, my fears diminished, as they, too, made it to the base of the trees.

"Ready Box?" I asked.

"As I'll ever be. Let's do it."

We stormed down the hillside, forking off as we neared the wooded barrier. We darted through the trees, screaming "Miranda," directing our weapons at the Campesinos in the clearing. They appeared more reticent than aggressive. We boldly compressed them from two sides, pinning them against the front of the building. Rick and Steven closed ranks from the sloping right side of the hill, bringing with them a cluster of non-belligerents who preferred not to be present during our visit. They grouped their captives with ours as Box and I inspected the containers that the Campesinos had intended to airlift out. Piled high and wide were about two thousand drums of ether.

Then, a foreboding sound. The sound of a gun firing ripped through the air.

I instinctively dashed to the rear of the structure, only to find Joey prancing up and down with his M-16 pressed to the base of a man's skull. I didn't see Debara. I had run past her and failed to take notice. Joey appeared to have everything under control. After all, these were but transplanted farmers, right? Someone must have fled, and Joey surely fired over their head. I was confident that was what happened.

"Joey! Joey!" I shouted. He looked at me. "Calm down. It's okay." I assured.

He frowned and then stared past me. His face shuddered, and his knees buckled slightly. He began to whirl like a fidgety child.

"What's wrong?" I asked.

"Ahhh!" He screamed, beating the man about the face with the butt end of his weapon.

"Stop it!" I hollered. He did so immediately, and collapsed to the side of the beaten man.

"Oh, sweet Jesus. Look at her. I was just … Oh, God, look at her." He staggered over his words.

Box came up behind me, gently placing his arm on my shoulders. "Don't turn around, man. Come on, let's go for a walk." He directed me away from the building, giving some final orders to Joey.

"Blow it up. Blow it all up."

I spun out of Boxer's arm catatonically, my eyes collapsing on Debara's mutilated body, her green and black jungle boots the only discriminating features still remaining. Her smooth olive skin and emerald eyes diluted in the blood drenched earth, pooling with the recent rain. Her skull, wedged in the gutter pipe, crumbled and dangled by the attached skin, her milky brown hair still sheened as it flowed gently in the breeze. I traced her body with my eyes, attempting to imagine the person who had become this ambiguous glob of organs and body parts. The blasts must have come at extreme-close-range. A complete side of her waist was torn away, the pellets embedding whole chunks of flesh into the wall. Her blood covered the structure like paint from a spray gun. Debara's shoulders snapped inward, contorting her elbows and back, the apparent force of the impact with the pipe and building. Her chest folded, causing the bones therein to give way. This was no longer Debara Allen.

I stood over her for a time, my hands folded to my face, trying to decide how to extract her from this impossible place. I reached out and then pulled back. In shock, I couldn't bring myself to help her. Rick responded to my numb desperation by yanking down the pipe and balancing Debara's remains with his knee. Everyone except myself assisted him when they realized that she would crumble if not supported in three sections.

I don't remember much after that. What I do recall is that I could vividly see her comforting smile as I ascended the hill enroute to the helicopter. I waited, looking to where she stood, and saw her still smiling at me. Reality soon slammed its door on my reflection when Rick passed by, Debara piled in his arms. I climbed aboard in a trance, vaguely recalling Borda's offer of sympathy when he saw what had happened.

The hill exploded into a distant memory.

I cried off and on on the return trip.

One of the basic axioms of this business is never to return home with the mortally wounded. The maxim was ignored.

The flight out of Colombia was the loneliest time of my life. Though the others tried, their words of encouragement and sympathy were no help. Only now, as her dead body was flown home, did I realize how many plans I'd made for our future together. In my own vacuum, I refused to admit the extent to which the others had suffered her loss. My selfishness and alienation would eventually have detrimental effects far more reaching than even I could fathom. But, for now, there was only this whirlwind of emotion to deal with.

We landed in the Darien Valley of southern Panama to have the tail of the C-123 repainted with its former United States registration number. Just prior to landing at Howard Air Force Base, Box informed me that we would leave Debara's body with CIA agents stationed there for proper disposal.

When the aircraft set down, Mack explained the situation to an Air Force OSI agent who was there to debrief him on transportation issues only. After Rick had prepared Debara's remains, I tenderly took her from his blood stained arms and carried her onto the tarmac. I was met by two OSI agents and a CIA representative. All were hyper-frantic about our having brought back the body. Responsibility for disposing of her remains became a topic of argument. I stood, broken, as they battled like children.

Suddenly, as the CIA agent attempted to gently take her from my arms, the two OSI agents yanked her heartlessly in the opposite direction. Her body separated, and my memory of the remainder of that day was gone.

Box told me I simply fell to my knees and cried.

Chapter 24

It was late May and I was home in Bellingham. My parents had informed me that the Army recruiters had been calling, but had been unable to reach me. My mother had been concerned that she had no way of knowing if I had been in an automobile accident while on the road if I didn't check in with her occasionally. A fictitious military career was beginning to make more and more sense.

I called the recruiter in Boston and told him I couldn't accept their Officer's Candidacy program unless I was offered a career in the Army's Central Intelligence Division (CID). I figured the slots were so coveted that they would never be able to agree. I was wrong, they agreed and I now had a major predicament.

It would look rather odd for me to turn down such an opportunity, especially since I had majored in Criminal Justice and was unemployed. My only chance was to tell them I would accept their offer if the Air Force turned me down. I was counting on the CIA being aware of events and ensuring the Air Force slot.

I received a call the next day. I had been selected for their next Officer's Training School (OTS) class in San Antonio, Texas. I had legitimately qualified for the class, even without the CIA's assistance.

My father and brother saw me off from the recruitment center in Springfield. It was the only time in my

life that I can recall my brother telling me that he was
proud of me. It lifted my spirits and made me realize
that I needed to succeed in San Antonio. Regardless of
the underlying reason for my going, doing my best
and succeeding became paramount. Like Tonopah,
OTS was to become my only reality for the next several
weeks.

Although there were no torture boxes or walnuts, OTS
was in many ways more difficult for me than Tonopah.
A poignant revelation in my life came when, after four
weeks of training, my flight commander called me
into his office and told me that I was by far his most
natural leader, but that I had to learn to follow. Under
his tutelage, I learned to listen to more than spoken
words. By the end of my training, Captain McKinney
expressed his belief that I was one of the finest young
officers he'd ever met, and that I had excelled in many
different categories of leadership, including counsel-
ing. Later in my career, I would become an effective
couselor and leader, translating to many Outstanding
Unit Awards and personal decorations.

Officer's Training School culminated with graduation
ceremonies on Friday, September 13, 1985. I felt I was
an officer in the Air Force, sworn to defend my country from threatening nations. A part of me wanted to
fade into CIA obscurity, while another part wanted
desperately to continue making a difference in the
drug epidemic. I was torn. I missed my friends and
worried about their well-being. I hadn't heard a thing
about the operation for four months.

I drove my Corvette to Chanute Air Force Base in
Rantoul, Illinois. For the next six months, I was to
receive training in the Aircraft Maintenance Officer's
Course (AMOC). I decided to enjoy the down time

before returning to the dangers of *Pseudo Miranda*. What I hadn't expected was to fall in love once again.

Her name was Christine Burnam. I met her in Champaign, Illinois, where she was a waitress at a local night club. She was in her final year of college, and a part of the Air Force ROTC program. She was quite a looker, and very personable. During my six months at Chanute, we grew extremely close, but I was still haunted by memories of Debara. In almost every manner possible, excepting intimacy, I was open and sharing with Christine. I just couldn't seem to get beyond my love for Debara.

In November, I received my first contact since May. Box personally came to Illinois to tell me that we were both to meet with Noriega in Panama and persuade him to talk to Ochoa at the CIA's request.

The topic of discussion would be money. Noriega was piggybacking drugs onto *Pseudo Miranda* shipments. Piggybacked drugs were subject to a higher rate of confiscation than the prescribed fifty percent. The reason was simple, piggybackers didn't have the luxury of spreading their production equally over all shipments. They took space as it was afforded them, whenever it was afforded them.

Noriega was to inform Ochoa that, as a condition of flying through Panama, the pilots would need to be given half their money up front, in cash, and would carry it with them throughout their mission. Noriega would sell this proposition as an incentive for the pilots to avoid detection by *Pseudo Miranda* intercept pilots. Under the umbrella of *Pseudo Miranda*, there was no incentive for a pilot to avoid contact. He was no longer subject to arrest, and he would be paid irrespective of the results.

The only real loser would be the pilot, and he would still receive the second portion of his labor's fruit upon return to Panama.

The theory was that the pilot, upon capture by the

Pseudo Miranda pilot, would drop the money first, as it is valued at far less per pound than cocaine. If we on the ground reported no money seizure, the *Pseudo Miranda* pilot would escort the drug pilot to a pre designate area, forcing a landing, where the money was then liberated to the CIA. The pilot, it was decided, would not attempt to fly out of the country after being escorted indefinitely by the *Pseudo Miranda* intercept craft, because his load (money) would cause a high consumption of fuel, making a safe landing highly unlikely.

The base commander forecasted five days of free vacation time for all the students during the week of Thanksgiving, so this was logically chosen as the week for Panama.

I drove to Murray, Kentucky, and joined up with Box. We flew to Kelley Air Force Base, Texas, where we boarded a jet bound for Panama.

Box went through a laundry list of problems that they'd been having with the operation. Over the past six months, they had only hit Colombia three times, and were never able to hit a laboratory with any sizable amount of cocaine. Box said they were jerked around continuously and delayed beyond reason. He told me they sorely missed my presence. He also told me that team members had been made to train in second occupations, impeding their ability to deploy to Colombia as often as they would have liked.

We finally arrived in Panama City late that evening. We were alone on this trip, because Noriega had demanded that his own translator conduct a two-way translation. We were met by a chauffeur at the airport and driven to the bay, where we waited for an armed military escort to arrive. Next, we boarded a small speed boat bound for a large yacht anchored in the bay. The warm air gushed passed my nostrils and down my throat. The water rippled smoothly as we glided over the surface. Lights from other vessels glowed in the distance as we raced toward a lone effulgence on the blackened evening canvas. The water surrounding the large yacht appeared oily, the ships lights unable to penetrate its evening darkness. I felt adrift and secluded. The shear isolation seemed designed to give the General a psychological edge.

Box and I soon found ourselves below deck, in the air-conditioned comfort of Noriega's den. With its wood finishing and marbled floor, it was more tasteful than I'd expected. I was seated on a couch that contoured two adjoining walls. Mauves and pastels accented the room. Not a place where bad things happened, I surmised.

When Noriega entered the room, Box and I stood, if for no other reason than to pay respect for his de facto leadership of this nation. He was dressed in full military honor, and wore the uniform well. Even more disarming was his manner of speaking. Of all the important people I'd met, he was surely the most articulate. Not so much in the words he chose, but rather the manner in which he used them. He was clear and uncluttered. His pattern of speech was polytonal, holding our attention. What he said, however, reminded me that these were the orations of a thug, and not a Martin Luther King.

His physical proportions were soft and his face would lead anyone to believe that dart teams do indeed have goalies. The rest of his features were nondescript. But his eyes, cold and calculating, were steely and fixed. He could speak endlessly without moving them. A man who could lie in this manner was without conscience.

"I wish to establish a large lab on the Rio Quindio."
The General was blunt.

"Is that into the Gulf of San Miguel?" Box asked.

"In the Darien jungle. Near Colombia." He explained.

"Why would we wish to add to our problems?" I

asked him, hoping to lead him into suggesting that it would be an easier way of controlling the flow of drugs. This would be a lab that we would be unable to strike, for fear that he would use it to gather evidence of our complicity in the drug trade, and later use the knowledge against us.

"You would have an easier time controlling your borders with so much cocaine coming from here. Don't you agree?" He argued diplomatically.

He knew of the deal we had struck with the cartel, but we couldn't even insinuate that we understood what he spoke of. We acted confused, and told him that we would make his demands known, no matter how outrageous, to our superiors. He knew that he would get his lab, and he seemed to know why we could not answer.

"General? The money issue. Can you do it?" I cut to the chase.

"The Don is just a short distance from where we last met. I will speak with him tomorrow. He will do this. But without my lab — safe from your DEA mind you — it won't last very long I'm afraid."

"Yes, sir, I understand. But I can not make a decision of such gravity without first consulting my superiors. You understand that?" I repeated.

"Yes, I do. But you must understand that I have a country to run. It takes money."

Neither of us acknowledged that he was asking for money to do what it was we needed him to do.

"Just so I understand though," I began. "This lab. The one in the Darien jungle... Do you intend for it to produce cocaine above and beyond what's already being produced in Colombia? Or will it replace other labs? Or do you even know yet?"

"No. This will be the only lab north of Antioquia, I assure you."

I almost choked. If he was even partly correct, this would make things infinitely easier for our team. I wanted so much to agree, especially because I knew he would be speaking with Ochoa tomorrow. As I made mental notes, he spoke again.

"You've already destroyed several labs. If I'm wrong, you'll destroy this one." He laughed.

"Protection of the Panama Canal is still paramount with our government. If you set up a lab in the Darien valley, do you intend to resupply ether through the canal? Because, I'll tell you right now, no one will go for it. We can't protect you if it's discovered that you're doin' that." I said.

"Then what do you propose? If you allow me this one thing that is?"

"Re supply through Colombia. That way we're assured that your lab isn't producing cocaine above and beyond what we've already got." I answered directly.

"Agreed." He stood up to shake our hands. "I will expect to hear from you soon then. Feel welcome to stay anywhere in Panama this evening at my expense. Thank you for coming."

❖   ❖   ❖

We were bursting at the seams, but were unwilling to show any emotion until we were in the air, bound for Howard. We had declined Noriega's offer to stay overnight in Panama City, unwilling to benefit from the dirtiness of the drug trade.

"Do you believe it?" Box was exuberant. "With that ether agreement, we'd wipe out a quarter of our problems for sure. What the hell do you make of that?"

"I'm really not sure. I think you mentioned something about the Panama Canal being used for ether shipments in the past. I figured if all his efforts in shipping ether went to supplying his own lab, it's got to have some effect on them down there. The problem is there's probably a million things I didn't think of."

"Yeah, but we got much more than we thought we

were going to get. If the money starts flowing in, and we take far less trips to Colombia, then it's been a grand slam, I think."

"I suppose," I said.

As we taxied in at Howard, I was disturbed to see other team members sitting in three jeeps, waiting for us to touch down.

"Not again," I said solemnly.

Almost the whole team was present: Christina, Joey, Quinn, Lourdes, Rick, Steven, Jesus, and even Tina. Tina was now Debara's permanent replacement.

Rick briefed us on a gigantic shipment of cocaine that was being gathered in the mountainous region just south of Medellin. According to intelligence reports, young Fabio intended to ship several tons simultaneously, in hopes of pushing more than fifty percent through our safe channels. Our mission was to intercept it prior to shipment and take half.

We would have to strike quickly if we were to have any chance of success. This would be our most precarious endeavor to date, and, arguably, the most important.

Chapter 25.

We flew out immediately, although Box and I had had very little sleep. I was told the aircraft was a C-60. It was old and narrow. Its green flat paint was oxidized and cracking and it had the same trailing tail as the C-47, but it was significantly smaller in every way.

I was tired of complaining about the inadequacy of the transportation, so I kept my fears to myself. We flew directly to the Ochoa ranch in northern Colombia. From there, we boarded two Titan-like aircraft and flew unobstructed to a grassy field just north of Medellin. The ground was saturated, and the planes slid sideways before coming to a complete stop. There was no resistance to our movements.

I had the aircraft serviced with fuel, to give the appearance that we intended to fly elsewhere in them, and had Lourdes instruct the pilot to radio for a helicopter. She was to explain that we wanted to fly as one group to Llanos. The pilot was eager to assist, deciding that we were not headed for a place called La Loma.

Our friction-free flight was most likely because most of the laboratories did not have a substantial amount of cocaine, due to the enormous stockpile in La Loma. Therefore, no matter where we struck in Llanos, not much damage would be incurred.

We waited at the edge of the woods for our helicopter to arrive. The Titans, along with the servicing truck, were pulled off the grass runway and covered with green and brown tarps. Large pools of water spotted the grassy runway, while droplets hung from trees that girdled the clearing. Our feet sloshed or swished, dependent upon the speed of our path. A light mist clung to my face. I was beginning to feel miserable.

When the chopper arrived, we scurried across the open field without delay. Quinn climbed in front, while the rest of us dove into the rear. My legs were still dangling in the open air as we lifted off for La Loma.

Quinn quickly gave the pilot the coordinates to our real destination. He balked.

"He won't go," she radioed back on the intercom.

"Don't let him on the radio." I desperately demanded.

"How? What should I do?" She said, somewhat panic stricken.

"Can you fly one of these things?" I asked.

"Yeah, I think so."

"Can you or can't you?" I yelled over the microphone.

"Yes!" She demanded.

"Put your gun to his head and tell 'em to fly us there or you'll kill him. Make sure to tell him that you can fly this damn thing, or he'll consider it to be an empty threat."

"Is it?" She asked, worried.

"No!" I said emphatically.

The pilot took her threat seriously and flew us to La Loma. We were soon in ascent above Medellin. Although our climb was brief, we were soon hidden in the dense wilderness. It was already daylight as we landed onto a large ranch with exotic animals running freely about.

"Oh, my God." Rick said with an astounded voice.

"Would you look at that. Would you just look at that." Box added.

"There's got to be fifty tons of cocaine there. Or more." I said in astonishment.

"I think more." Rick said.

"I don't like the way this feels," warned Lourdes.

Our presence was neither expected nor welcomed. About twenty vehicles besieged us, toting automatic assault weapons. As the pilot informed the leader that we were there under the auspices of a bilateral agreement with Don Fabio Ochoa, he was struck in the face with the butt of a rifle. I attempted no further conversation.

We were all pushed to the ground and seated back-to-back in a circle. Another pick-up truck soon arrived with Don Fabio and young Fabio. When I detected their presence, I rose to my feet and demanded answers from the bandit who injured the pilot. He immediately raked the stock of his gun across my face, snapping the bridge of my nose. I did this deliberately to gain a sense of indebtedness from the Ochoa's. With my nose gushing blood, I was helped to my feet by none other than Fabito himself.

The Ochoas walked with us to the long pile of pure cocaine stacked beneath a hundred and fifty feet of tin roofing. It was crammed into duffel bags, and piled six feet high by four feet wide. The sideless structure was supported with 4x4's and wooden poles, camouflaged under grass and brush. It was obviously temporary, and served the main purpose of protecting the drugs from the elements. We walked slowly down the length of it.

At the half-way point, I paused.

"We'll take it from this point on."

Long-winded gasps could be heard from behind me.

"Never." Fabito said. "This is not a single shipment, or a production lab. This is a storage facility. Several smaller shipments will emanate from this location."

"It doesn't matter at what stage of shipment or production we find the product. We have an understood agreement that we can take half. This is half, and we are taking it." I said clearly.

"No!" He shouted, now standing in my face. He reverted back to Spanish and continued to yell.

"This is our country! This is our resource! We are sovereign."

I stared directly into his eyes, yet addressed my response to *Don* Fabio.

"Are you changing the rules Dona Fabio? Because I wouldn't want to bring such news back to the States."

"We are men of honor. It has been agreed upon. You've outplayed us this time, so take what you can." Dona Fabio said, knowing that it would be theoretically impossible to carry half the cargo in the helicopter. By the time we returned, the drugs would be gone.

"Okay, everyone," I said to my people. "Let's load the helicopter as tight as she'll pack. Leave room for two people in the back. We'll fly loads to the coast or over the jungle. Split the bags and let it fly."

Fabito pleaded with his father to stop us. "They will now intercept half of the remaining cargo when it enters their country. They will cheat us as they always have."

"Will you intercept half this coca when it comes to America?" Don Fabio asked quite innocently.

"Don Fabio. You have my solemn word this will not happen." I answered earnestly.

"They will inform the DEA, and they will steal our coca!" Fabito yelled while stabbing his finger at me. "They will then say that it was not taken by them!"

"If you fly it through our safe zones, it will go untouched. But if you don't trust me and fly it elsewhere, you will undoubtedly lose it all, because I will personally tip off the DEA." I firmly contended.

Don Fabio began to laugh vociferously. He told his son to accompany him as he departed. They both drove off, leaving us to labor over the destruction of this massive amount of cocaine.

It had occurred to me that the Ochoa's might be pulling one over on us. By our dumping half this shipment, we were in essence guaranteeing safe passage for an equivalent amount. So, what if most of what we were dumping wasn't, in fact, cocaine? Or, even more insidious, what if it were only half pure? Then they would be cheating the United States out of tons of cocaine seizures.

We had an insufficient number of testing kits. I needed a way of positively identifying each bag. I knew the answer, but didn't know how to go about implementing it. Then it struck me. I would get volunteers.

"Who wants to test the remaining one-hundred bags or so of cocaine. We can test about one-hundred and fifty bags with the kits, but the other hundred need to be tested orally. I'll need four people to test in shifts." I could hear myself saying it, but I couldn't believe it was me.

There were no shortages of volunteers. I selected Lourdes, Steven, Quinn and Tina. I needed Joey to remain completely sober because of his shooting ability. Christina had been an addict in the past, so I didn't want to subject her to a possible relapse. And Box didn't volunteer.

"We've got a bunch of coke heads!" Box spouted off.

"We're just making the necessary sacrifices for our country." Lourdes said all too altruistically.

"Sacrifices!" Box replied with a sarcastic shrug.

"I want no more than five bags tested per person, per trip. Get it!" I demanded. "Place only an infinitesimal amount above your teeth. Just like you were taught in training." I paused at their snickering. "I'm not fucken' around here! This is some serious shit! I don't want anyone getting high and doin' somethin' stupid that might endanger the lives of the rest of us!" I calmed a bit. "Now. Does everyone know what it's supposed to feel and taste like?" They began to chuckle once again.

"Great. I want to know the general quality. And don't test on the same spot in your mouth more than once in a short period."

I had the Titans flown in to assist us. After a trip to the coast and two to the jungle, we decided to simply fly over the local wilderness and pour the cocaine into the air. The swirling wind tended to blow the local anesthetic back into our porous faces, so we were forced to wear masks and shield our eyes. We slept and worked in shifts, never for a moment leaving the drugs unattended. The entire campaign took the better part of two days to complete.

The disposal went well. The Ochoa's were remarkably hospitable, bringing us food and drink every day, and offering us comfortable quarters to sleep in. We refused the quarters, because the rules of engagement would have allowed them to remove the cocaine while our backs were turned, provided they were not forcibly removed from us.

With the Herculean task completed, the Titan's were refueled one last time as we prepared to depart La Loma. Fabito made his way back from the Ochoa family home to bid us farewell. His attitude had changed. He was not the same man that had lambasted me days earlier. He offered his hand in friendship.

"My father's word is his honor, and I trust that yours is also."

"I assure you." I said.

"This is all just business." He said with his arms thrown open. "I'll ship all this by the end of the year."

"We'll be watching this area very closely. If it comes from this stock pile, we won't touch it." I pointed up to the heavens. "We have very sophisticated satellites up there. We will know absolutely if a shipment comes in from this particular batch of coca. Any further build up in this area will be detected, also. So I ask you, Fabio, please ship all of this immediately, and none other."

"Agreed." He said with a nod and a smile.

The flight home was satisfying, but unusual. Everything had gone perfectly, but the group was not the talkative bunch that we once were.

"So? What's everyone been up to?" I asked jubulently. "Doesn't anyone want to know about the Air Force?"

"Oh, yeah. It's Lieutenant now, isn't it?" Christina said with relief. She seemed happy that the silence was officially broken.

"Oh, don't be so formal. My friends call me sir."

"Too bad Box is in the other plane. He'd be calling you LT and shit." Joey said. "Vietnam, right?"

"I'm not sure, he's never quite said." I answered.

"How was it?" Christina impatiently inquired.

"You know. I never thought I'd be thinking this, albeit saying it. But most of these Air Force guys are pretty on the ball. Too bad I'm not actually gonna be one of 'em."

"How've you been dealing with Debara's death," Lourdes asked.

The smile ran from my face, as I tried not to let my pain show through.

"I'm fine." I responded. "So what have you been up to, you little shit."

"I'm so sorry..." Lourdes began.

"So, you're an officer and a gentleman now. I bet you're a handsome boy in that uniform." Christina insightfully changed the direction of the conversation.

We gradually fell back into our familiar ways. But there were still lingering issues not yet dealt with, Debara's being the principal one.

I awakened on Sunday in Rantoul, Illinois, with every muscle in my body aching with pain. It was bizarre, sitting there in my appartment, knowing that my body ached from the cocaine I'd wrestled with in the Colombian jungle, only the day before. It was then that I realized that it was to become more difficult to keep my lives seperate. This Air Force stuff and my new girlfriend were going to complicate things. I had no choice about the Air Force, and I wasn't about to shed the girlfriend.

As I relaxed and watched the football games, I found myself laughing at what my life had become, and not regretting it for a moment. I smiled when I thought of how proud my parents would feel if they could see what I'd accomplished. And I cried when I thought of how my parents would feel if they could see what I'd done. I sat alone, and watched the football games.

Chapter 26.

When I finally met Christine's family, I was pleased to discover that her father was a Senior Master Sergeant in the United States Air Force. It was a relief to know that her family would also understand the nature of the military, and in turn, the nature of my job. I expected that, eventually, the CIA would have me on secretive missions throughout the world for the Air Force. Christine's parents would not be likely to ask many questions. Of course, I'd decided that I would eventually tell Christine everything if she would become my wife.

The Christmas season arrived, and the students of AMOC were to be given several unofficial days off. I went home to begin loading the Corvette for an unexpected Christmas in Kentucky.

My car was packed when a courier arrived with a message for me to meet Box at Paducah Airport that evening.

I made it to Paducah in about five hours. It was late afternoon when I pulled into the main terminal parking lot, expecting to be immediately greeted. Two hours later, Box arrived.

"Let me in." He said, outside the window of my car.

"Not enough room. Just tell me what you need." I was abrupt.

"I'm freezing!"

"Good. Then you'll be short."

He looked in at my crammed passenger seat, his breath fogging the window.

"Damn, man. It's cold out here."

"Cold! Are you crazy." I said. "You want cold! Try

Chanute this time of year. I'm freezing my cannolis off up there. Now, what is it you want?"

"You need to fly out of here after Christmas. They need to speak with you at Langley."

"Headquarters'? Why the hell do they..?"

"No. I'm sorry. I mean Langley Air Force Base."

"What! Why there? What's goin' on, Box?"

"I don't know exactly."

"Do you know generally."

"I don't know exactly."

"What's goin' on, Box?"

"They spoke to me in Washington. At the old Executive Office Building. Spoke? More like interrogated me. About our meeting in Texas, remember? I don't know what's happening? Whatever it is though, it appears we're smack dab in the middle of it. I wanted to tell you, but I didn't want you to appear coached. You know, you need to tell 'em that it was my responsibility to tell Casey, not yours. You tell me things, and I'm supposed to tell them. Okay? Okay!" His speech seemed pressured.

"No. Not okay. I'm not leaving you to twist in the wind. Screw 'em. I don't owe them jack shit."

"See! That's why I didn't want to tell you in the first place." He spoke rapidly. "I knew you'd start worrying about me. Just do what I told you to do!" He changed direction. "Damn it I'm freezing!"

"Why you so up tight about this? It's just a stinkin' meeting for cryin' out loud."

"Take this stuff serious." He said gravely. "These guys can be meaner than the Colombians."

"Where's my plane gonna be?" I asked, steering him away from advising me.

"It'll be in the same place. The twenty-seventh. T-39." He redirected. "Do you understand what's goin' on here?"

"Quite frankly, Box. No, I don't. But I really don't care. It sounds like a problem bureaucrats worry about, not field agents. You see. I'm goin' there because I have to, not because I think it necessary or anything. Can't you see? The Vice President was only positioning himself back in Texas. He's a good man, I think. A smart man, who wants to take a bite out of crime. He's not gonna finger point if this hits the fan. He's simply gonna clam up. If he wanted us stopped, he'd have done it. Dammit Box! He could just do it! Boom! Just like that. Everyone running around covering their asses, really sucks. And I'm not about to cover mine with yours. I believe in what I'm doin', Box. And, dammit, you should too. I hide what I do because it would be impossible to do otherwise. But, if it's discovered by the public at large, I'm not gonna defray responsibility for what I've done. Look, Box, if you can't defend it right now in your own head, you sure as hell won't be able to later in public. If you asked me, the CIA's so involved in things closely related to *Pseudo Miranda* that they can't defend themselves. And that's why they're running scared."

"Yeah. I guess you're right. But, please, for God's sakes, don't give that speech to the bureaucrats in Langley."

"Don't worry. I'm just gonna sit and listen."

"Good."

My aircraft was landing in Langley Air Force Base before I knew it. By this juncture, I was the only passenger on board. There had been others, but they must have had other stops along the way while I slept. I was scratching my forehead and rubbing my face when a late model Lincoln, black on black, pulled up beside the plane.

"Time to go!" The pilot called back.

The driver of the car actually held the door for me. I felt kind of important arriving in what appeared to be my own personal jet and then being whisked away

by chauffeured limousine. Of course, I had the presence of mind to know that a convicted criminal's door
is held open for him, also. Just before he's carted off to
death row.

I was under the impression that the drive would be
short. However, after traveling the I-17 for about
thirty minutes, I had determined I was headed back to
Maryland. Probably some remote location, where the
DEA had confiscated a house or something. I woke up
about an hour later, and discovered we were on the I-
95, still headed north. Langley, I thought. That must
have been why Box didn't say "Air Force Base" when
he first mentioned Langley. I wasn't in the least bit
worried, I wanted to stroll the hallowed halls anyway.

I fell asleep, and didn't awaken until I heard the
gate guard ask for identification. When he handed it
back to the driver, I noticed little red tags clipped to
notches that were cut out of the card. We were entering from the side, across from the old Executive Office
Building. I pressed my face to the window for a better
look. The Marine guard spoke on the phone, and then
asked me to surrender my military ID. I passed it
through the window. We drove around a winding
driveway, stopping about three quarters of the way to
the building. Two men approached the car, and discretely escorted us across the lawn and down a walk-
way. I paused momentarily to look at the Washington
monument aglow in the distance.

We quick-stepped it up the "L" shaped widened
staircase, and into the south end of the building. From
the main hallway, located at the middle of the house,
we passed by an elevator and descended to the first
floor via a straight flight of stairs. With the Library to
our side, we continued our descent into the basement.
The basement corridor seemed narrow, and featured
an arched, low slung ceiling. To the right, there was a
small walk-way, and a door. I entered the room turning left, and was surprised to find such a confining

room in all the White House. It was called *The Situation Room*, but it was not all that impressive. Aside from being cramped, the furnishings were strikingly plain. There was a computer on each end of the long and narrow conference table, and an easel at the head; that was basically it. Both walls were draped, concealing what I'd guessed to be maps and diagrams. Just as I pulled back the curtain to take a peak, Mr. Casey walked in.

"Leave that alone." He said sternly. He looked as crumply as ever. He wore no glasses this evening, and was without that massive school ring. He appeared tired. Not in the conventional way, but as though he was running out of the energy to live.

"Director." I acknowledged his presence.

"Mr. Bucchi." He took a seat at the head of the table, beside a Marine Colonel.

"We've got a problem." He then mumbled something imperceptible. "This Texas meeting. Why did you keep it from us?"

"He's your boy, sir. Claire George. I—I don't fill him in on anything. As for the Vice President... He should be talking to you, not me."

"The... You didn't speak with... You don't... You didn't see him. I'm asking about the man you spoke with."

"Yeah. Claire George. I said that."

"So why didn't we hear about it?" The Colonel asked. He was a CIA agent's worst nightmare. He was, in essence, a tightly groomed man, attempting to play in an no-holds-barred world, often called the Company. I, on the other hand, was a no-holds-barred man, playing in a tightly groomed company, otherwise known as the military.

"You didn't hear about it because you're just a schmuck, Colonel. And I don't answer to schmuck Colonels."

Bill Casey laughed briefly.

"No you don't. But you do answer to me."

"Give me your telephone number, and I'll call you next time." I said facetiously.

"You can reach me at the (703) 482-7676 number or the 6363 number simply by saying 4PM." Casey said. "Call secure."

I couldn't believe he actually gave me a number. I had just been kidding him.

"So. Did you bring me all the way out here just to harass me?" I asked.

"We're not harassing you! We're just trying to hold this thing together, while idiots like you keep tearing it apart!" The Colonel condemned.

"You're right. You're not. Because it takes a hell of lot more than you to shake me. So just keep your mouth shut when it comes to me or I'll slap you around and stick a dress on ya."

"Excuse me, Lieutenant." The Colonel said.

"Only in name." I replied.

"No. I'm afraid that's not quite true, Mr. Bucchi." Casey added. "You'll be stationed at Randolph Air Force Base, San Antonio, Texas, after this assignment. It offers a very convenient location for *interceptions*, and your close proximity to Kelley Air Force Base will allow you to readily fly out on *intervention* missions. Also, your position as an Aircraft Maintenance Officer will provide you with certain benefits that other career fields don't. For instance, you'll have easy access to a T-39 if we need you to leave suddenly. And, we've had that squadron deploying to Hondo for some time now, offering you the perfect excuse for going there from time to time. So, you see, it's the way it needs to be." He made a grumbling noise and leaned backwards.

"You should buy a house as soon as you can. In San Antonio. If you marry that girl…" He searched through a file with a **Top Secret** cover page. "Christine. That's her. Lovely choice. That would be a nice touch."

" A nice..?" I started with a disbelieving frown. I had begun to tell him where to stick it, but then remembered where I was and who I was talking to. "Great. Two full time jobs." I said in frustration.

"No, I don't think so." Casey said. "You'll be tapering off on the drug exchanges. I want to concentrate you on the diplomatic stuff. Maybe an occasional tough seizure. But, for the most part, diplomacy."

"Diplomacy?"

"Yes."

"Sounds good to me." I responded. I was relieved. I loved what I was doing, and would never have slowed down, unless forced to do so.

"Oh. Mr. Bucchi. Before I go, one last thing. This whole thing. *Pseudo Miranda*—Mena—Noriega... It doesn't go any higher than here. Okay?"

"As far as I'm concerned, sir, it doesn't go above me."

"Good—very good. Oh, and by the way, excellent job in Colombia and Panama last month. Excellent work. Superb." Casey embellished.

On the way back, I began to piece together the pattern of events for the past several months. The operation was becoming more entrenched than I had believed possible. My original impression was that, after we performed this operation for a few years, we would have enough tactical information about South American cocaine trafficking that we could persuade them to significantly draw back their production. The theory was that they would have made in four years what would have otherwise taken twenty, and, with our significant threat to their personal security, they would gladly scale back their efforts by at least half.

This may have been a bit idealistic on my part, but, certainly, it was not unreasonable. We were to become a living, breathing organism that exists for the purpose of self perpetuation. We were becoming welfare-like, forgetting our original motivations, and growing bigger and more important than that which we served.

I arrived back in Paducah the following morning, tired and confused. It suddenly struck me while walking toward my car, that I was an Air Force Officer, an aircraft maintenance one at that. I couldn't change the oil in my car, and now I would be supervising hundreds of people whose main job was to perform maintenance on multi-million dollar jets. I knew then that I would need to do more than get good grades over the next few months, I would actually have to learn something.

I was surprised to bump into Box on my way out into the main parking area of the airport. He had one eye closed and a concerned grin as he tentatively approached me.

"So. How'd things go ace?" Box asked.

"Well. Fine I guess. I'm officially a full time officer. I'm getting married and we'll be living in a new home I'm buying in San Antonio, Texas. I wasn't told how many kids to have yet. Maybe the next time you see Bill, you could ask 'em for me?"

"How 'bout the games? You didn't find that unbelievable?"

"The what?"

"The games." He saw that I was unresponsive. "The... Oh boy." He walked around the other side of my car and got in.

"Okay. Get this. They want us—as a team, mind you—to travel to Colombia and play some drug trafficker reps in sporting events. Somethin' to do with building better relations and cutting down on violence. It's crazy. It's fuckin' loony bin."

"Play games?"

"Yeah. Believe that shit?"

"In Colombia?"

"Yeah. I mean it's crazy."

"What...what..." I shook my head and cast my hands to the roof of the car. "I don't have a response to that." I was flabbergasted. "What sort of..."

"Soccer, football, bull fighting, and I think base-ball." He answered my question. "Those are the ones decided on so far."

"I guess they forgot to mention it. When do these games... God, I can't believe I'm saying this. When do they..."

"Soon. But no dates yet. Oh yeah, another thing. You and I have also got a date in Medillin at the Intercontinental Hotel. Roof Top Lounge or something. In a couple weeks. It'll be on a weekend, so don't worry. You may have to call in sick one day, though. We'll see."

"Any other surprises before I leave."

"No. That's about it." He looked at me, his hands pulling on his hair as he grinned and growled. We both began to laugh at the absurdity of it all, and didn't stop laughing until we said goodbye.

Chapter 27.

I didn't hear from Box for several weeks, but he showed up on a day that I was supposed to take Christine into Champaign for a day alone together. I wanted to call her, but neither Box nor I could come up with a sensible excuse. I decided to spin the wheel and wait until I saw her next to explain. Big mistake.

"It's the company's way of keeping me single, isn't it." I said to Box, as he shuffled into my apartment.

"I'm sure, with your track record, it's not much effort."

"I'm serious, man. I might as well be dating you. I see you more than anyone I've dated."

"Come on, now. You know the company's policy on dating people you work with." Box said, tight-jawed. He then pivoted back around toward me and smiled. "She'll understand. Whatever you tell her. Hey, look at me. I'm married."

"I'm sure, in your case, the agency felt there was nothing to worry about. I guess they just didn't count on anyone being desperate enough to sleep with you. But I suppose if they were caught off guard by the Berlin Wall, how much greater a surprise could this have been." I spoke as I gathered up all my gear.

"Are you done?"

"Yeah, I think so."

"Good, because my wife wasn't desperate! She's very pretty and quite smart." He defended her honor.

"If she's quite smart, why is she married to someone in this screwed up profession." I became serious. "Why would anyone, Box? You tell me that, because I want to know. Why would anyone marry me? Look what the hell I've become."

"It hasn't always been like this for us. I've never come home with nightmares." He took in air through his nostrils. "She's scared. She doesn't want me to leave the house any longer. She knows what I'm doing now isn't the same as before. It's so obvious. I can see it in her face now. I hate what I'm doing to her." He paused to drink some water. "But I've got to see it through, you know?"

"Oh, I know all right. But at least you're married. I'm either gonna die doin' this, or be too old to marry when it's over."

"Hey! Let's not get all down and shit. We're goin' to a party and then a bull fight. When's the last time you had a weekend like that?"

Box drove to a small airstrip outside of Chicago, where we boarded a small twin engine prop bound for Mena, Arkansas. We transferred to a T-39, as we hooked up with some of the others en route to Howard Air Force

Base. Soon we were all together, flying the smoothest course to Colombia imaginable.

We landed in that same grass air strip outside of Medellin. This time, however, we flew the C-60 all the way in. When we slammed down, I could feel the struts bottom. The aircraft's nose darted left and then gamboled right, jolting us about in our nylon strap seats. I could hear the brake disks grind, as we snaked through the field to an eventual stop. Tina was visibly shaken by the episode.

"Rookie." Quinn teased.

"What? There have been worse landings than that?" Tina asked.

"Oh. I guess we may have had one or two that rivaled that." I added.

"Well, it could have been worse." Tina comforted herself. "We could have crashed."

We all exploded in laughter.

We flew a minor jaunt to a runway on the border of Medellin. There were a number of hangars and some expensive aircraft just outside the doors. We left the aircraft and traveled, aboard trucks, to the southern most part of Medellin. We moved rapidly along a curving dirt path, high into the mountains. The drivers appeared confident that no one would be traveling in the opposite direction, as they haphazardly slung their vehicles across the road through each turn. The landscape widened, a result of the trees being pushed back from us.

"Are we...?" Rick started.

"Looks like it." I said.

"What?" Box began. "Oh yeah. La Loma."

The sun had set on Colombia when we arrived at the palatial estate at the peak of a hill, overlooking Medellin. It was like a castle looking down upon the

kingdom. I was feeling uneasy about getting too cozy
with our enemy partners.

The estate didn't appear as colossal as Hacienda
Los Napoles. Rather than sleeping 120 people comfortably, this modest home could seemingly accommodate only fifty or so.

We slept in very exquisite quarters in the main
house. My bed was Victorian, raised from the floor so
as to make falling into it impossible. The furnishings
were all hand crafted, and delicately sturdy. Drawers
slid heavy and without slippage. A Jacuzzi was sunk
flush into the floor close to the fireplace. The bathtub
was raised above the Spanish tiled floor, oyster col-
ored, and three feet deep. It stood alone at the center
of the bathroom. Staircased in the corner was a shower
that permitted no privacy for its occupant. The bathroom window offered a picturesque view of a flower
garden.

Each of us were given our own room, all in the
northern portion of the home. The day (Saturday) was
spent eating traditional Colombian cuisine, horseback
riding, and perusing the countryside. We were capti-
vated by the dwarfed horses which roamed freely
about the ranch. I spent hours petting and playing
with the cuddly fellows.

It was soon time for us to attend the party at the
Intercontinental Hotel. Box and I were the only ones
invited to attend this lavish affair. From the moment
we walked into the *Roof Top Supper Lounge*, we were
like celebrities at a Hollywood premier. Although the
Ochoas were lightly complected for Colombians, and
Box and I were quite dark for gringos, we nonetheless
stood out.

We were a curiosity, and were treated as such. Box
was noticeably uncomfortable with the spotlight. Con-
trarily, I thrived under it. I didn't stand on pedestals
when they were offered, I performed somersaults on
them. I never shied from the light, I shone beneath it.

I was, and still am, best when the pressure valve is turned fully clockwise.

It was here that I met Jose Ocampo. Of average height, his big, curly hair made him seem much taller. He was obviously a working man, pretending to be of the aristocracy. But all the coke money in the world couldn't turn his blue-collar into blue-blood. He didn't impress me as a leader or a sophisticated businessman. Too frequently, he would slide into his native slang, often too crude for interpretation. The advantage to dealing with Ocampo over the others was the fact that he couldn't help but speak his mind.

Pablo Escobar was extremely personable for a nefarious killer. He introduced me to *Crystal* at this affair, and laughed grandly when I told him that it tasted no better than *Martini and Rossi*. Ocampo had provided the bountiful spread which included delights for all palates. Escobar found amusement in my very particular eating habits. I devoured the beef and crustaceans, avoiding altogether the wide array of plant life and appetizers.

We all sat at the head table along with the Ochoa clan, overlooking at least a hundred of their closest friends.

The evening was moving along quite nicely, until many of the gallery tables began to raise their glasses in salutation to the aristocracy.

"To the gringo coke mine!" One of them cheered.

"The coca crop!" Another followed.

I stood naturally, extending my glass outward before speaking. I looked about at their curious faces as they leaned inward.

"To extradition!" I shouted.

Box literally fell over in his seat.

There was no reaction. I continued to hold my glass of *Crystal* into the silenced air.

"The extraditables!" Escobar first proclaimed in

English. Everyone cheered, and Box heaved a sigh of relief.

Box and I soon found ourselves becoming friendly with the lot, even though we were conscious of what we knew them to be. Somewhere near the witching hour, I saw a man move to the center of the room, where there were no tables, and raise a hatchet above his shoulders.

"He's got an ax!" Box cried out.

I grabbed a large carving knife and vaulted over the table. The man squared to face us, as now Box joined ranks with me to do battle with the assailant.

"No! No! No!" Fabito screamed. Through translation, we were told that the man was part of the entertainment.

"Oh. Sorry." I said, feeling quite foolish.

The laughter that ensued amused us as much as it did the cartel. We returned to our seats and awaited the hatchet demonstration.

"I hope he juggles them." Box said.

It soon became evident that this would not be an innocent juggler's act. The two men rotated about the room no more than ninety degrees opposite one another, stalking methodically for an opportunistic shot. Their backs were always to the side tables, never approaching where we were sitting. As they shuffled about, the guests would lean away or crawl over one another to avoid the eminent path of the hatchet. The obscenity of the game was the perverse laughter the drunken crowd maintained throughout.

I knew that Box was feeling deceived and violated, because so was I. We had temporarily deluded ourselves into believing that these people could still appreciate the innocence of life.

The man to our right jabbed his weapon into the air repeatedly as a means of trickery, then heaved it at his competitor, missing him entirely. The hatchet gashed the wall and fell to the floor. Everyone started to pound on the tables, three quick raps and then another. As the intensity of the pounding increased, a fever's pitch was reached, and held for at least a minute. With no baiting lunges of the ax, the man whirled it forward, missing the man by a Lilliputian centimeter.

The hatchet didn't fall on deaf ears, however. A woman, no more than twenty-five years of age, was restrained behind the intended victim by the shoving crowd, and in the direct path of the rotating trajectory. It struck her to the front of the shoulder blade, virtu- ally pruning the arm from her trunk. Needless to say, her laughter turned to screams of pain as she col- lapsed to the alcohol drenched floor. My instincts were to help her. By the time I reached her, they were sprinkling cocaine on her wound to deaden the pain. A butcher knife, used to carve the prime rib, sliced the final membranes holding her arm to her body. She smiled and giggled through the ordeal, a result of the cocaine going up her nose before I arrived.

Box and I requested that we be driven back to La Loma, and Fabito politely complied.

Chapter 28.

The next day, Box and I took our hangovers and the rest of the team to Vera Cruz. Along the way, we had to decide who would take part in the bullfighting extravaganza. I volunteered myself and Box. Box took immediate exception, as I'd anticipated.

"No, thank you. I've already had my fill of bulls chasing me."

"Okay. I need a couple more volunteers." I said.

"Sure. I'll do it." Joey said without hesitance.

"Me too." Quinn followed.

"Sorry. I forgot to mention — no girls. Colombians don't like that sort of thing when it comes to this macho bullshit sport." I explained.

"Hell, I'll do it." Rick said. "You just hold a thing out for the bull to run through, right? How dangerous could that be? I just don't see how they grade such malarkey."

"Well, Steven. I guess it's yours my friend." I said.

"All right, already. I'll do it." Box complained. "Steven. Great. It'd take me a month to explain that one."

"Hey!" Jesus shouted from a tucked away position in the plane. "What am I, chopped liver?"

"No! Don't even think about it, Box!" I explained. "You've already volunteered. Case closed."

"You tricked me." Box acted betrayed.

"Yup."

Several trucks were deployed to greet us. It was a ritual that I had grown quite tired of. Not that I was opposed to getting chauffeured around, I simply wanted to be more in control.

"Oh, my word!" Christina reacted with consternation. "Elephants!"

"What?" Lourdes began. "You've never been to the zoo? It's an elephant, for Pete's sake. Don Fabio's got all kinds of animals. Zebras, giraffes, buffalo, Llama, you name it."

"Lamb." I said sarcastically.

"Yeah, lamb..." Lourdes caught herself. "Funny."

"What?" Christina, and then the others asked.

"It's too complicated to get into. Just don't ask what keeps the carnivores on that island out there." Box pointed to the lake in the distance.

There were many people, men and women, mostly spectators, gathered at the bullring. We hadn't any bullfighting attire, so we opted to wear what we had on, camouflage fatigues. Had we known they would

make such a big deal of these games, we would have
come more prepared for the event. As it was, I didn't
think it mattered whether we won or lost any of the
events. I just wanted to get them over with.

I had been led to understand that young Fabio had
collaborated with Mr. Casey on setting up the events.
He was soon at our sides.

"Are you ready?" Lourdes translated.

"We just let the bull run through a towel, right?" I
forecasted my ignorance.

Fabito's laugh told me that he must have thought I
was kidding around. It also told me that I was in some
deep manure.

"What do you suppose was so funny about that?" I
asked.

"I think you have to jab them with little arrows,
don't you?" Christina sounded unsure.

"Oh no!" Boxer's blood pressure began to rise. "I
almost got killed when I shoved one of those bad boys.
Now you want me to prick n' prod one. You're crazy!"
Box directed his anxiety toward me. "You're nuts. I'm
gonna get in there, make an appearance, and run
around a little bit. Then I'm right over that fence. It's
not as if we can win anyhow."

"So who's asking you to do anything else?" I stated.
"You won't see me throwing my sombrero to the
crowd. Let's just make an effort and have some fun."

"Hey, Ves." Christina grabbed my attention. "Looks
like your fun has arrived." She was marveling at a
bull, rippling and bulging with muscle. Its monstrous
head bore protrusive horns that jutted out like batons.
Its flaccid lips hovered low about the ankles, dripping
saliva and collecting dirt. Each pant aroused the soil
beneath its face. He wavered, and then burst forward
without warning, circumnavigating the horse that
Fabito commanded. Fabio was El Torero, frustrating
and confusing the bull, as he whisked lightly about the

ring, elegant and sophisticated in his sprayed on white pants, and red on black vest. It gave him a British flavor, with his long blondish hair adrift in the gentle breeze.

The bull was soon persuaded to its pen by a single horse. Fabio patiently strolled his horse over to us, and politely asked if we would prefer to go first. He explained that the bull would be more difficult to contend with after he is stabbed three times by the first rider.

"Rider?" Box asked, pressure reaching maximum allowable limits.

"Yes." Fabio answered. "This is equestrian bull-fighting." He then galloped away to the other side.

Box stared me straight in the face. "I've never fought a bull, and I can't ride a horse! And now someone's asking me to combine them both into one event! Why don't we just add climbing and swimming to the damn thing!"

I stood solemn for a moment and then answered. "You can ride."

"That was a parking lot, you moron!" He quickly returned.

The rules of the game were simple. There were four riders per team. Each rider was given three needle tipped arrows, about the length of a lawn dart. The arrows were yellow with either green or red feathers, depending upon what team you represented. The riders had a minute and a half to insert their arrows (one at a time) into the bull, forward of the shoulders. Fabio assured us that this would not do any permanent harm to the bull. Needless to say, this was never a concern to any of our players.

"Everyone shut up!" Box yelled about our chatter. "I want to see what he does." Box leaned over the railing to watch Fabio fight the bull. "That's it?" Box wondered aloud, as young Fabio hastily placed three arrows strategically into the neck of the bull.

"The bull hardly did shit!" Box strutted to the horse he was supposed to ride.

"Like taking burgers from a drive-through."

We all cheered him on with encouragement. "Go get 'em Box!" We yelled and cackled, attempting to squelch the applause for Fabio.

"Stick it to 'em, Box!" I called in support.

"All right, Box!" Lourdes wailed. "Think he'll get 'em all in?" She asked me.

"Hell, no. The bull might, though." I said with a smile. "Go get 'em, Box!" I hollered.

Box moved the horse out to the center of the ring. He kept perfect rhythm with the animal. As the horse sank down, he went up, when the horse popped up, he dropped down. The bull tore from his pen and charged past him. Boxer's style was the converse of Fabio's, preferring to remain still rather than move about the ring. As the bull ran by his mount, Box awkwardly leaned over and stuck it in the ass. When the bull reared about for a second run, Box was still facing the other direction. He acted imperturbable, almost to the degree of insanity. He hummed softly while removing another arrow from his belt. The bull attacked. It passed him once again, taking another arrow to the butt. The bull was annoyed. The horse was becoming jittery, sensing something that Box obviously was not. The bull gored the horse in the chest, knocking it to the ground. I never knew a bull would do that.

Boxer's leg became trapped under the horse as the bull readied its next assault.

"Holy shit!" Joey yelled.

"Get up, Box." I repeated softly.

The bull charged with malice. "Help!" Box screamed. "Help me!" He continued, terror in his voice.

My eyes flashed between Box and the bull like a strobe light, knowing that there was nothing we could do. "For God's sakes, somebody help me!"

Two ear drum damaging blasts, and it was over. We had lost the round, but they had lost an expensive bull. Young Fabio seemed to take pleasure in destroying the bull under such outrageous circumstances. Like the hatchet incident, it was entertainment. If it hadn't been one of our team, he would probably have let the bull mutilate him.

The next game was baseball. We were a little more prepared for this, I had my glove and spikes with me, they provided the rest. The field was completely make-shift, baselines of grass, and an outfield of unleveled turf, made for some rather stopgap play. The mound was perfectly grated and curved. I hadn't thrown a baseball in earnest for over a year now. We warmed up for about an hour, before finally taking the field.

Lourdes, with her lank and flex body, played first base. I was on the mound with a ninety mile-an-hour fast ball and a slight tendency to clock people with it. Rick played center field, his prior baseball experience came in handy between two lesser experienced play-ers, Christina in right field and Tina in left. At third base, we were rock solid, Joey could snag anything that came his way. He was a virtuoso, the Venus Fly Trap of ground balls. Filling in the rest of the infield with some fancy glove work of their own were Quinn at short, and Jesus at second. The sad recipient of my ninety mile-an-hour palm inflater was Box. If you were to switch Box with Christina and Joey with Tina, you would have the makings of our batting order.

I assumed we would annihilate them as they would had annihilated us in bullfighting. That is, if the bull had not died. But it was the fourth inning and neither side had gotten a hit. They did have a player advance to first base, however. Actually, he wobbled to first. He had the audacity to laugh when Box took one in the cup. I kind of forgot to shake off a fast ball that I'd changed to a curve. Anyhow, he would neither laugh at our misfortune or hug the plate again.

It was now the fifth inning and we had yet to get a run. Jesus led off with a blooper single over second base. I took the first pitch to deep left, and was already around first base when the dope head made a no-looker over his right shoulder. Jesus was picked off before he could make it back to first base.

I was now in a groove, picking the corners of the plate at will. We still hadn't scored, though. I was amazed, these guys were the equivalent of the high school pot-heads that wore army boots to gym class, but we couldn't score on them. Several of us tore the threads off the ball, always to have it caught in some unorthodox manner. They, on the other hand, had yet to hit the ball out of the infield. And that was good, because, except for Rick, I had little confidence in our outfield's talent.

It was the top of the seventh, the final inning in our regulations. I struck out the first two batters, and beaned the third, purely by accident. My arm was exceedingly tired and sore, but I knew I would never pitch another day, so it didn't matter. By this time, I was counting my blessings that the sole umpire was better at calling balls and strikes than they were in high school. I was pitching to the number five batter. After two consecutive fast balls that went for called strikes, I became lazy and pulled a sophomoric move. I threw a change-up curve. He hung on it, and plastered a frozen rope to deep, deep left. Tina snapped up from her crouch, hesitating for a fraction as she judged her angle. By the time she closed in on it, the lead runner had rounded third for home. When she left her feet for a horizontal plane, I knew it was a home run.

"Damn-it. Why did I throw that." I grunted.

"I don't believe it!" Joey declared, as Tina arose from the playing field with the ball in her glove.

"Throw it in!" I called to her, the runner having not tagged up. "Holy Cow! I can't believe you caught that!" Everyone was jumping up and down, as she lobbed it in, easily catching the runner, who made no real effort to return to first. It looked like we had just won the pennant. It was good for us to cheer together this way. There was so little to cheer about. It also did a lot for Tina, who had felt like an outsider for so long.

The games took on a whole new meaning with that catch. We finally realized that we had to win. We had to show them that we could win, and that we would always endeavor to beat them. That they indeed were the enemy.

I led off the bottom half of the seventh. I brought a face of determination to the plate. My whole team was up and cheering. It was the biggest baseball game of my life, yet there would be no trophies, no offers of scholarships or contracts, not even a picture in the newspaper. It was more important than all that, it was as if we played for our country's honor.

I waited for the count to go three and one, when I leveled my bat on a low, inside fast-ball. I croaked it down the left field line, only to have the third baseman leap out and grab it. Rick was next. He drilled one to the gap between short and third, to yet again have the third baseman dive into the grass and snow-cone a one hopper. The ensuing gun to first nailed him by a half-step. Box was up next, and hope for avoiding extra innings fell off.

Box swatted for the trees at the first two marginally good pitches. The next toss, which was surely out of the strike zone by at least a foot, saw Box teeing off. He barely nicked the top of the ball, as it trickled toward the third base line. The third baseman charged the ball, bare-handing it and throwing it all in one motion. The throw was perfect, arriving at its destination about the same time Box did. Box rammed the Colombian in the same manner as the bull, bowling him into the grass and mashing down upon him. Safe at first.

Joey now stepped up to the plate. All I could think of was that I wished I had placed Rick in the fifth batting position and not little Joey Bali. He was a gifted infielder, but not much with the stick, I thought, having already watched him fizzle some ground balls to the pitcher and second base. He did all the things that give the appearance of knowing what you're doing, like clicking the dirt from your cleats with a bat, and rubbing dirt in your hands, but the results were always the same. I sat back down from my enthused cheering.

The first pitch was a hard outside fast-ball, about waist level. It would be the last pitch. Joey clobbered it with an inside-out swing, knocking it into the only field that had a defined home-run line. The line was drawn by a stream that darted across right field, wherein the ball fell. I was in complete shock. Everyone but Box and I stormed Joey at home plate.

"Hell of a hit my man." I said with a grin.

"Ditto." Box added.

"You two and your generalizations." Joey said.

I brushed his shoulder lightly and said sarcastically: "Let me get that chip off there for ya."

"What's that suppose to mean?" Box asked.

"I'm not sure. But, to be honest, I don't care. He hit the homer. Can you believe that?"

"I got a hit, you know." Box said.

"A what?" I said loudly. "You're not calling that a hit. Please! You fight bulls better than you play baseball."

"What do you mean? I stuck two darts in that thing!"

"In his ass!" I explained.

"Bull! Right in the throat! 'In the ass'? You're crazy."

"You know. Joey may be confused about his sex, but you're confused about everything else. Throat? Gimme a break. I'll give you throat."

Joey called to us.

"Are you two gonna stay and argue, or come back to the states with us and celebrate!"

"Ask the matador!" I replied.

On the way back home, we levied superlatives and accolades on each other. It had been one of our better days, that's for sure.

"Does anyone feel as strange about all this as I do? Playing sports against the Colombian drug traffickers?" Rick asked.

"Here, here." Jesus reacted. "I like it, but I don't. You know?"

"If it'll stop people from dying, I'm all for it." I said.

"Is that what it's supposed to do?" Christina asked. "How?"

"I don't know." Box said. "But I guess it can't hurt. Maybe if we know each other better, we'll be less likely to — shit I don't know. Let's just seek our own reward. If we leave Colombia feeling this good anytime, don't question it."

"Good point!" I agreed.

Silence prevailed on the last leg of our journey together. We were exhausted, so we huddled together like puppy dogs in slumber. My eyes remained open as I thought of Debara. How I wished she could share in this victory. I closed my eyes and could still see her smiling back at me. I missed her — now more than ever.

Chapter 29.

By the time April rolled around, Christine and I had been with each other almost every day since January. I was so sure of this relationship that it actually frightened me.

These past couple months were virtually *Pseudo Miranda* free. Of the interceptions I went on, only one had what might be considered negative results. While in southern Texas on a milk run, Steven had his femur bone snapped in half.

We were sitting around, out of harms way, awaiting the arrival of a cocaine shipment. Steven had just received word that the aircraft had been intercepted and was heading our way. Quinn was holding our only pair of night vision glasses.

"We're dead! Run!" She suddenly screamed.

"What's wrong!" Steven asked. While the rest of us fled without question, Steven fuddled with the ComCord. He quickly freed himself, only to have a two-hundred pound bag of cocaine strike him in the right leg.

He didn't scream during the entire ordeal, even when I placed a rifle under his chin to restrain him, while Rick popped the bone back into place. He groaned and grunted, but he never once cried. It was a painstaking task to deliver him from the field in this condition. Had it occurred in Colombia, we would have been prepared with morphine. As it was, we had only the coke to give him. However, that luxury didn't occur to us until we had already put Steven through several excruciating bouts of pain.

My graduation date was set for the first of April. Christine had already decided to put in for Randolph Air Force Base as her first station, post graduation. If she was unable to get stationed there, we had already discussed the possibility of getting married to ensure our lives together.

After graduation, I took about a week's *leave* time. I had been informed by Box that I would need to accompany him, Rick, Christina, Joey, and Quinn to a large *finca* east of Medellin, on the Pacific Coast.

The contemporary lines of the house curved fluidly along the hillside. Adorned in white luster, it capped the mountain like snow, as it ruled over the ocean shore.

The guarded entryway had a gun-check girl, who politely relieved all guests of their weapons. This honor system made me feel trusted, even as I walked through the metal detector on the way into the house. The black marble floor glided through the house like ice, ironing out the natural jaggedness of the terrain. Our steps were crisp and snappy as we passed directly through the center of the mansion. The art was contemporary, and was designed specifically for these walls. Vases and sculptured arrangements were invariant to their surroundings, conforming in size, shape and color. The rear of the house was of continuous glass, and looked out upon a large pool and an enormous patio.

I was disillusioned with the number of Americans I saw there, some I recognized from the entertainment industry, but could not place their names. The women were the most beautiful I'd ever seen gathered in one place at one time.

Don Fabio, young Fabio, and Jose Ocampo were our hosts, and were essentially the only ones with whom we mingled. As the music played on and the guests consumed large amounts of cocaine and alcohol, Box and I concentrated on some diplomatic efforts to enlighten Don Fabio on the inevitable course of *Pseudo Miranda*. Once they were all billionaires, we would seek a voluntary discontinuance of cocaine trafficking. Ochoa seemed amenable to the premise.

We were all relaxing by the pool when suddenly a man, dark skinned and tall, came over to Don Fabio and whispered something in his ear.

"If something happens," I said to Christina. "You give me all the English."

Two men then stormed into the party, dragging a third. The man being flung about was much older, probably in his fifties, and bore an unthreatening physique. His soft body recoiled with every poke and prod. The man that whispered to Don Fabio now approached the tormented man, and began to beat him.

"He's saying something about theft." Christina advised. "Shouldn't we do somethin'?"

"What? Want me to jump 'em and wrestle their guns away." I said sarcastically.

"They all get what they deserve." Box said.

The tall man drew his handgun and stroked the man's face softly with the barrel, teasing him with the device that might soon cause him intense grief. The old man begged from his knees, insisting he had done nothing wrong.

"Don't anybody panic," Box said. "He won't kill 'em."

The tall Colombian capped off a single round to the man's forehead, spilling his brains to the cement. He then grabbed his feet and twisted him into the pool. I watched in absolute dismay as several women jumped into the pool and began to play with the floating body.

"Time to go." I said. I then nodded my head at *Don* Fabio. I had heard the murder's name, a name that I had heard once before. I was frightened at what it was I was thinking about doing. On the way out, I knelt inconspicuously to pick up a single shell casing.

At the front of the house, the gun-check girl handed back our weapons. I pressed the empty casing into my clip. Although it was the wrong size shell, it looked authentic enough from the rear of the clip. I then showed her the rear of the clip and snapped it back into my Colt 45. Placing it to her head, I had Christina tell her to give us back our bullets. She promptly unlocked the safe and we loaded up.

"What the hell are we doin'?" Box said angrily.

"We can't let this pass. I just can't." I said. "You do what you want." I said, determined to make right that which couldn't be.

The moment I crossed through the metal detector, bells began to ring loudly. We were swarmed by security forces before we could make it to the outside. I continued walking until I reached the patio. The others had been cut off inside, as I was now.

"Don Fabio!" I called.

He said something, and I was allowed through, without my weapon. I was able to convey to him that I needed the assistance of Christina for translation. He had them get her. I asked him permission to meet this killer squarely. Ochoa informed me that the man was his production chief, and that he was doing what was necessary. While I discussed the matter with him, caretakers were busily cleaning the blood at my feet with something that smelled like gasoline.

"This is the way we do things." He said.

"I understand, Don Fabio, but this is the way *we* do things also. You wouldn't want a coward working for you at such a high level, would you?"

"What if you are killed?"

"So be it." I waited. "No retribution whatsoever."

The Don backed away, symbolic of nonintervention. Something I remembered from my classroom training in Nevada. I intended only to destroy the man's credibility by bluffing him into displaying his true cowardice. After all, I thought, nobody duels anymore. The man acted confused as he stood with his back to the swimming pool. "Don Fabio? What is this? Who are these people, Don Fabio? Are they your friends? Can I kill your friends?"

Don Fabio did not answer.

The man's gun was tucked in the front of his pants.

"What!" He screamed at me. I didn't respond. "I'll kill you!" He yelled. "You — you — you are dead!" He shuttered in Spanish.

I controlled the gun at my left side, muzzle pointed upward in his direction. I depressed the safety grip mechanism with my pinkie, and placed my index finger over the trigger. With my hand straight down on the weapon, the untrained eye could not recognize that it was ready to fire. My fingers were stretched, and I could feel the cramping pain between them. He went for his gun.

I squeezed off a single round, striking him in the

chest. My gun recoiled, snapping the bone in my hand.
The back of his chest exploded with blood, spraying a
mist halfway across the water. He launched over the
corner of the pool, his head bouncing as it met the
concrete. I picked up my weapon in my right hand
while cradling my left, and walked over to where he
lay. By now, he was mired in a pool of blood. I grabbed
his shirt, and dragged him across the corner of the
pool, releasing him as he bent at the waist into the
water. His apparent girlfriend, one of the women who
toyed with the other floating corpse, attacked me with
flailing arms. I grabbed her by the hair, and twisted
her into the pool.

"Play with that." I said, and walked away.

I couldn't look any of my teammates in the eye on
our journey back. I felt evil, and dirty. I didn't mean
for it to happen, I kept telling myself. But I couldn't
deny how good it felt, and that's what scared me. I
would soon find out that sin has its own judgment.
Punishment brought on by our acts, and not by God.

The man I had killed went by a name, when loosely
translated, means Hitler's Savior. The name I carried
with me for the many months following Debara's
slaying. The name Joey kept repeating. The name of
the man who vanished from that lab on the hill. The
name of the man that killed Debara.

I decided to divert the aircraft to England Air Force
Base. We had already stowed our weapons in Arkansas, so I wasn't at all concerned about any problems
we might face there. The pilot complied without argument, calling in a fictitious In-Flight-Emergency (IFE)
as we neared the base. We taxied to the Transient
Aircraft Parking area and called a taxi from Base
Operations. Box quickly rented a car, and we were on
our way to New Orleans for a little R & R.

My attitude over the past few weeks was not in

keeping with team unity, and I was rapidly widening the ethical grey area of my life. No one was adamantly adverse to this spontaneous decision to go to New Orleans, but they seemed analytical about my motivations.

"Partying on Bourbon and Canal Street." Rick said, sounding up. "Any particular reason?" He directed his question at me..

"No. I just wanta party until I drop." I answered. "I have a lot of good memories about that place."

"Sounds good to me!" Joey seemed excited.

"Yeah. Real good." Christina dampened the mood.

"What's with you?" Quinn said in a snotty way.

Christina switched gears. "Nothing. Let's have some fun. We've earned it, darn-it."

"You're darn tooten' we have!" I acclaimed loudly. "Bourbon Street!" I yelled till they all joined in.

We stayed at the Holiday Inn. Sometime during the evening, we hooked up with a crowd of people, mostly women, and took them back to our hotel. With four rooms, we were able to party on through the morning in the two that adjoined.

As the party raged on, I retired alone to the room across the hall. I sat at a desk, and removed a kilo of cocaine that I had emancipated from the party in Colombia. Staring down at it, I wondered why I had taken it in the first place. I then pondered what mysterious grip this innocent looking powder had on so many millions of people. I carefully sliced the thick cellophane to get a whiff from afar.

Suddenly Christina barged in unannounced.

"Don't let me stop ya." She said, swatting her backhand in my direction before sitting on the bed. "Your first time?"

"It might have been if you hadn't stormed in here."

"Oh, please. Go ahead, knock yourself out. Don't let me ruin your indulgence." She walked over to me and said loudly: "Go on! Go on, you hypocritical bastard!" She then grabbed the kilo and smashed it in my face. "Here! Get a big snoot full."

I smacked her arm and grabbed the fallen kilo, heaving it against the door. "What the hell's your problem! You psycho bitch."

"What's my problem? You. You're my problem. Ever since Debara's death you've been acting as if you had a license to do whatever the hell you want to do."

"What are you talking about? I haven't changed... Have you been sniffing any of that *Rush* junk from the French Quarters?"

"You didn't have to kill that man."

"He murdered a defenseless old man! In front of us no less! We allow that—even once—and they'll have us—they'll have us forever. I don't know what shooting you witnessed? But I sure as hell didn't see it that way. Killed? You say it like I committed a crime. The only crime I'm guilty of is running a sanitation service without a license."

"I don't care what he did! Or what you call it!" She pleaded. "Don't you see? It's not about justice. If that were the only standard we had to achieve, fine. But we have to be above that. This crazy operation requires that we *be* above that. Above equal. Above instinct. You killed that man. And then you threw his girlfriend in the pool after his dead body? My God, Ves. What level did you seek there?" She paused to back away from me.

"No matter how fair and just it was to challenge him, you met him—you met them—at their level—on their playing field."

"That's easy for you to say. You stand behind God as an excuse not to act. Well, I acted, dammit! Right or wrong! Good or bad! I did something."

"Walking away *is* doing something! And don't you dare lecture me about doing! Every day of my life now—and in the future—I ask if what I'm doin' is right. And then I go out and do it! It's easy for you. You don't have to wrestle with a conscience every minute you're out there. Well, I do! And it's hard." She thought for a moment.

"Do you think that I didn't want to kill him? Do you think any of us didn't get sick when he toyed with that man before killing him? You didn't kill that man because it was right! You killed him because it made you feel better!"

"Who the hell do you think you are! You wanta be judge and jury? Take it somewhere else, because I don't need it! You want reasons..."

"Yeah!"

"Good! Because I've got plenty of 'em! He was a cold blooded killer! They're all cold blooded killers!"

"That's right!"

"That's right! And that's why Jerimiah and Debara are dead!"

"And what's that make you?" She shouted.

"His name was the Savior! Hitler's Savior!" I shuttered and trembled.

"What?"

"Hitler's Savior! Hitler's...Oh God. Debara." I fought back the tears, as my voice faltered.

"You mean — he was — the guy that killed...?"

"Yes! What does it matter! What does any of this matter!"

"It matters. You're not the only one hurting over her, you know. We all miss her. Not a day goes..."

"A day? Not a day? Not a second goes by that I don't die inside." I paced about the room. "I see her smiling on that hill. I smell her hair — in the jungle. I hear her voice — her voice — constantly! Right now — I hear her. I'd waited my whole life for her. And now..." I swallowed tightly and then switched momentarily to thoughts of my new love.

"And now I've found the most perfect girl. And I can't let her in. And I don't know if I ever will. You miss her every day? Is that what you said?"

"Go on feeling sorry for yourself."

"How can you be so..."

"But remember there are people that count on you."

"Don't! Don't give that about needing! How 'bout me! Huh! What do I get! Who can I count on! I've got nothing! Nothing! So take your..."

"Nothing! You selfish little prick! While you're there..."

"I don't wanta hear..."

"While you're out there venting your anger, the rest of us are looking over your shoulder, making sure you're safe! So don't tell me you've got no one! There are fifteen..."

"Thirteen."

"...thirteen people who are counting on you! They'll go anywhere with you! They trust in you! And no matter what you think! They'll die for you. So don't tell me you've got no one. Because there's a VesBucchi I would have died for. And I think I still would."

"Save the pep-rally speech for Lourdes. I've grown up a lot in the last few months."

SMASH! Christina whacked me over the head with an empty beer bottle. I collapsed to one knee, half hurt, and half shocked that she would do such a thing.

"Oh my God. What'd I do?"

Box flew into the room. "What the hell happened?" He asked.

"Christina broke a glass." I said.

"What?"

"Just leave, Box." I was short with him. "Everything's fine. Really."

I stumbled to the bed, and laid my head upon the pillow. "Nice wrist action." I said.

"A misspent youth, I guess." She said mildly. "I'm sorry." She touched my head.

"Ow!."

"Well, it serves you right."

"Yeah, I suppose it does." I sighed deeply. "I guess

I've made a debauchery of this whole thing, huh? Don't answer. I know I have. Everything has just gotten so damn confusing. It seems like only yesterday that we were just a bunch of trainees trying to get through camp. All of a sudden people are dying, and you can't tell the good guys from the bad guys. If anything, you're right about that. If we don't exceed normal standards of behavior under these trying circumstances, then we'll never be able to tell the good from the bad. It's just sometimes — I think about her — and I forget how to do what's right."

"You don't forget. You just choose not to."

"Damn, girl. You don't let me slide on anything. Okay — you're right. I know when I'm screwing up. It's just that it's so easy to screw up out there in the jungle. You're right, you're right — more excuses." I exhaled loudly. "God. How do I put it all back together?"

"I don't think you can put it back together. But I agree that asking God is the place to start. And finish, for that matter. Do you want me to get some ice for that. Okay?"

"Yes. Please." As she started out the door. "Seedy?"
"Yeah?"

"God? You know, Jesus? His father? Do you ah…? Do you think he approves of anything we're doin'?"

"I think you have to ask yourself what your motivation is. I don't think anything done with pure motives can be bad. And I don't think anything done, that appears to be good on the surface, can actually be good if done for the wrong reasons. It removes the powerful hand of God, which can make ten fold your labor, from the picture."

"Like Mafia money to the church."

"Exactly…I think."

"Are your motives pure?"

"No. But I think they're as close as they've ever been on anything. How 'bout you?"

"I don't know."

"Wait there. I'll fetch some ice."

Numerous successful interceptions and interventions were made over the next several months, some that I was a party to, and others not. We had become expert in the field, developing preemptive techniques and strategies that made such delicate matters seem perfunctory in nature.

It was now the Summer of 1986. I was in the house that I was told to purchase, but the girlfriend had disappeared. She gave no reason. She simply cried and said that I couldn't call her any more. Though I tried and tried, I never got my answer, nor spoke to her again.

With Summer passing, I readied myself for another milk-run to Colombia on the Labor Day weekend.

Chapter 30.

"Hey Ken," Robert asked, speaking on the telephone, "Are we on for Labor Day weekend?" Robert was, and still is, a good friend of mine (non-government type) from San Antonio, Texas.

"Oh crap! Robert. Man, I forgot all about Corpus Christi. The damned Air Force man. They've got me going TDY (Temporary Duty) to Shepherd (AFB) for some bogus training."

"On the holiday?"

"Yeah. You believe that, man?"

"That's cool. Don't worry about it. I'll probably head to Austin."

"I'm sorry man. We'll grab a limo and do the town when I get back. All right?"

"Sure. Sounds good to me. Hey, look. Don't worry about it. When Uncle Sam calls, you've got to answer. That's what we pay our taxes for."

"Thanks for understanding, man. See ya when I get back.

"Have fun."

Robert was the type of friend I could hold on to through these complicated times because he was so understanding. I had a few other male friends with that same selflessness, but never once a girlfriend.

I hung up the phone and was out the door in minutes. I drove my De Lorean to the Hondo airstrip at well above the legal speed limit the entire way. A desperate search for my keys had made me tight for my appointment. I sped into the almost abandoned airport, sliding my car's back end as I peeled down the taxi way. My car barely cleared the partially opened door. I skidded short, throwing the car door upward to permit my hasty egress. Box hung outside the Cesna 400 twin prop, slapping his thigh like a drum roll, as testimony to his heightened exasperation.

"You're gonna be late to your own funeral!" He vented.

"That sounds good to me," I said, pulling my gear from my car. "Hurry!" He demanded, looking back into the aircraft to speak with the pilot. "Hurry! Come on!"

I slipped past him in the doorway, and went directly to a seat in the cramped rear quarter of the aircraft.

"Let's go!" Box called to the pilot. "Where have you been?" He snapped at me.

"I had to wait around for an FCF on a CND." I answered, knowing it would drive him mad.

"A what on a what!"

"Oh, I'm sorry," I taunted. "I forgot you've never served in the armed forces. A Functional Check Flight for a Can Not Duplicate discrepancy on a jet. You know, like the CND aircraft we handed the mechanics in Alexandria."

"What CND?"

"Remember? We faked a problem to get them to allow us to land at England Air Force Base."

"Oh yeah. Man, you've really corrupted me."

"Yeah, right. You were such an angel when I met you."

"Well... I just hope we're not late or nothin'."

"Why? Are we on some sort of an unusual deadline or something?"

"No, not really. Well. Sort of." He collected his thoughts. "We've got a big shipment of paste just sitting in southern Colombia."

"Oh, I get it. We need to strike it before it gets divided up to several labs."

"Correct. One problem though."

"What's that."

"It's right near a river called the Piranha. And you know our luck with those little critters." He said. It seemed quite prophetic at the time.

In Panama, we met up with the others: Christian, Joey, Rick, Quinn, Lourdes, Steven, and Tina. We were all sporting darker complexions and leaner figures. The result of too much equatorial sun and too many jobs. Not to mention the nervous stress. We didn't appear withered, but there was an emptiness in our eyes. We were now veterans of the drug wars, whether we liked it or not.

With the aid of a second Cesna, we journeyed to Colombia. I sat comfortably in the copilot seat as we contoured the landscape tightly, through jungle and green pasture, jarring on pockets of air and souring like eagles on heated updrafts. Every now and then, we would catch the eye of a lonesome farmer waving as we dropped to tree-top level for insulation.

When the clouds rolled in over the Saturday morning sky, they blurred the varying landscape, causing mountains and lakes and jungles to meld. The torrential rains of central Colombia enabled us to blend in with the radar ground clutter, while, at the same time, heightening the chances of us becoming ground clutter ourselves.

Our planes finally touched down for transference somewhere in the Llanos. Colonel Borda climbed into the cockpit with the pilot, as we didn't need a navigator of our own to direct the pilot to the first stop. We would soon be in Leticia once again.

Now, all packed aboard a helicopter, we joked about our ride thus far, and loosened up for the pending mission. We were roughhousing in the back of the helicopter to suggest we bore no concerns about our immediate future. In the act of laughing, I looked around at my friends and wondered how long I would have them. I worried about how their loss would effect me.

The commotion that occupied our cramped cabin inexplicably deadened as we landed in the shantytown section of Leticia, as if in homage to Jerimiah, and Debara as well. The partially dried surface of the ground infiltrated the cabin, eddying about the aircraft like a whirlpool. We waited, somewhat poised, somewhat crouched, for the right moment to exit. With our faces thinly coated in dirt, and the rotor blades at a weathervane's pace, we strolled out to greet the children. Borda was already doling out the coins when Rick gave him a guilty, somewhat intimidating stare. The bag was immediately turned upside down and shaken. When Borda demonstrated that the bag was indeed empty, Rick nodded and walked back to the group.

"It's good this way!" Borda bellowed. "I won't miss the trip!"

I had no intention of shedding him this time while he indulged in some desperate woman, so I was glad to see Rick honor Jerimiah that way.

Fuel was brought to the helicopter in large drums pulled by a pack team, making me extremely nervous about the possibility of fuel contamination.

"How do you think we fueled you the last time you were here?" Borda said through translation.

We ate cornbread and some unusual form of chicken soup before readying ourselves for departure the following morning.

"Let's go." I said, sitting beneath some trees, soup bowl in hand.

"Where's Christina?" Lourdes asked.

"What's she doin' over there?" Box asked, as he gazed across the street. Christina was chatting with a young girl, maybe fourteen, who appeared to be pregnant.

"Seedy! Come on! Let's get a move on!" Box yelled.

"No. We can wait." I quickly interjected.

"What? She's just shooting the shit with some chick." Box explained.

"Some pregnant chick." I emphasized.

"Okay. Some pregnant... Oh yeah. Right." He remembered. "Well. I wouldn't give her long," he advised.

"No. But we can spare a minute or two." I turned back to Christina. "She sure is a good person, huh?"

"Not again, okay." Box said.

"Not again, what?"

"You know."

"What, I can't compliment a woman without there being some sort of implication?"

"Exactly."

"Shut up. Here she comes."

The course heading would take us the shape of a "7", with each leg consisting of approximately a hundred miles. The first leg up the handle would not tip off our intended destination, but the second leg would. The key was to invite Borda to transmit messages at will by not placing anyone in the cockpit with him and the pilot. We would then run slightly above the second leg

so that Borda would be lulled into believing that we
were steering away from the coca paste storage site.
After we were convinced that Borda gave notice to the
Campesinos at the target site that they were in the
clear, we would then radio forward to the cockpit and
advise the pilot to set down near a lab in our immediate area, one that had been plotted out earlier by CIA
intelligence. Quinn then moved to the front, and Borda
to the rear, in turn, reversing our course from a north-
erly to a south-westerly heading.

Borda was furious, spitting with each profane ut-
terance of disdain for my character. "Box." I said
unemotionally. "Shut him up."

Box scooted over on his butt and grabbed hold of
Borda's military shirt. As he reared back with his fist,
Borda submitted and shut up. Our game faces slid
over us like fine silk linen. "Ves! Trouble!" Quinn
radioed back. "Pilot says we've got a GOES unit on our
ass. Advise."

I studied Colonel Borda for facial expressions when
I told him of the warning. He didn't impress me as a
man concerned about going to jail.

"Ignore it!" I told her. "Drop down to tree top and
increase speed! Roger?"

"Roger, sir!"

"Lower Quinn!"

"Copy that lower, sir."

"Max throttle!" I demanded, my eyes affixed on the
Colonels.

"Copy that max throttle, sir! Max throttle!"

Moments later the skids scraped the canopy. "Pull
up, sir?" Quinn suggested.

"No! Well, maybe just a hair!" I answered.

<ind>Box pivoted his posterior across to my side of
the aircraft, plopping down beside me.

"What do we do if the pilot is telling the truth?"

"Go to jail."

"Good. I thought you were gonna say shoot 'em down."

The second leg of the journey was quick. The helicopter slowed on its approach, as it turned sideways per Quinn's instruction, offering those of us in the rear a clear vantage point by which to view the site. A faceless structure was squarely before us, its perimeter protected on three sides by a snaking river, and by the jungle on its fourth. Barrel upon covered barrel spilled out from the structure, engulfing most of the clearing. Their contents: a thick, sticky, grey substance called coca paste.

I placed Joey and his M-60 machine gun at the center of the helicopter's doorway. The pilot descended parallel with the storage facility, keeping us in constant eye contact with the site's occupants. We left the chopper on either side of Joey, breaking outside his direct line of fire, while covering the perimeter.

I was in the lead position this time, cantering past the Campesinos to the left-rear of the structure. "Clear!" I called to the others.

Rick now crossed to the opposite side to face me. "Everything looks hunky-dory here."

"Good," I said. "Let's dispose of this shit and get the hell outa here." I searched the forest for any immediate signs of danger, and then quickly refocused on Rick.

"Stay back here. Be on the look out for anything out of the ordinary. We'll dump all the paste in the river and be on our way."

"Wouldn't I be more useful up there? Those containers look kinda heavy."

"Good point. I'll send someone back to replace you."

I moved hastily to the front and told everyone to pitch in and start moving some barrels. "Lourdes. Go to the rear and replace Rick."

"Could you send someone else. I sort of forgot my contacts." She explained.

"You sorta forgot your... How far can you go before you realize something like that?"

"I'll go." Christina volunteered.

"Fine. It doesn't matter. Just go. We need to get this shit done already." I grabbed Lourdes by the shoulder. "Under no circumstances do you fire that weapon. Understood?"

"Yup."

Box and Rick stood knee deep in the river and dumped the goop into the rushing water as we passed the barrels to them in assembly line fashion. The empty barrels were spun to the rear as the full ones passed to our front. Barrel upon barrel rolled by, and then suddenly Lourdes grabbed hold of an empty one.

"Steven." She said. "You're getting them confused."

I had a real bad feeling. "Tell me you haven't been rolling the empty ones to the rear of the full ones. Please tell me that."

Steven searched frantically for a full barrel, yet found none.

"We emptied them all, didn't we?" I asked, with the answer already known.

"Shit!" He yelled.

"Box! Don't pour out the rest of those!" I then said softly. "We may have a problem."

"What?" Box shouted. "Have we reached half already!"

"Oh yeah." I said, barely audible. "And then some."

"You hear that?" Joey called from the chopper.

"What?" I asked.

"That!" He replied.

I began to hear what sounded like the faint purr of a cat. The sound grew and became more distinct.

"Take cover!" I yelled.

We scattered to one side of the structure, with Christina still in the rear. Now hidden in the brush, we watched nervously as the chopper approached. "What the hell is that guy doin'?"

"Who?" Box asked.

"Borda." I directed his attention to the storage building.

"He's near the IFF, I think." Steven advised.

"Shit! Joey!"

"Got 'em." He said, firing one bullet to Borda's skull.

Borda had attempted to change the IFF codes, in turn telling the occupants of any *Pseudo Miranda* aircraft that we were not a part of *Pseudo Miranda* and, therefore, the enemy. We would then have been forced to wage war with the cartel. Borda knew the consequences of such a decision, but I'm not sure I did, even as I called to Joey for help. Whatever Joey's actions though, he did it because he believed I wanted him to, and, therefore, I was ultimately responsible. To this day I'm not actually sure if I wanted him to kill Borda, but I'm reconciled to the fact that I ordered it.

The small Huey helicopter passed directly over head, toward the rear of the building, at a high rate of speed. With so many barrels strewn about, and the Campesinos tucked away in the structure, I was sure that our uninvited guests would be alarmed. If the codes were changed, which we weren't sure of yet, there would soon be trouble.

"Check the IFF Steven!" I said.

"It's changed." He called. "Damn, Joey. Good shot."

"Hey!" Joey shouted. "Listen! No sound! I think our visitors are on foot."

"Okay! Let's go!" I demanded.

"Look!" Steven pointed to the river. It looked like tons of paste had collected on the bank of the river, against a fallen tree. "Joey! Blast that shit outa there!"

As he shredded the tree and blew apart the paste, I cornered Box.

"Where the hell could they have set down?"

"On the bank of the river? I don't know. They probably just flew out of ear's shot."

"I hope you're right."

Joey completed his task, and we were ready to leave.

"Let's get a lift off."

"Bap! Bap!" Two shots were capped off from the side-rear of the structure. Then some return fire. It was Christina fending off the intruders.

"Let's go!" I shouted. We scurried for cover, firing into the wooded area on the bank of the river.

"We need support cover for Seedy! Rick! Box! Get there!"

"Lourdes! Steven!" Box called. "Follow us!"

I fired my modified 30-06 at anything that moved, in an attempt to suppress fire as they made it around to the other side of the structure. Christina had positioned herself on the point, and was unable to seek refuge near the building. "Joey! Joey!" I called out.

"Yeah!"

"We're assaulting! Let's go!" I didn't need to look for him. Joey knew no other gear than overdrive. He was ready to give his life on every mission, especially if it meant saving one of us.

My feet struck the dank shore rhythmically, almost without sound. They moved without command. Shots were being fired toward the others, but none toward us. I stopped, my legs became real to me again. I could hear my breath and feel my heart. Joey broke left and took position behind a tree. We fired, striking three of them before they surrendered. Only one of them had been killed, the one Joey struck.

"How are we?" I hollered, keeping a watchful eye on the prisoners.

"It's Christina!" Box replied.

"Oh, no." I dashed toward them, leaving Joey to guard the assailants. They were all huddled around her. I gently pushed through, and found Christina cradled in Steven's lap. As I knelt beside her, Steven placed her in my arms and said that he would radio a distress to Langley.

"Oh Seedy." Tears fell. "Is heaven calling you?"

"Yes."

"Heaven's been getting much prettier lately." I nervously laughed.

"I'll say hello to her." Her eyes began to close.

"Don't go. Stay and talk a while. Please."

"I'll see you again some day, Ken. Please don't blame yourself. I've been ready for this day for the longest time. Remember. Only the dead bury their dead."

"I don't understand."

"I love you." She said, gently closing her eyes as she went limp in my shivering arms.

"I love you too." I whispered.

I carried her body to the chopper, and laid her carefully inside.

"Lourdes." I said, still choked up. "Stay with her." As she past me, I hugged her, feeling the barrel of her .22 rifle. It was warm. Christina had been struck in the abdomen by a small caliber bullet, and I could tell by the sound of the return gunfire that our adversaries used assault weapons. "We'll get through this, Lourdes."

I went back behind the building and told Joey to lend me his weapon. "Rick. Line 'em all up against the wall. Tie that asshole (Mandoza) to the overhang." Mandoza had replaced the man I killed at the party in Colombia, as Ochoa's new production chief.

Box stood before me as I prepared to implement a form of jungle justice. "What do you plan on doing with that? I hope it's not what I think. We're not about that."

"Step aside, Box." I turned to the others. "Everyone step aside!" Box reluctantly moved backwards, probably hoping that I was merely scaring them. I could hear the silence. "Let the dead bury their dead." I thought, my finger clenching the trigger. Shell casings expelled like popping corn, demons exorcised from my spirit. With each ejection came release. I felt exalted, taken above my hideous intent, my soiled motivations. The gun finally stopped cycling, but my body did not. It was done.

Box and Joey came to my side, the dim sounds of moaning and crying in the backdrop. Joey pulled firmly on the gun a few times before I could release it. "I hope we don't run into any more problems. That's the last of the sixties." Referring to the ammunition.

"I knew you wouldn't kill them." Box said.

"How could you? I didn't know myself."

"Because I know how much you wanta see them again some day."

"Yeah. Let's go, my friend." I walked to Rick and said to him, while facing Mandoza, "Cut this piece of shit down."

Mandoza never cried, and hardly flinched throughout the ordeal. The building behind him was destroyed. The Campesinos were covered in rubble, but none the worse for wear, excepting some abrasions caused by flying shrapnel. I must admit, I came dangerously close to killing some *innocent* people that day.

"We can't take her, you know." Box advised.

"I know." I responded. "Get the windscreen cover."

I carried her to the river. We shrouded her in the cover and stood, waist deep, in the running water. After everyone said their farewells, I added, "Lord. Into your arms." And left her to find her own way, her own grave, somewhere down stream in the Colombian jungle.

Chapter 31.

"Ves." Box said on the phone.

"Yeah, Box?"

I could hear a tremor in his voice. "I've got somethin' bad to tell ya."

"What?" After all we had been through, I sensed this must be bad. "What's wrong?"

"It's Rick." He sobbed. "He's dead."

I couldn't speak.

"Did you…"

"Yeah. Yeah, I heard you. How? How Box? Oh, for God's sake, Box. Oh God. I can't take it anymore."

"Suicide. They're telling me suicide." A lull. "Are you still there?"

"Yeah, I'm still here." Another lull. "Where is he? Can we see him? I want to see him" We need to see him, Box." I said in a glum tone.

"I know. I've already set somethin' up. We'll have to be blindfolded. You know, knowledge about each other and all. Anyhow, call in sick tomorrow and I'll see you in the morning at your house. Okay?" He spoke despondently.

It was only a few months after Christina's death when Langley began putting pressure on Box and I to withdraw the team from the operation. Withdrawal could only be accomplished, per the rules established in Zurich, by transmitting, via satellite, the phrase "Miranda Is Alive And Well." This would be accompanied by a code word, also sent by satellite, from Mena and changed weekly, verifying that the operation was indeed terminated. The code word had to be likewise issued during the final interceptions themselves. This combination was established on the outside possibility that someone apart from *Pseudo Miranda* would attempt to pirate a shipment.

Box and I agreed to drag our feet until all the fears

of our disclosure subsided. Casey was more than a bit concerned that the Contra affair would destroy the anonymity of *Pseudo Miranda*. I felt no direct personal link, and, therefore, no allegiance to its cause. Box and I did not act within a vacuum, however. After consulting each of the remaining members, we found everyone to be of one mind.

After we conducted this unauthorized "family meeting" in New Orleans, I came home to find that a couple of uninvited guests had dropped in. I parked my De Lorean in the driveway, choosing not to pull it into the garage and immediately detected the garage door which leads to the house, ajar. I had been meaning to fix the problem I was having with it not closing properly, but now I was glad I hadn't.

Entering the house, I made my way back to my bedroom where my Colt 45 lay beneath my pillow. On my way past the kitchen, I smelled aftershave. In the bedroom, I pulled the slide back on my gun. My hands beneath the pillow and a sneeze muffled the distinct sound. I crept back down the hallway, turned on the kitchen lights from outside, and got the drop on them through the serving window that led to the dining room.

"Games over boys." I said smugly. "Drop the guns. Drop 'em!"

"There's two of us. You drop the gun!"

"You're a very stupid man." I paused. "Okay. Let's play that hand. Raise your fuckin' weapons. Come on! You want me! Raise 'em! You think you can beat me! Huh! Raise 'em!."

They kept the guns at their sides.

"That's what I thought. Now drop 'em."

"You'll kill us."

"I could kill you both four times over, so what's it matter."

"I don't wanta die for this." One said, his voice stammering.

"I'm not gonna kill you." I said sympathetically.

"Really. Thank you." He sounded surprised. He then looked at the other guy.

"Drop it." They placed their weapons to the floor.

"Hands where I can see 'em."

They raised them above their heads, blaming one another for their obvious ineptitude.

"Shut up." I said. "You talk when I tell you to talk."

And talk they did. They had been sent as messengers to demonstrate the Company's ability to reach out and touch me. We were to make every effort to finalize the operation as soon as possible. My deadly mistake was equating the CIA's resolve with the caliber of people they sent to intimidate me.

I met Box at my home and we drove to Hondo. Our flight, in a Cesna, afforded us no way by which to see out the windows. We landed twice, probably to affect our ability to calculate the distance traveled, before finally touching down at our destination. We were blindfolded and driven to Rick's apparent residence, where the blindfolds were then removed. It was a very modest home, and, although it was night time, I could tell that it was in a southern state. We were directed into the living room by two men who were already in the dwelling. There he sat, his head leaned over the top of the recliner and his arms casually at his side. The blood had long since dried, clumping together his long silky hair. The entry wound was to the right temple, it was small and sunken. Like the mouth of a toothless old man, the wound folded inward. The exit was clean and precise, the result of a small, fast moving projectile fired at close range. The blood sprayed decidedly downwards and in a tight controlled pattern, slightly off kilter with the present placement of the body. He looked so peaceful, so calm.

"Could you leave us alone please." I asked the men.

"Sorry sir. We have our instructions."

"It's funny how people chose to do things differently when they kill themselves, isn't it, Box?"

"I'm not sure I..."

"You know. Like sitting higher in the chair than would be normal." I turned my attention back to the agents in charge of disposal. "For God's sakes, can we be alone here!" I needlessly cried in their presence. "Couldn't you have at least had the decency to check to see what hand he used first? Do you know what you've done here. Do you know what form of man this was? Of course you don't. How could you? You don't run in circles where people actually sacrifice themselves for something. You have no idea what sacrifices this man has made. Sacrifices which afford you the privilege of being here today to kill him!"

"Step outside, gentlemen," Box started. "Before I kill you with my bare hands." They left the room.

Box and I sang what we could of the *Cheyenne Anthem* song, and then kissed him good-bye.

"Good-bye my friend." I said, barely able to see through the tears. "You deserved to go out with more honor than this. Oh God, I'm sorry."

Box and I were totally silent throughout the return trip. When we were finally back at my house, Box said, "They wanted us to know they killed him, you know."

"I know." I said. "It's over you know. We've gotta end it."

"I know." He looked me in the eyes. "Are you gonna be all right?"

"Huh." I sighed. "Yeah. I'll be okay."

"Damn-it!" He screamed.

"I known, Box." I sobbed. "I know, man."

"Well. I'll be in touch."

"Box." I called. "Are they gonna kill us all?"

"I don't know."

"Let's vow now — today — to go down with dignity

and honor. I don't wanta go that way—the way he went. I don't want any of us to. Will you promise me. If you know before me. You'll give me—us—that chance."

"What is it you think?"

"I don't know anymore. I don't care. Promise?" I talked with a deadness in my voice.

"Get some sleep. You don't know what you're saying."

"Promise."

"Promise what! What do you think! That I knew about this! That I let him die!"

"Did you?"

"Are you serious? My God, you are."

"I don't know what to think anymore."

"As God is my witness, I swear that I would never allow anything to happen to any of you. My God, what has this done to you?"

"I believe you." I bowed my head. "Good night Box."

"Good night, Ken." He said hesitantly, and then walked off.

"Box!" I called to him. "I know you didn't."

Over the next several months, there were only four intervention missions. Langley wanted us to concentrate on making *interceptions* that had already made it to the first level transfer. Their reasoning was complex, but, in its simplest terms, it went as follows.

With the cartel already in possession of the first half of the code that released the United States government from its commitment to the operation, they were very reluctant to have us pass on the second half of the code which officially terminated the operation altogether. They were able to elude us in Colombia by having their labs vacated upon our arrival, leaving us no way to confirm the end of *Pseudo Miranda* with the drug lords. They were also careful not to tag any of the pre-shipped cocaine with the individual drug lord's identification symbols. These ingenious tactics came as a result of our catching Ocampo's people at a lab in Colombia and discontinuing his participation in *Pseudo Miranda*. However, because he was still able to piggyback shipments, it essentially had no affect on the amount of cocaine coming into America, it simply put us one step closer to ending the operation. Because shipments coming in had to be tagged, *interceptions* at the first level made more sense. We would have people to give codes to, and, based on the tagging symbols, we would know where those codes were going.

I was informed of two simultaneous shipments that, if they reached the mules on the ground, would serve our purposes. That is to say, we could easily distribute the code words to the traffickers, informing them of the official termination of *Pseudo Miranda*. I had been adamantly against such an interception, but I was weakening beneath the stress and coercion of Langley. The threats had become more and more intense with the passage of time, and, on one occasion, had Box and I fleeing for our lives in a 308 Ferrari. Box would take half the team to Florida, and I would take the other half to southern Texas.

Chapter 32.

"Joey!" I called in utter desperation. I got no response. I heard gunfire outside the house. The ambush had begun.

We were in the Texas hill country, where gunfire, often multiple, is commonplace. From a distance, I'm sure it sounded like a bunch of drunks blowing apart an unsuspecting deer. "To them, we're just sheep." Box once told me. And here we were, like lambs to the slaughter.

Quinn, Jesus, Lourdes, and Ming were fighting for their lives outside, while Joey and I scrambled to survive inside. The guy I called Fossil? Well, he was probably already dead, the likely result of having his head separated from his shoulders by Quinn—she was one to take orders quite literally.

"This way!" Joey yelled. He fired his M-16 for suppression, and continued to call for me as he made his way up the stairs.

I ran toward him, tripping on the raised floor as I scurried in a semi-crouched position for the staircase. I could now see Joey clearly, as he leaned over the railing and continued to riddle the room with bullets.

"Go!" I screamed, almost at the top of the staircase. He darted down the hall, and out of sight. Return fire gained on me, following my path up the stairs. I knew now the caliber of murderers I was dealing with. I traveled the hallway nearly halfway, then dove into a side corridor, slapping a preloaded clip into my weapon.

The shooting ceased inside, and I could now hear clearly the frantic cries of my friends and the sporadic gunfire that sought them.

"Joey! Ves! Joey!" Quinn hollered.

"Run! Get outa here! I demanded, although I knew they wouldn't.

"Joey?" I said softly, peaking around the corner for our assailants. "Joey?"

"Mmmm."

"Joey?"

"Hhhh. Yeah. Over here."

I glanced down the hall before scooting across it to the corridor on the opposite side. I saw his legs first, his feet were turned outward, more like a person resting than under fire. I stood up, turning my back to the opposing wall, and sliding downward. I now had a good vanish point by which to detect our assassins, and face Joey at the same time.

"What's up buddy?" I asked, drawing back his protective vest. A bullet had penetrated the seam, and tore through to the front of his abdomen. His pants were already drenched in blood, and he was fast losing consciousness.

Gunfire erupted once again down the hall, but it didn't seem to matter any longer. I numbly leaned out with my head, and fired two consecutive shots into the attackers stomach with my 45 automatic. He fell back on his ankles, and sat, somewhat perpendicular, in the middle of the hall, with his shotgun only a few feet in front of him.

The gunfire outside had all but stopped. I was sure my friends were gone.

"Joey? Hey buddy. I'm gonna take you out of here." I bore no illusions about our present state of security, and said this only to ease his suffering. "I'm gonna lift you now, okay?"

"Give me your gun," he mumbled. "So you can grab me better and I can cover your ass."

"You're the expert in these matters." I said. "Hey, Joe? We did the right thing, you know. And I wouldn't—I couldn't have had a better man at my side when it ended."

"Go out like James Cagney, Ken."

I handed him my Colt 45, and threw his M-16 around my shoulder. I gently lifted his weakened arm, placing my head under his shoulder. As I positioned myself for leverage, I heard another shot. The ensuing burst of blood and human debris led me to believe that I had been killed. I jolted backwards, pounding the wall with my head and back. The M-16 was firing down the hallway, and I wasn't sure how. The gun emptied and blood poured down my shirt, but I wasn't yet sure what had happened.

"Joey." I said, spirit finally broken. I hugged him, pressing my face to his. His blood was all so very warm. I could feel sanity slipping away. Wiping his blood from my eyes, I removed the Colt from his grip, wrenching back his still depressed trigger finger. He had made the ultimate sacrifice.

Now, at the center of the hall, I stood tall and ready. I wasn't there to do battle, I was there to die.

I walked wearily to the staircase, wondering why no one had come to kill me. The man kneeling in the hall was still alive. In my half-lucid mind, I bent, kissed him on the top of the head, and said that it would be all right. His hands stretched to the floor and he attempted to pull himself to his weapon. "You need to kill me that bad?" I asked, and handed him the shotgun. I backed away and faced him. "Top of the world, ma." I said softly, already missing life.

He fired, striking the side wall.

He gasped several times, attempting to build up the resources to fire once again. "You're gonna die, and you still want to kill me?" I was debilitated, the fight gone out of me. "No greater love." I thought. Or did I think it? "Joey." I said scrupulously. I knew now that I couldn't give up. A thought that would have served me better had it occurred a few seconds earlier.

As I went to relieve the broken man of his shotgun, he fired. At extreme close range, the pellets didn't have a opportunity to expand, slamming the brunt of their force to my torso. I launched several feet in the air, bouncing off my back and tumbling to my face. It took time, precious time, to catch my breath. Hoisting myself up by gripping the hole in the wall which was created by the first shotgun blast, I laughed painfully as I sensed the sweet taste of blood on my tongue.

I aimed at his head, sadness in my heart. I couldn't kill anymore. He could. He fired again, this time with an empty weapon. Shots fired blindly from around the corner, struck the wall next to me. Instinct prevailed over honor, and I fired three shots into the corner of the wall leading to the staircase. I heard the sound of a person tumbling down wooden stairs.

A vision of my mother crying at my funeral started
me toward the window, located at the opposite end of
the hall. "Into your hands, Jesus." I said lightly, and
then crashed backwards through the window. My
right shoulder collided with a solid object, ramming it
into my chest as I flipped a hundred and eighty degrees en route to the unpardonable ground. My left
knee, which was already less than perfect, buckled
inward. My vision became blurred and unreliable. I
was feeling less than human, a twisted and contorted
pile of incongruent limbs.

A dull pressure formed at my shoulders, my legs
dragged roughly across the grass. I was being pulled,
Quinn on one arm and Jesus on the other. Was it over?
I didn't know for sure.

We came to rest at the back of the yard. I faced a
metal fence, my chest still held above the ground.
"Whata we do?" Lourdes asked, quite scared.

"Run." I heard myself gurgle.

"We're in charge now, Ken." Quinn said. It only
now occurred to me that they all seemed to know my
real name. A strange thought for a man slipping away.

I then heard a lot of voices chattering in the distance. I couldn't tell if they were Spanish or not. My
body was gently lowered to the ground, my face turned
right, in the direction of Lourdes. I saw, as if in slow
motion, her weapon fall to the ground. "No!" I yelled.

I heard no sounds but the sounds of their bodies
crashing the fence. My eyes were clamped shut, but
when they opened, I could still see Lourdes standing
there. Two men, speaking Spanish, threw her to the
fence and began stripping the clothes off her. Though
I tried and tried, I couldn't move. My mind somehow
did not seem connected to my limbs. I was fading in
and out now. Lourdes never once screamed, nor did
she resist. But that didn't matter to these animals.
They began to do unspeakable things to her, things
born from the pits of hell. I heard laughter from

everywhere, as they continued their abominable acts.

"Please don't forsake me." She cried softly. Or did she?

I had my left hand tucked beneath my body, and in it, what felt like a gun. My hand was completely numb, so I wasn't sure whether it was actually still there. It was as a man with severed legs who still perceives sensation where his feet once were. I just wasn't sure.

When they began to slice her skin as a prelude to death, I grunted loudly, forcing my rear-end off the ground and arching my back. I squeezed what I prayed was a trigger, and watched in relief when the bullet struck my dear friend in the side.

The angered men hurled me into the fence and beat me about the face repeatedly. I hardly felt a thing, even as they tore off my vest and jabbed me several times with a knife. I simply wasn't there any longer.

Faint, dull sounds of gun fire reverberated in my mind. Or were they just fired? My tormentors lifted me higher, piercing my forearm with the fence, like a side of beef hung on a hook. My skin quickly tore, releasing my carcass to the earth once again. More Spanish voices, and then loud blasts. The two men hurled against the fence, painting it with a rich shade of scarlet.

The muffled sounds of rotor blades filled the temperate air. I counted my breathing and remembered how I'd listened to my uncle George and Christina take their last breaths. I was dying, I knew that, but how would it feel the moment my heart stopped? Hands squeezed me and slid me along the morning dew. I saw the bodies of my friends and enemies, steam rising up from their gutted corpses. Now on a stretcher, I was lifted above the crawling fog. The condensation was like a thin veil, softening the horror that lie below the surface.

I could hear a hollow thump, and then another, and

another. I checked my breathing. It was me. The thumping—it was me. They were attempting to resuscitate me. But I wasn't dead? A bright light shined in my eyes. "Come on sir! You can make it!" Someone said. But I have made it, I thought. It's over now. I listened to the soothing sounds of the rotor blades, and felt warmly about the faceless people who were doing so much to help me. And then, darkness.

I opened my eyes, a brightness rushed in. I drifted back to the darkness.

I opened them once again, this time fighting back the pain. I sunk back to the darkness.

I reemerged moments later—I thought. Three days had elapsed since the ambush. "Ves! It's me, Mr. Dix!" Mr. and Mrs. Dix often took care of us whenever the team gathered in Florida. At first I had trouble deciding what I was, never mind who I was. My faculties returned in an avalanche after about a half hour of listening to Mr. and Mrs. Dix. "Oh, my God." I cried with a scratchy, dry throat. "They're dead. They're all dead." I drew my hands to my face and screamed from the pain.

"It's your arm. Don't move it. You've received a lot of injuries. It'll take time." He said.

"Time? Time for what? I've lost everything." I caught my breadth. "How long before they come for me?"

"Who?" Mrs. Dix asked.

"The people who did this!"

"It's over now." She answered.

"Mr. Casey passed away while you were—well you know." He said.

"Where am I?"

"The Galloway's—Lake Austin." He stumbled on his reply.

"The Galloway's? What's that?"

"Fine patriots. They've helped keep you alive, and they ask no questions." He explained.

"What happened to Box — and Tina — and Steven — the others?"

"I don't know. I swear, I don't know." He said truthfully. "Get some rest. You need to build your strength. Oh! And don't worry, it was arranged to extend your leave by two more weeks."

"That's a real fuckin' load off my mind." I said sarcastically.

"Goodnight."

For the next few days, a nurse came in twice daily to refill my intervenes, check vitals, and administer cortisone shots as needed. She told me that I received some internal injuries, but that she wasn't sure how extensive they were.

"Don't you wonder why I wasn't taken to the hospital?" I asked curiously.

"I'm paid not to ask. Now, you just do your job and get well."

She also said that my knee and shoulder would be permanently deformed with arthritis. And that some day, in the not too distant future, I would be tormented with back problems. Just the kind of bedside manner I needed at this point.

After about a week's time, I was allowed to sit in a wheel chair and was taken outdoors. It was only then that I realized I was in a mansion that sat immediately on the lake. The lot next to it was empty, and directly behind us was a tall hill made of sheering rock that stood perpendicular to the ground we occupied. There was a boat garage that appeared to house at least two vessels, perfect for fast getaways.

I was filling my lungs with the refreshing air when I noticed an American flag hanging from the front of the house, and I wondered what it now meant to me. I was slowly regaining my strength and had stopped taking my meals through an arm straw.

I was in my room resting when Mr. Dix came in with some news. "There's some people out front who'd like to see you."

My heart churned like a locomotive. His smile told me what I wanted to hear for days.

"Box." I whispered.

"Hi, Buch." He said gently.

Tina and Steven were with him. They had all survived. But how?

"You remember that guy in Panama with the wigs? Butler?" Box said.

"Yeah, I do."

"Well. He heard about this plot to ambush us, so he phoned someone in Langley. Whoever he spoke with, I'm guessing Lauder, knew only about those of us in Florida. When we got the warning, we told the courier about you guys. Before we were able to get someone to you, well…" He paused with a saddened voice. "You remember that guy Mandoza?"

"I saw him." His face flashed in my mind. "He was the one who saved me, right? Why?"

"Ochoa."

"Why?"

"Escobar's people were sent to kill us, and for some—crazy reason, Don Fabio didn't want it done. I have no idea why."

We talked into the late afternoon, no one wanting to say good-bye, but good-bye it was to be. "Well KaBuch," Box started. "We've gotta be off."

"Where? Why so soon? When will I see you guys again?"

"It's over for you, Ken. You've given more than ten people to this country." His voice weakened. "It's over."

"Oh, Box. We've lost so much. And what did we

accomplish? There's got to be more. How can I walk away like this?"

"Don't do this." He said, weeping lightly.

"What? What am I doin' Box? What happened over the past three years? Did they die for something? Did they?"

"Damnit! Look at you. You're all busted up. You're not the same VesBucchi that started this operation. None of us are. But you have a chance. You're out. They've given you a new lease. Pick the pieces up and start over." He then said: "Someday, this will all seem much clearer. Give it time."

I turned my attention to Steven. "You made it through. Who'd of thunk it?"

"I'll miss you. More than anyone, I'll miss you." He said, all welled up.

"I'll miss you too, scarecrow. You're a brave man, Steven. I just wished I'd told you that before, when it mattered."

"It matters." He replied.

"Tina." I said. "We could never have won the football game without you." We both strained a chuckle. "I wished you'd of been with us from the beginning. We could have used you, and you really would have liked Debara."

"I know I could never fill her shoes." She said.

"You did fill her shoes. And she'd be the first to tell you that. God bless you for saying that, though."

Box wheeled me to the end of the dock where their boat was tied. He sniffled profusely, and brushed back the tears. "I know I can be real pig-headed, but I want you to know that I have never met a finer, more qualified agent. I mean that. Huhhh!" He sighed. "I'm never gonna work with anyone like you ever again. I know that. And I tell ya, not a day goes by that I don't think about that."

"Thanks, Box. And stop calling me a *daigo*." We all laughed, still strained. "You're the best, Box.

Pure and simple. I pray we meet again some day."

"Hey!" He whispered loudly. Do you hear that?"

"What?" I asked.

"The music?" He said, a great big smile rolling across his face. He then began to dance. Even Tina joined in, though she had no idea what he was doing.

I spread my arms and swayed back and forth, not hearing music, but happy to have been associated with such people. As they cruised away in the boat, they saluted me with the sign language for *Pseudo Miranda*.

EPILOGUE.

In 1989, while stationed in Korea as a Captain in the United States Air Force, I was contacted by representatives of the CIA, and told to feed disinformation to reporter Carl Bernstein. I did as I was *asked* to do, and met with Mr. Bernstein at his New York home. After myself and a close friend, namely Mark Rizzo (who was not cognizant of the true nature of our visit) met with Mr. Bernstein for what turned out to be a four hour meeting, I was satisfied that my job was done.

When I was told that Bernstein had spoken with Frank Rubino, then Noriega's lead defense attorney, about our visit together, I became quite concerned. I then notified the DEA and told them what had transpired. Dan Moritz (the agent who convinced the attorney to prefer charges against Noriega) immediately took my call from Korea, and had me speak hypothetically about *Pseudo Miranda* as he taped our conversation. He then sent DEA agents out to speak with me on four occasions about the operation. Agents Tom Raphenello, Steve Grilli and Dave Sir assured me that they had extensive knowledge of the operation, and that they wanted desperately to head off any attempts on the part of Rubino to introduce this operation in court. In no uncertain terms, Dan Moritz stated that if Rubino were to prove the existence of *Pseudo Miranda*, General Noriega would walk.

Months later, after receiving my second Commendation Medal for meritorious service, the DEA (Agent Ed Wezain and one other), CIA (Agent Sutherland), and OSI (Agent Ron Humphrey) interrogated me for six hours while I was a student at Squadron Officer's School. The gist of the conversation revolved around their demands that I sign a perjured statement, that in essence said that *Pseudo Miranda* never happened. When I refused, the OSI threatened me with a psychiatric discharge, even though I had a highly decorated and flawless record. Essentially, the psychiatrist found that I tested normal on all empirical tests and interviews, but that, if the OSI found what I was saying not to be true, then I was suffering from delusions. A perfect military circle jerk.

Throughout the following year, the OSI pressured everyone in my chain of command to leave well enough alone, as they continued to pervert an already perverse military psychiatric profession. At the end of my year long humiliation, the final review board (the only one I actually got to physically meet) rendered a diagnosis of sane in my case. The OSI, concerned about the implications, went behind closed doors in Washington, DC with the review board that is only supposed to decide if the final review board was conducted fairly, and supposedly gave them some new *evidence*. I was never given the opportunity to see this supposed new evidence, and was drummed out of the Air Force with a fifty percent disability.

During all these events, I was able to acquire some very persuasive evidence that demonstrated my veracity in this matter. Evidence, I might add, that convinced the final review board that the OSI had indeed been lying about my state of health.

The DEA, in a response to a Freedom of Informa-

tion (FOI) request concerning *Pseudo Miranda* and
my connection to the same, initially sent me a reply
that said they had no records pertaining to it. Later,
when they became concerned that I would be called
to testify in the Noriega trial, they reissued a response, in writing, to the original request. They admitted this time that such an operation indeed occurred, but that they could not release said documents to me. They cited several reasons for their
denial to release these records.

In November of 1990, Frank Rubino, while appearing on the *Larry King Live* television show, evoked my
name and the operation as being closely tied to his
client.

Carlos Lehder, in a letter to me from his prison cell
in Marion, Illinois, identified *Pseudo Miranda* as a
"...drug proyect (sic) of the United States."

I have since passed an extensive polygraph examination, administered by a highly recognized expert in
the field, and a retired FBI agent. I also prevailed after
a battery of psychological tests, which were likewise
administered by a recognized leader in the field.

I interviewed on camera with *Prime Time Live*'s Sam
Donaldson, but, when things got too hot for everyone
involved, the effort to air the show was discontinued.

A woman by the name of Pilar Rivas contacted me
several times on behalf of Carlos Lehder. She was, at
that time, speaking directly with Manuel Noriega,
attempting to get him to tell her things that would
provide Lehder with enough testimony against
Noriega so as to help him strike a substantial deal with
the government. Frank Rubino did not know of these
conversations with his client until I informed him of
them. Noriega surrendered critical information to
Rivas, which Lehder used in Noriega's trial.

This has been a capsulated version of all that has
happened, and does not include the numerous threats
of bodily harm I was forced to endure.

Political Current Events
from SPI Books

☐ **Compromised: Clinton, Bush and the CIA** *by Terry Reed and John Cummings.* This shocking first-hand exposé, by a key CIA operative, reveals that Bill Clinton was up to his saxophone in illegal arms manufacturing, gun running, drug trafficking and money laundering as Governor of Arkansas. Are these mere allegations based on circumstantial evidence? NO. Author Terry Reed was there with CIA ringmaster Colonel Oliver NORTH and he saw Bill CLINTON directly involved in the illegal activities going on his jurisdiction. The chain of command clearly led back to former CIA chief and Vice-President George BUSH, his associates William BARR (later Attorney General) and William CASEY (former CIA director). Implicated, too, are lesser players like the murdered ex-Green Beret and CIA operative Barry SEAL and the president's brother Roger CLINTON.
(ISBN 1-56171-249-3) $23.95 U.S.

☐ **Target America: Terrorism in the U.S. Today** *by Yossef Bodansky. Intro by Congressman Bill McCallum (R-FL)* The World Trade Center bombing was only the beginning. International terrorists from Iran, Iraq, Libya, Syria and successor states from the former Yugoslavia are plotting against not only Israel, but also against America, the world's remaining superpower. Now, for the first time, Yossef Bodansky, Director of the Republican Congressional Task Force on Terrorism and Unconventional Warfare and Terror documents these new sources of terror and how they have set up powerful and widespread networks to strike at targets in Israel, as well as here in the U.S. and Canada. (ISBN 1-56171-269-8) $5.99 U.S.

Great S.P.I Books
Fact and Fiction

SPi.
BOOKS